THE GREATEST
U.S. OPENS

ALSO BY DAVID BARRETT

Golf Courses of the U.S. Open

Golf's Dream 18s

Miracle at Merion

Golfing With Dad

Making the Masters

The Story of the Masters

THE GREATEST
U.S. OPENS

HIGH DRAMA AT GOLF'S MOST CHALLENGING CHAMPIONSHIP

David Barrett

TATRA PRESS

The Greatest U.S. Opens
Copyright © 2024 by David Barrett

Library of Congress Cataloging-in-Publication Data application has been submitted.
ISBN: 978-1732222779
First Edition: October, 2024

Tatra Press LLC
Distributed by Independent Publishers Group, Baker & Taylor and Ingram
Cover designed by Mimi Bark
Interior designed by Maria Ilardi

Media, special sales and permissions:
Chris Sulavik (Tatra Press) at tatrapress@gmail.com or 646-644-6236

Printed and bound in the United States of America by Sheridan Group (Chelsea, MI).
Tatra Press, 4 Park Trail, Croton-on-Hudson, New York 10525, www.tatrapress.com

TATRA PRESS

For Luda, Michael, and Sophia

CONTENTS

INTRODUCTION

The U.S. Open has implicit importance and prestige because it is the national championship. From a global perspective, it is one of golf's four major championships. Winning—or not winning—the U.S. Open is one way we measure the careers and records of the game's elite players.

Additionally, the championship is considered the toughest test in golf because of the extremely demanding course setup favored by the USGA—with narrow fairways, deep rough, and firm and speedy greens. It also showcases some of the greatest courses in the U.S.

With so much attention focused on the event, and the importance of its outcome, the action of each U.S. Open becomes part of golfing lore and is stamped in the memories of the golf-watching public. When the circumstances are right, and the drama particularly intense, the story of a U.S. Open becomes epic. In this book, we tell the stories of 20 of the greatest U.S. Opens.

The selections were made based on a variety of factors. The identity of the chief protagonists makes a difference—many of the greatest U.S. Opens were battles between the greatest players of their era. In some cases, they determined who was at the top, such as the Jack Nicklaus-Arnold Palmer duel of 1962. In others, there were memorable giant-killing upsets, such as Francis Ouimet in 1913 or Jack Fleck in 1955.

The drama of the tournament action is another factor in selecting the greatest U.S. Opens. The back-and-forth thrusts of the final round and the uncertainty of who will emerge as the winner down to the very end make a U.S. Open memorable. Or it could be the greatness of the performance. Tiger Woods's 15-stroke victory in 2000 lacked drama, but inspired awe. Johnny Miller's 63 in 1973 is one of the greatest rounds in the history of the game. In some cases, great shots have determined the outcome and become part of the game's lore, including Tom Watson's chip-in in 1982 or Payne Stewart's putt in 1999.

It could be a back story that heightens a U.S. Open's resonance, such as Bobby Jones's pursuit of the Grand Slam in 1930. Sometimes the venue itself is a co-star. The 1972 event was especially noteworthy as the first time the Open visited California's Pebble Beach; in 1986, it went to the Long Island gem Shinnecock Hills for the first time. In each case, the drama of the event matched the staging.

Every U.S. Open has a deeper story that extends beyond the well-known narrative. While these championships have been chosen largely for that narrative, research turns up further layers that are also compelling, illuminating, and sometimes surprising. Herewith are the tales of 20 great U.S. Opens.

1913

LOCAL KID MAKES VERY GOOD

The great English golfer Harry Vardon toured the United States in 1900 for a series of exhibitions and to play in the U.S. Open, which he duly won. His next appearance in America came in 1913, when he embarked on another exhibition tour, this time with fellow Englishman Ted Ray.

In 1900, Vardon and another Englishman J.H. Taylor, who was in America on his own business, finished nine and seven strokes, respectively, ahead of the nearest American. The standard of American golf had risen considerably in the ensuing 13 years. Still, Vardon and Ray won every exhibition match before running into John McDermott at the Shawnee Open in Pennsylvania three weeks before the U.S. Open.

In 1911, McDermott, at just 20, became the first American-born player to win the U.S. Open, 16 years after its establishment. Previously, it had been won only by America-based Scottish- or English-born pros, except for Vardon. At Shawnee, McDermott won by eight strokes, finishing 13 ahead of Vardon and 15 ahead of Ray. At the award ceremony, in the presence of the Englishmen, he said he was sure they wouldn't win the national open. The remark stirred controversy when it was reported in the press, creating consternation for McDermott as he headed into the championship.

Despite the Shawnee result, Vardon and Ray were the favorites for the U.S. Open at The Country Club in Brookline, Massachusetts, near

Boston. Vardon, after all, had won five of what would be an eventual total of six British Opens. Known for his deadly accuracy, he was the best golfer the game had ever seen. Ray was not only an accomplished player who had won the 1912 British Open, but also a gallery draw because of the prodigious length of his tee shots.

The duo attracted the lion's share of the attention leading up to the U.S. Open. Receiving a slight bit of attention—and that only because he was local—was a 20-year-old amateur named Francis Ouimet who was beginning to show promise.

Ouimet had grown up on Clyde Street, across the street from the 17th hole at The Country Club, and still lived there with his parents and siblings. He and his older brother had become fascinated with the game, passing the time by observing golfers across the street. The brothers built a makeshift three-hole course behind their house when Francis was just seven, using balls that the young lad found on The Country Club grounds on his shortcut to school and a couple of clubs his brother had been given by members after he started to caddie.

Francis also began to caddie at The Country Club at the age of nine and he'd sneak onto the course to play a little at twilight or on rainy days, when the course was empty. A couple years later, Francis was caddying for a member playing alone who asked him if he would like to join him in play. Young Ouimet played so well that word got around and he was allowed to play the course, though most of his rounds were played at a public course that was a couple of streetcar rides away.

In 1910, the U.S. Amateur came to The Country Club. Francis was 17. Club membership was then required by the USGA to play in the event. Ouimet came from a working-class family, and with member-ship not forthcoming at The Country Club, he applied to the nearby Woodland Golf Club, which charged him $25 for a junior member-ship (he borrowed the money from his mother). However, he failed to qualify for match play by a single stroke.

The next year he took a job at the Wright & Ditson sporting goods store, where his boss, ex-major league baseball player George Wright, encouraged him to work on his game. Francis was runner-up in the Massachusetts Amateur in 1912 and won it in the spring of 1913.

Ouimet was ready to try his hand at the U.S. Amateur again, and Wright gave him a week off to compete at Garden City Golf Club in New York. Francis was second in the 36-hole qualifying for match play, then had the bad luck to draw Jerome Travers in the second round. Ouimet impressed observers by making it a tough match before Travers prevailed and went on to win his fourth U.S. Amateur.

The USGA was so impressed that they entered Ouimet into the U.S. Open that was to begin two weeks later at The Country Club. Francis hadn't been planning to enter. He assumed he would not be able to take another week off from work. Wright, however, urged him to play.

The Country Club was founded in 1882, before golf even came to America. It would add golf in 1893, making it one of the earliest sites for the sport in the nation. The original course was six holes, with many modifications and additions made to the layout over the next 16 years, all carried out by members or host pro Willie Campbell. It had evolved into a test worthy of the national championship—one that Ouimet knew like the back of his hand.

A total of 162 players came to compete at The Country Club. Only 69 would be in the field for the U.S. Open, however, after qualifying earlier in the week. There were no exemptions from qualifying—even the great Vardon and two-time defending champion McDermott had to go through it. Half of the entrants played 36 holes on Tuesday and the other half on Wednesday, with the low 32 and ties each day making it through.

Vardon led the field on Tuesday with scores of 75-76—151. Perhaps more noteworthy was the performance of Ouimet, who finished second with 74-78—152, and would have been first if not for a double bogey on the 14th in the afternoon. The local kid, who merely had to walk across the street each day to reach the course, would bear watching in the championship.

On Wednesday, Ray topped the field with 74-74—148, followed by another Englishman, Wilfred Reid, at 72-79—151. While Vardon and Ray were bankrolled on their U.S. tour by British newspaper magnate Lord Northcliffe, Reid had come on his own for the U.S. Open, with hopes of possibly finding a club to employ him in the States.

The tournament was framed largely as a battle between Great Britain and the U.S., with that angle receiving more reporting and analysis than on which individuals would prevail. The championship consisted of 36 holes on Thursday and 36 on Friday. The first day saw a reversal of fortunes for the U.S. contingent.

Americans held the top seven spots in the morning 18, with foreign-born players based in America now being universally counted as on the U.S. side in the face-off against Vardon, Ray, Reid, and Louis Tellier of France, who, like Reid, had arrived with hopes of gaining employment. Vardon and Reid were in a tie for eighth place after 75s, with Ray lagging far behind at 79.

The co-leaders with 71s were a pair of Scottish-born pros, Macdonald Smith and Alex Ross. Smith was a 23-year-old of great promise who had lost to his brother Alex in a three-way playoff for the 2010 U.S. Open (with McDermott as the third participant). The three-under 71 was a course record and would have been even better if Smith hadn't missed two three-foot putts with mud on the ball. Players were not allowed to lift and clean their ball on the green under the rules at the time.

In fact, the rules were even harsher than that. There was no recourse if a ball plugged on a soft green; it had to be played as it lay. That's what happened to Boston pro Tom McNamara on the par-three 10th. He hit his tee shot within two feet of the hole, but it remained lodged in its own pitch mark. He had to use a niblick (an iron club) to dig it out. That shot didn't go into the hole, nor did the next short putt due to mud on the ball, so McNamara made a four instead of a two. He ended up with a 73, so the bad break cost the 1909 and 1912 U.S. Open runner-up a share of the lead, though it ultimately didn't matter, as he limped to an 86 in the second round.

Ross's 71 was the result of an outstanding 32 on the back nine, which included a near ace on the 10th and an eagle on the par-five 12th. Par was a relatively new concept at the time, and hadn't really been considered when the course was being designed and laid out. When par for the holes was established for the U.S. Open, the 12th hole was designated a par five at 415 yards, though it was reachable in two for most of the field, even in the hickory-shaft era. The course played to a par of 74 with five par fives and three par threes.

Newspaper accounts of the event, while not completely ignoring par, often just mentioned the score a player made on a hole (i.e., a four) instead of saying they made a par or a birdie. There were two other reachable par fives, both early in the round, with the first and third holes playing 430 and 435 yards.

The first hole posed an interesting choice of whether to lay up short of the horse racing track/polo field situated in front of the green (and also extended into the adjacent fairway short of the 18th green) or go for it in two. Drawing the bulk of the gallery, Vardon laid up but ended up making a putt for a birdie on the opening hole and added a fairly routine birdie on the third. Soon, however, the putting woes that often plagued the 43-year-old at this stage of his career reared their ugly head. Vardon three-putted the fifth for a bogey, three-putted the sixth from six feet for another bogey and made a third consecutive bogey on the seventh.

McDermott was in the twosome just behind Vardon. As the Englishman started to struggle, word was spreading of a spectacular start by the American. For a two-time defending champion, McDermott had received little attention in the press in the run-up to the tournament, which had been dominated by the anticipation of the Vardon and Ray show. McDermott felt overshadowed and was also annoyed about what he saw as an overreaction to his post-tournament remarks in Shawnee, which had drawn a reprimand from the USGA.

Perhaps taking his frustrations out on the course, McDermott made birdies on the first three holes, a par on the fourth, and birdies on the fifth and sixth to go five-under. Two of the birdies came on putts of 12 and 20 feet, while the par-five birdies were relatively routine.

Could McDermott be on the march to a third straight Open title to match Willie Anderson's feat of 1903-5? Just as quickly and brilliantly as he had started, McDermott's round suddenly plunged with bogeys on the seventh, eighth, and ninth. Whatever frustrations he was feeling now had solely a negative effect. McDermott went two-over on the back nine. He was described as not bothering to aim on a two-foot par putt on the 13th, which he missed. He drove out of bounds on the par-five 14th, leading to a bogey with the distance-only penalty then in effect. He had no birdies on the back nine, failing to take advantage of the vulnerable par-five 12th due to a topped drive and missing a four-foot birdie putt on 17. McDermott finished the round three strokes behind with a 74.

Ahead of him, Vardon steadied himself after his three-bogey stretch with eight straight pars, a bogey at the 17th, and a pleasing birdie on the 18th, where he made a 25-foot putt for a 75.

Another young American off to a hot start was a 20-year-old from Rochester, New York, described in the *Times of London* as "a home-bred American player of whom no one seems to have heard much." Walter Hagen was indeed little known at the time, evidenced by the fact that his name showed up as "Hagin" in every published report, because that's the spelling the USGA had provided. A couple of newspapers compounded the error; one had him as "Hogin," another as "Willie Hagin."

Hagen would make a name for himself soon enough, winning the Open a year later, in 1914, and adding another in 1919. He had dropped out of school to apprentice at the Country Club of Rochester and had recently become the head pro there when his mentor moved to another club. Hagen was inspired by attending the 1912 U.S. Open at the Country Club of Buffalo as a spectator and played in his first event as a pro at the 1912 Canadian Open.

The raw competitor was threatening to lead the way through the first round at The Country Club, going three-under through 14 holes with birdies on the three short par fives and two birdies and two bogeys elsewhere. Bogeys on 15 and 17, however, left him at one-under 73.

Ray was one of the late starters and wound up disappointing. He was out of sorts with all aspects of his game. His lone birdie came at the first hole, and he had six bogeys due to errant drives, misjudged irons, or missed short putts. After signing for a 79, he declared he needed a 70 in the afternoon to get back into it.

A 70 would represent the course record—and that's just what Ray shot. A big man, weighing 220 pounds, with a big moustache and an ebullient personality, the 36-year-old Ray spiced his round with an eagle on the 12th hole, where he launched one of the long drives he was known for, reached the green with an iron, and holed a 12-foot putt. That got him to five-under, having already birdied Nos. 1, 2, and 6, the latter on a chip-in. A bogey-free round was a rarity in those days, and Ray ran into one on the 15th, where he three-putted from 20 feet. Still, he had a good chance for a five-under 69 when he rifled an excellent approach to the 18th, leaving a five-foot putt for a birdie. It veered slightly off course at the last instant, leaving Ray with a 70 and a 149 total.

Earlier, the other two Englishmen, Vardon and Reid, had finished at 147. After trailing in the morning, England's finest had climbed to the top of the leaderboard, as the Americans were falling back. Vardon and Reid were tied for first, and Ray tied for third with the top U.S. representative, Herbert Strong, who added a 74 to an opening 75.

Vardon still looked uncomfortable on the greens in the afternoon, according to Bernard Darwin's report in the *Times of London*, but, with his unerring accuracy, was grinding out regulation par after regulation par. He also made a two-putt birdie on the 14th, where he reached the relatively long par five with what Darwin called a "grand" brassie (two-wood) shot. For the round, he scored three birdies and one bogey for a 72. Reid also had a 72, with five birdies and three bogeys.

The American retreat included a disastrous 44 on the front nine by Smith, who double bogeyed the sixth and triple bogeyed the seventh. He recovered on the back nine, but still it was a 79 for 150. That was one stroke better than fellow 18-hole co-leader Ross. Little-known Jack Croke went from 72 to 83 and McNamara from 73 to 86.

Hagen started out promisingly with an eagle on the third. That was his only subpar hole; he had six bogeys, including 17 and 18, to card a 78 for 151.

The man who was supposed to be the American leader, McDermott, fared no better with a 79—153. The culprit was awful putting, and he didn't have Vardon's excuse of age. It almost seemed like a case of the yips, though McDermott hadn't been afflicted with that malady before. The round started with three-putts for par and bogey on the first two holes, missing a two-footer in both instances. It didn't get any better. In fact, it got worse with a four-putt triple bogey at the fifth. The litany continued with, incredibly, six more missed putts from four feet or less, a couple of them birdie tries. McDermott did manage a couple of birdies along the way, enabling him to break 80 on a day when his confidence on the greens was utterly shattered.

There was one bright spot for the Americans in the afternoon. The lad from across the street, Ouimet, shot a 74 to move into a tie for seventh at 151. He had gotten off to a nervous start in the morning with sixes on the first two holes for a bogey and double bogey. He settled down nicely to play even par the rest of the round with one birdie, one bogey, and plenty of solid pars to boost his confidence as he proved he belonged on the big stage with the best of American golf and the famed international guests.

In the second round, Francis handled the opening holes with ease, getting birdies on Nos. 1, 3, and 4. He was three-under through 12, recovering from bogeys on the seventh and eighth to birdie the ninth and 12th. At that point, he had birdied all four par fives. Ouimet ran into trouble on the last par five, No. 14, and bogeyed after finding a bunker. Another visit to a bunker on the par-three 16th cost a double bogey when it took two strokes to extricate himself. It was a disappointing finish, but, in the broad scheme, a pretty good day.

Friday's conditions for the third and fourth rounds were anything but ideal. It started raining overnight, and the rain continued to come down all day. The turf was getting saturated, which meant almost no roll on tee shots—perhaps an advantage for a long hitter like Ray. It would be hard to keep the clubs' grips dry, which could lead to hands slipping and wayward shots. The greens were holding, but they would become slower and sloppier all day. Often, players putted balls splattered with mud.

Despite the weather, thousands of Bostonians turned out to watch the festivities, sludging through the mud and sloshing through puddles. Curiosity about the intriguing game of golf and the publicity surrounding international stars Vardon and Ray drew the throngs to Brookline. It helped that there was no admission fee.

The Country Club was well prepared to handle the multitudes and guide the many among them who didn't know much about golf or how to watch it. Teams of marshals shouted through megaphones and waved red flags when quiet was called for. Most players and observers, even those from Britain, commented that the crowds were well behaved. British writer Henry Leach did have one complaint: "I do wish these American golfing congregations would restrain themselves more in the matter of their applause, which becomes very wearisome and trying in its frequency." He, and some others, were particularly concerned with cheering that occurred for one player while a fellow competitor still had a stroke to play.

Ray was in the first twosome off the tee in the morning, with the leaders spread throughout the field (the pairings and order of play would stay the same in the afternoon round). He was off his game early, slicing his first two shots well to the right. He managed to hit the par-five green with a third shot and make a par, but his ball-striking didn't improve on the front nine and he also missed a couple of short putts. He bogeyed the short par-five third and added bogeys on Nos. 5 and 7 for a three-over 41 on the front nine.

The big Englishman played like a new man on the back nine, where he swiftly recovered precise shotmaking. Eight pars and a birdie on the 12th gave him a 35 on the back nine for a respectable 76 in the tough conditions. Ray told Darwin that he liked the back nine holes so much that he "would like to carry them around with me and use them instead of the first nine."

Vardon was next, and he didn't fare any better on the front nine. His trademark accuracy was absent on the first few holes, errant shots leading to bogeys on the first and third. A short putt missed on the fifth meant another bogey, with Vardon duplicating Ray's 41 on the front nine.

Harry got a terrible break on the 10th, where his tee shot came to rest three feet from the hole—sitting in a depression made by another ball. Much like McNamara's first-round debacle, he dug the ball out with an iron, then missed a short putt. Instead of letting the bogey throw him off his stride, Vardon seemed to take inspiration from his fine tee shot and his game turned decidedly for the better. Eight pars coming home left him with a 78 and the same 225 total for 54 holes posted by Ray.

American hopes were kindled by the lackluster third-round showing by Vardon and Ray. The first U.S. contender in the order of play was Hagen. He double bogeyed the third hole, then made up for it by holing his second shot for an eagle on the 300-yard par-four fourth. Walter went two-over the rest of the way to make up two strokes on Vardon with a 76 and pull within two strokes of what would turn out to be the 54-hole lead. Perhaps this previously unknown homebred had what it took to follow in the footsteps of McDermott.

McDermott himself created a bit of a stir by being one of the few players to head out in the steady rain without a coat. His 38 on the front nine made up some ground on Vardon and Ray, but he slipped at the finish. Yet another missed two-foot putt gave him a double bogey at the 15th and a bogey at 18 left him with a 77. His 230 total was five behind the leading Englishmen—not out of it but undoubtedly wondering what might have been with merely an adequate showing on the greens.

Jim Barnes would go on to win the 1921 U.S. Open, but the tall, 27-year-old wasn't well known at this point. The Englishman had settled on the West Coast of the U.S., working at a club in Tacoma, Washington, and this was only his second U.S. Open. He was tied for fourth at 150 through 36 holes—and at even par for the third round through 15 holes, thanks to a surge early on the back nine. At that point, he could finish one ahead of Vardon and Ray with pars on the last three holes. Instead, he bogeyed 16 and 17 and double bogeyed 18, going over the green in two, pitching nicely to six feet, and then three-putting (mud on the ball was probably a factor). A 78 left Barnes three back at 228. Smith and George Sargent clung to hopes at 230 after 80 and 79.

The third Englishman, Reid, shot himself out of it with a 46 on the front nine and a round of 85, which would be followed by an 86. The reason was clear. As reported in the *Boston Globe* that morning, Reid had gotten into an altercation with Ray in the bar of their hotel the previous evening. An argument over British taxation policy turned into insults about their respective regions of England, and Ray lost his temper and punched Reid twice in the nose before a waiter stepped in between them to break it up. Reid, his nose bloodied, returned to his room, didn't sleep a wink all night, and was hardly ready to take on The Country Club in the morning.

With Vardon and Ray on the back nine when he started at 10:45 a.m., Ouimet's early gallery was a gathering of acquaintances and a scattering of Bostonians curious about this apparent prodigy. He gave them a great show at the start, later saying that he "played as I never had before for seven holes." He birdied the first three holes without having to sink a long putt, handling the two par fives with ease and hitting a great approach on the par-four second. Francis bogeyed the fifth but got back to three-under for the round by holing a long putt for a birdie at the seventh. Vardon and Ray had each played the first seven holes in three-over, so, at that point on the course, the amateur had gained six strokes on each of them and was two ahead of Vardon's pace and four ahead of Ray's (in the days before electronic scoring and leaderboards, a reckoning was generally made by comparing players' scores through the same hole).

Ouimet couldn't keep it up. He made sixes on the next two holes, a hooked drive leading to a double bogey on the eighth and three putts causing a bogey on the ninth. Another bogey came at the 11th after an approach shot ended in a bunker. He drove into a bunker on the par-five 12th, had to play out sideways, was short of the green in three, and pitched to 25 feet. The bad stretch would have shattered many players' confidence, but Francis, despite his soft-spoken, friendly demeanor, was made of sterner stuff. As the *Boston Evening Transcript* described the long par putt: "He hit the ball as if there was no doubt in his mind as to what would happen. It hit the back of the cup and dropped."

Ouimet thought his second shot to the par-five 14th was on the green, but it had hit a mound and deflected into a bunker. He settled for a par there, but hit his approach on the par-four 15th to six feet and made a birdie. His swing now grooved, Francis nearly birdied the 17th, just missing a 10-foot putt. His birdie attempt on 18 rolled four feet past, and he holed the knee-knocking comebacker eliciting cheers from the swelling gallery. With a pair of even-par nines,

Ouimet's 74 was the best score among the contenders and lifted him into a tie for the lead with Vardon and Ray at 225. That was nice. But the English pros would take over in the final round, wouldn't they?

Maybe not. Just as in the morning, the distinguished visitors hardly played like great champions on the front nine, with Vardon carding a 42 and Ray a 43. Ray had two birdies, but also two double bogeys and three bogeys. He double bogeyed the short par-four fourth when he chunked a 50-yard pitch shot into a pot bunker short of the green and ended up three-putting. Adding to his woes, he three-putted for double bogey on the seventh and missed the green with a short iron to bogey the par-five ninth. After not making a single birdie in the morning round, Vardon continued birdie-less on the front nine of the afternoon and made four straight bogeys on Nos. 2-5. It wasn't what the spectators were expecting. Yet, they weren't exactly displeased with what was unfolding—the Britishers' misadventures were opening the door for the U.S. representatives to keep the trophy on this side of the Atlantic.

Similar to the third round, Vardon and Ray righted themselves on the back nine, Ray with a 36 and Vardon a 37. Ray had dug himself a deeper hole with a bogey on 10—making him five-over on a four-hole stretch—so it was a welcome sight for him when a 60-foot birdie putt dropped on 11. He didn't birdie either par five, 12 or 14, but did birdie 13 before a bogey on 16. Vardon bogeyed 11, then finally got his first (and only) birdie of the 36-hole final day on 12, bogeyed 13, and came home with pars on the last five. Both were in with 79 for a 304 total.

"We were guilty of bad golf," Vardon wrote in a commissioned column for *The Evening World*. "Putting was my downfall. My awful score of 42 on the outward trip was entirely due to missed putts, and many of them very easy."

The Englishmen didn't think their score would hold up. Vardon, in fact, speculated that it might be beaten by as many as four players.

Rumors were circulating of Americans making a move on the front nine. The word through the grapevine was that Hagen was out in 35, Barnes in 36, McDermott in 37. Fans rushing out to follow those players home learned that the rumors were false: Hagen actually had a 40 on the front nine, Barnes a 41, and McDermott a 39. Granted, that was better than Vardon and Ray on the front, but all lost ground to the Englishmen on the back, Hagen finishing with an 80, Barnes a 79, and McDermott a 78. Smith's 77 also was not good enough.

Out of nowhere, it suddenly seemed the U.S. vs. Britain battle could be won by—of all things—a Frenchman. Tellier was the sole contender to successfully handle the muddy slog of the front nine, going out in three-under 35. Starting the round six strokes behind, he made the turn one ahead of Vardon's and two ahead of Ray's scores to that point on the course. The back nine gobbled up Tellier, who bogeyed both par fives and three other holes for a 41. His 76 matched the best score of the final round under the thoroughly soaked conditions, but left Tellier three strokes behind Vardon and Ray, as were Barnes, Hagen, and Smith, with McDermott one stroke further back.

As player after player dragged themselves into the clubhouse, shaking the rain off their drenched clothing, it appeared more and more likely that Vardon and Ray would square off in a playoff for the title.

Only one man remained with a chance—Ouimet. It was an outside chance at that, after he struggled to a 43 on the front nine. He double bogeyed the fifth, taking two to get out of a bunker, and bogeyed the sixth. His ball found another bunker on the eighth, coming to rest in a depression made by another player that had not been smoothed out. He had to play backward and ended up with another double bogey.

The round went from bad to worse with another double bogey on the par-three 10th. The conditions were a factor. In an attempt to avoid lofting a high shot to the soaked green and risk the ball plugging in its own pitch-mark, he took more club and tried to hit a low shot. He couldn't properly execute the finesse shot, however, topping it well short of the green, and then three-putted.

Through 10 holes, Ouimet was seven-over for the round. He would need to play the last eight holes in two-under, hardly a likely prospect in a round with an average score of 82.1.

The *Times of London*'s Darwin later wrote that "as I splashed out in the mud and rain to meet Ouimet, I was already composing sentences to telegraph home, to the effect that he had fought a great fight, but the burden had just been too heavy for him to bear."

The best birdie chance was the par-five 12th hole, and Ouimet had to settle for a par there after hitting his second shot into a bunker, leaving him little chance to get the third close. He then missed the green to the right on the 320-yard 13th—and chipped in from 30 feet for a birdie.

The gallery—with all of the other contenders finished—was now following Ouimet and trying to root him home. When the chip shot dropped, they let out a tremendous cheer. Vardon and Ray, having changed into dry clothes, heard the commotion from the clubhouse and decided to head out to watch Ouimet finish.

They saw him make a routine par on the 14th, then find trouble on the 15th when his approach shot drifted to the right, leaving a pitch over a bunker from muddy rough. A bogey here would virtually sink Ouimet's chances. He judged the lie and the green perfectly, sending the pitch within three feet of the hole to save the par.

When Francis contemplated the situation early on the back nine, he figured the 125-yard 16th hole as a place he would get one of the two necessary birdies. He misjudged the tee shot, however, knocking it to the back of the green 40 feet past the hole, perhaps powered by adrenaline. It was a tough putt to gauge on a soggy green, and he left it nine feet short. For a second consecutive hole, he stared a crushing bogey in the face. Calmly, though, he knocked it in the hole for a par.

Now Francis headed to the 360-yard 17th, the hole where he had become enamored with the game at a young age by watching members play it. He drove into the fairway and hit a nice approach to 15 feet from the hole. Darwin later related this exchange between a spectator and Ray. "He can't do it," said the spectator of the birdie putt. "I'm not so sure about that," Ray replied. "It's on the map, you know. He's a really fine golfer and I shouldn't be surprised at anything he might bring off."

Ouimet brought it off indeed, knocking the ball into the hole. "I struck that putt as firmly as any putt I ever hit," he later wrote in his autobiography, *A Game of Golf.* Pandemonium ensued.

"[The spectators] could not control themselves," Herbert Warren Wind wrote in *The Story of American Golf.* "They yelled, pummeled each other joyously, swatted their friends with umbrellas, and shouted delirious phrases they had not thought of since boyhood."

Still, nothing was assured. The 410-yard 18th hole was one of the most demanding on the course, playing across the racetrack on the relatively long second shot to an elevated green. Ouimet's approach landed near the top of the bank in front of the green. A mite farther, and it would have hopped onto the green and given him a chance for a birdie. A mite shorter, and it would have rolled down the hill onto the muddy racetrack. As it was, he faced a 40-foot chip from the fringe.

He rolled it five feet past the hole, leaving a par putt in the same range he had made in the morning. This one was even more pressure-packed, with a spot in a playoff on the line. Ouimet tapped it, the ball rolled slowly toward the hole, caught the edge, and dropped.

Again, the spectators could hardly contain themselves. When Ouimet walked off the green, they lifted him onto their shoulders and carried their new hero to the clubhouse. "Many not realizing that Ouimet was an amateur and not a professional, thrust bills of large denominations at him only to be met with a smile and a shake of the head," the *New York Times* reported.

Darwin sung the American's praises after watching how he handled the back nine. "The picture that remains to me is of the young hero playing all those last crucial shots as if he had been playing an ordinary game. He did not hurry; did not linger; there was a decisiveness about every movement, and whatever he may have felt, he did not betray it by so much as the movement of an eyelash. He was just entirely calm and entirely natural."

The young American had stood up to the game's greats and the pressures of his first U.S. Open. Now he would have to do it again the next day. What he had going for him was an enthusiastic gallery cheering him on—and a spunky 10-year-old caddie by his side.

Ouimet had stopped caddying at age 16 to preserve his amateur status, but he still had friends in the caddie corps at The Country Club, and one of them had agreed to caddie for him. On Monday morning, however, that caddie told Francis he had an offer from Tellier to caddie, and he had accepted. Caddying for a pro with the wherewithal to pay seemed like a better deal, not to mention that Tellier was accorded a reasonable chance of a high finish.

Now without caddie, Ouimet walked out of the clubhouse and saw Jack Lowery, a 12-year-old who had caddied for him at Woodland Golf Club. Jack and his little brother, Eddie, had come out to watch Vardon and Ray, but Jack agreed to caddie for Ouimet in that practice round, with little Eddie walking along.

Jack said he would caddie for Francis in the next day's qualifying. However, when the Lowery lads got home, they found a truant officer waiting for them for missing school that day. The championship was being held in the third week of September, delayed from its originally planned June dates to accommodate Vardon's and Ray's itinerary. Kids weren't supposed to skip school to caddie in or watch the U.S. Open. The Lowery boys agreed to go to school the next day. But in the morning, Eddie decided to take his chances and skip school again. He caddied for Francis in the qualifying, and vowed to do so for the week, no matter the consequences.

Eddie weighed only 70 pounds, but players were carrying less than 14 clubs in those days, and the boy was able to manage just fine. As he handed Ouimet a club before each shot, Eddie would say, "Keep your eye on the ball."

"A brighter or headier little chap would be hard to find," Ouimet wrote in *The American Golfer* magazine. "His influence on my game I cannot overestimate."

Before each round, Eddie would tell Francis that he was going to shoot a 72. For Saturday's 18-hole playoff, Lowery didn't have to skip school. And he wore a red, white, and blue ribbon on his lapel. "You've just got to beat those fellows, Francis. They never can take the championship across the water with them!" Ouimet wrote in the *Boston Globe*, revealing what Eddie had said to him before the round. "Those words from a 10-year-old boy inspired me to outdo myself," Ouimet wrote.

Tellingly, that thought didn't cause the moderately tempered Ouimet to become overhyped. It only intensified his focus. "I determined then and there, before a stroke had been played, that I would forget my opponents throughout the round and play the game that I felt I was capable of playing," he wrote.

He did just that, hitting his shots with nearly unerring accuracy and recovering well from his one poor stroke. Instead of the veterans grinding down the young amateur with relentless play, it was the other way around.

All made relatively routine pars on the first two holes, with only Ray requiring a one-putt after a fairly easy chip shot on the first hole, where he had driven to the right. Ouimet later admitted he was nervous on his second putt on the first hole, a three-footer, but he knocked it in.

The trio struck the ball very well on the 435-yard, par-five third. Ray was on the fringe in two and Vardon on the green when Ouimet hit his second shot, finishing inside Harry. Ray chipped on and missed a four-foot putt, losing a stroke to the two-putt birdies of Vardon and Ouimet, the latter nearly holing his eagle try. All parred the fourth, Ouimet needing to make a four-foot second putt after leaving the first one short.

The fifth hole, a 420-yard par four, was perhaps the hardest on the course. Ouimet made it even harder when he push-sliced his fairway wood second shot out of bounds to the right. Crucially, after the distance-only penalty, he hit the right edge of the green with his third stroke. Vardon missed the green to the right; Ray was left and short. Neither got up and down, while Francis knocked his fourth shot close and tapped in for a bogey that tied the others. It must have felt like a win after the out-of-bounds shot.

Vardon birdied the short par-four sixth, holing an eight-foot putt, after Ouimet and Ray missed from inside 20 feet. Harry was in front at one-under, with Ouimet even, and Ray one-over.

It mercifully wasn't raining this day but, following 30 hours of precipitation, the course was still soggy. Ouimet, facing a 40-foot birdie putt on the seventh hole, thought the green would play very slow. It was not as slow as it appeared. He knocked the putt 12 feet past and missed coming back. Vardon missed the green and made a bogey, while Ray parred to pull even with Ouimet, one behind.

The 380-yard eighth hole played uphill to an elevated green. The surface of the green wasn't visible from the fairway, but when Ouimet's second shot elicited what Darwin termed a "wild war whoop" from the gallery near the green, those below knew that it must be close to the hole. It was, in fact, a mere foot from the cup, a magnificent shot. Ray then holed a 35-foot putt to match Ouimet's birdie. The trio were now tied at even par. The quality of the golf was excellent.

Vardon hooked his drive on the par-five ninth and laid up short of a creek, leaving a long-iron third. He hit a good one, but it bounded over the green. A chip left a three-foot par putt, the type he had been struggling with, but he made it for a par. The 520-yard hole wasn't reachable in two, even for as long a hitter as Ray, and he and Ouimet made two-putt pars.

All three hit their tee shots in the 25-to-35-foot range on the par-three 10th. As bad luck would have it, both Vardon and Ray had the pitch-marks made by their tee shots directly in their putting line. There was no rule allowing repair of pitch-marks, though the USGA had instituted a local rule for this day allowing players to lift a ball on the green that was stuck in its own pitch-mark. Forced to aim to the side, they left their first putts four and six feet from the hole, respectively, and both missed. Ouimet, with a two-putt par, led them both by one.

There was no change on the 11th, Ray narrowly missing a 15-foot birdie putt while the others also parred. Ouimet stuck a decisive blow on the 12th—two, actually. The first came with his tee shot, which he belted longer than Ray's. That left an iron to the 415-yard par five, and he knocked that one to within 12 feet of the hole. Vardon and Ray had both been in range of the green from farther away, but Vardon missed to the left and Ray was short and right. Neither got up and down, and Ouimet's two-putt birdie extended his margin to two over both opponents.

Vardon was too good a player, and too tough a competitor, to fade away quietly. He made a 12-foot birdie putt on the 320-yard 13th, and when Ouimet missed a 10-footer for a birdie, the veteran was within one.

With the tension mounting, all three messed up one of their shots on the par-five 14th. Vardon hit his drive into the left rough and had to lay up well short of the green. Ouimet half-topped his second shot, failing to carry a hill in front of him, and leaving himself a longer third than Vardon. Ray sliced his second shot into the trees short and right of the green. Ouimet and Vardon hit the green with their third shots, as did Ray, with a punch shot through a narrow opening between trees, earning applause from the gallery. The end result was three pars—but Ray's errant second shot gave Ouimet the impression that it was primarily Vardon he had to fear.

Ray proved the assumption correct on the next hole. His tee shot hit a spectator and fortunately deflected into the fairway. He didn't take advantage of the break, coming up short with his approach shot and finishing in a deep bunker. It took two strokes to get out, and a double bogey essentially ended Ray's chances. It still remained, however, a tight battle between Ouimet and Vardon. Both narrowly missed the green, then matched each other with good chip shots and short putts for pars.

Ouimet maintained his one-stroke margin when he and Vardon parred the 125-yard 16th, Francis two-putting from 20 feet and Vardon from 15, his birdie try just missing. The amateur's nerves were holding up better than could reasonably be expected. Now, he headed to the hole where he had made the clutch birdie in the fourth round.

It was Vardon who cracked. Trying to cut the corner and leave himself a shorter approach shot on the 360-yard hole, he hit his drive a bit too far to the left and not quite long enough. The ball came to rest in a bunker at the elbow of the dogleg, with no chance to reach the green. Ouimet played his drive safely into the center of the fairway.

While Vardon was on his way to a bogey, Ouimet hit his second shot to 18 feet. Fittingly, the kid provided the denouement on the hole across the road from his house, rolling in a birdie putt for the second straight day. Again, the gallery went bonkers.

Ouimet wrapped it up with a par on 18, while a dispirited Vardon hit his second shot into the muddy racetrack and made a double bogey. Meanwhile, Ray stroked in a moot birdie. The final tally read

Ouimet 72, Vardon 77, Ray 78. It was a decisive victory, though the final margin betrayed how closely fought it had been for most of the round. In the end, it was the pros who came undone, while Ouimet continued to deliver quality shot after quality shot—and posted the 72 that his caddie had been predicting, with a 34 on the back nine.

Francis earned another ride on the shoulders of his boisterous fans. When they finally brought him back to earth, they collected money to pay his caddie and came up with $54.10 for Eddie. As an amateur, Ouimet was awarded a plate worth $300 in lieu of first prize money of that amount. Vardon was paid $150 for finishing second and Ray $125 for third.

"When the tournament started, the thought of winning such an event never entered my head," Ouimet wrote in *Golf* magazine.

Nor did many think he could prevail in the playoff. "He was one David against two Goliaths," is how Darwin later put it. "Mr. Ouimet's 72 in that weather and on that muddy course was just about as good a single round as ever was played. I thought then and I think now that it would have beaten anybody."

Ouimet didn't go on to become one of the game's greats. He remained an amateur, winning the U.S. Amateur twice, and only played in five more U.S. Opens, with a best finish of third. But his storybook week in his hometown will never be forgotten.

TOP-10 FINISHERS			
1	Francis Ouimet	77-74-74-79—304*
2	Harry Vardon	75-72-78-79—304
3	Edward Ray	79-70-76-79—304
T4	James Barnes	74-76-78-79—307
T4	Walter Hagen	73-78-76-80—307
T4	Macdonald Smith	71-79-80-77—307
T4	Louis Tellier	76-76-79-76—307
8	John McDermott	74-79-77-78—308
9	Herbert Strong	75-74-82-79—310
10	Pat Doyle	78-80-73-80—311

*Ouimet won playoff, 72, Vardon 77, Ray 78

1923

BOBBY'S BREAKTHROUGH

With entries reaching 360 players, four days of 36-hole qualifying were held on Monday through Thursday at the championship site, Inwood Country Club just southeast of New York City near the south shore of Long Island. Ninety players competed each day, with the top 18 and ties qualifying for the main event, where they would play 36 holes on Friday and 36 more on Saturday. The qualifying rounds were an integral part of the week, drawing large crowds each day and previewing the contenders for the championship.

The qualifiers on Monday were led by 21-year-old defending U.S. Open champion Gene Sarazen, who had added the PGA Championship to his Open title in 1922 to stamp himself as a young phenom. The New York native, who grew up just north of the city in Westchester County, had rounds of 73 and 75 for a 148 total that led by three strokes. He avoided the embarrassment that he experienced earlier in the year at the British Open, where he failed to get through the qualifying at Troon, thus wasting a trans-Atlantic trip. His confidence regained, Sarazen told George Trevor of the *Brooklyn Daily Eagle*, "I think I'm going to win this."

Tuesday's action featured a course-record 70 by Joe Kirkwood, a 26-year-old Australian, whose 144 total led by a whopping 10 shots. He had played some in America in 1921 and 1922, and more extensively in 1923, when he claimed his first three victories on the U.S. tour early in the year. He also was making a name for himself giving exhibitions as a trick-shot artist.

Folks thought they might see a trick shot on the ninth hole of the second round, when Kirkwood's ball came to rest partly under a tall boundary fence with a small gap at the bottom. The ball was ruled in bounds, but Kirkwood had to go over the fence to be able to play it, which involved climbing up a tree and dropping over on the other side. He was just able to punch the ball into safety rather than trying for a spectacular shot at the green. Then, unable to get back over the fence, he had to wait for a car to take him up the road to the club entrance to return to the course.

Walter Hagen, the 1914 and 1919 champion and a vibrant person-ality, helped draw 12,000 spectators to the qualifying on Wednesday. He made it through, but in unimpressive fashion with a 156 total, just three strokes inside the qualifying line. "Hagen gave a dramatically realistic picture of a man exploring darkest Africa without a map or a compass in his possession," wrote William D. Richardson in the *New York Times*, noting that he wore a sun helmet in the afternoon round. Only Hagen's putting saved him. He played with Macdonald Smith, whose much less adventurous play gave him a 150 to lead the day's qualifiers by three strokes.

Amateur Bobby Jones was the attraction on the fourth day of qualifying, but he was no more impressive than Hagen had been, also posting a 156 total that was six behind co-leaders Jim Barnes, the 1921 champion, and Johnny Farrell, who would win in 1928. Jones had come to Inwood the previous week for practice and wasn't at all pleased with his game.

"My first practice rounds at Inwood were terrible," he wrote in his autobiography *Down the Fairway*. "I was continually in trouble from the tee, and it was hard to get under 80. I was fearfully depressed."

Jones had developed a reputation for not being able to win the big one. He had lost in the final of the U.S. Amateur in 1919 and the semifinals in 1920 and 1922. He was the co-leader through 54 holes of the 1922 U.S. Open before finishing T2, one stroke behind Sara-zen. He was still looking for his first national title, and the strain was wearing on him. "The full heft of responsibility seems to have hit me, at Inwood—the idea of being a great golfer (as people kept saying) who couldn't win," he wrote.

In retrospect, perhaps those critics could have cut Jones some slack—or maybe just acknowledged that he was only 21 years old.

Jones played with Bobby Cruickshank in the qualifying. The Scottish pro opened with a 73, so his blowup to an 84 in the afternoon round didn't keep him from making it to the championship proper. As it turned out, the two would battle for the title.

The first 36-hole day of the championship, however, belonged to Jock Hutchison, a 39-year-old native of St. Andrews, Scotland, who emigrated to America in 1905. Hutchison had overcome some near misses of his own in big events to win the PGA Championship in 1920 and the British Open in 1921. At Inwood, he birdied three of the first four holes and shot a first-round 70 to tie Kirkwood's recently set course record. Hutchison made six birdies in a more erratic round of even-par 72 in the afternoon, giving him 10 birdies in 36 holes, an extraordinary total for that era.

"Never have we seen Jock in a more confident mood. His chest was out like a pouter pigeon's," Richardson wrote in his *New York Times* report.

For his part, Jones regained some confidence in his own game, and shot strong rounds of 71-73—144 to claim second place. He had a two-under 33 on the back nine in the first round, the best of the day, with birdies on 14 and 18 to go with seven pars. He birdied 18 again in the second round, quite a feat since the 425-yard par four with a moat of water guarding the green was one of the hardest holes at Inwood. His second round was also highlighted by a jaw-dropping shot over trees to three feet from an adjacent fairway to birdie the ninth yet sullied by three three-putts.

Cruickshank was next at 145 with rounds of 73-72. He was steady in the morning with two bogeys and one birdie. In the second round, he overcame a double bogey at the second with birdies at the third and fourth on Inwood's unique layout with three consecutive par fives on Nos. 3 to 5. He bogeyed the seventh, then rebounded with two birdies on the back nine against a lone bogey.

The 28-year-old Cruickshank, who had escaped from a German POW camp during World War I, moved to the U.S. in 1921, one of many Scotsmen to see America as the land of golf opportunity. He became a pro at Shackamaxon Country Club in New Jersey, while also playing in the early days of a pro tour, which was then a hodge-podge of events under the PGA umbrella. So far, he had two wins to show for it, both in 1921.

Nobody else scored better than 148 on a tight Inwood course that punished off-line shots. It was a rough day for many of the favor-ites. Hagen, who won the 1921 PGA Championship at Inwood, was at 152 after uncharacteristic putting problems. The daily qualify-ing leaders were even further back—Farrell and Smith at 153, Kirk-wood at 154, Sarazen at 157, and Barnes at 159. It was looking like a three-horse race.

On the 36-hole Saturday, it became a two-horse race. Hutchison's game mysteriously abandoned him as he ballooned to an 82 with a triple bogey and two double bogeys in the third round and a 78 in the fourth. Hagen managed to pull within five strokes with a 73 in the morning, only to totally lose it in a final-round 86. Sarazen also had a 73 in the third round, but he had started too far back and, in any case, shot an 80 in the fourth round. Two months later, Sarazen would beat Hagen in a classic 38-hole final match at the PGA Championship. At this U.S. Open, Sarazen finished T16 and Hagen T18.

With Hutchison's retreat, Jones moved into the lead with a 76 in the morning for a 220 total that was three ahead of Cruickshank, who managed only a 78, and was four clear of Hutchinson. The lead-ing duo struggled on the front nine before recovering on the back to take control.

Jones was four-over through seven holes, with bogeys on Nos. 2 and 6, a double bogey on the tough, 223-yard seventh, and no birdies on the trio of par fives. He played even par from there with a birdie on 14 and a bogey on 15.

"As I now learned, the third round in an open championship is a great one for blowing up, and if you find yourself going a bit sourly under the pressure, the thing to do is to stick to your business and save all the strokes you can," Jones wrote in *Down the Fairway*. "I was surprised to find I was out in front by three strokes."

Cruickshank's start was even worse. He double bogeyed the second, then went bogey-par-double bogey on the par-five stretch from Nos. 3 to 5. On the latter hole, he hit a wild third shot from a fairway bunker that settled near a refreshment stand and he took two more to reach the green.

"I was ready to cry a bit after that, but something seemed to say to me, 'Keep on, you bloomin' bounder, there's always a chance.' So I grit my teeth and went on," Cruickshank told a newspaper reporter. The Scotsman finished the front nine with four pars, then three birdies and four bogeys in a wild back nine, with a birdie on 18 to end on a good note.

Jones's fourth-round tee time was an hour-and-a-half before Cruickshank's. With nobody else seriously in the hunt, it became a matter of the American amateur setting the target and the Scottish pro seeing if he could beat it or match it.

Jones bogeyed the first hole, then got the stroke back with a two-putt birdie on the fifth, nearly making an eagle. The long par-three seventh was a setback; his tee shot hitting a spectator and caroming out of bounds. He did well to escape with a double bogey.

Early on the back nine, it appeared Jones was moving within sight of his first major title. He birdied the 10th from 18 feet, saved par with a 10-foot putt at the 11th, got up and down for pars out of bunkers on Nos. 12 and 15, and made a fairly routine birdie on the par-five 14th. That put him even par for the round, and if he could finish that way there was almost no chance Cruickshank could catch him.

As Jones would admit in his autobiography, the burden of leading weighed on him down the stretch. He pull-hooked his iron approach on the par-four 16th out of bounds onto an adjacent road. The young amateur then caught a break when his next shot bounced off a mound next to the green and finished six feet from the hole. He sank the putt to survive the stroke-and-distance penalty with a bogey. Another bogey followed on 17, where he drove into the left rough, missed the green, pitched on, and two-putted.

The 18th was a disaster. Jones drove into the fairway, but relatively short. He carried the water with his fairway-wood second shot, but it went wayward, landing far left among the spectators and finishing between posts connected by a chain near the 12th tee. The chain was removed so Jones could play his third shot, creating a delay during which he "sat on the turf for five minutes and brooded over my rotten play," he later wrote.

He chunked the pitch shot into an intervening bunker, blasted out, and two-putted for a deflating double bogey. Jones looked crestfallen coming off the green. O.B. Keeler, who chronicled Jones's play for an Atlanta newspaper and was also a friend, tried to put a positive spin on things.

"Bob, I think you're champion. Cruickshank will never catch you," Keeler encouraged.

"Well, I didn't finish like a champion," Jones replied. "I finished like a yellow dog."

By going four-over par on the last three holes, Jones finished with a 76. Cruickshank needed an even-par 72 to win outright or a 73 to tie.

Cruickshank was on the front nine when Jones finished. He was even par for the round through six holes with a bogey at the first and an approach to one foot for a birdie at the sixth. He got a break on the par-three seventh, where his tee shot finished a yard from a water hazard, and he was able to pitch close and save par. Cruickshank put himself in great position with a birdie on the eighth from 10 feet and another on the 10th, a 295-yard par four. He drove near the green, and his pitch shot hit the flagstick to end up three feet away instead of well past.

On reaching the 13th tee at two-under for the round, and informed of Jones's finishing total, he knew he could go two-over the rest of the way and win. What followed was a stretch of four holes as bad as Jones's finishing collapse. Cruickshank missed the green on 13 and stubbed a chip, making a bogey. Another poor chip from the fringe on 15 and a missed 10-foot putt gave him another bogey.

Worse was to come on 16. The Scottish pro missed the green to the right and chipped weakly, leaving a 20-footer. "I could see his hands twitch and shake as he took his stance to putt, and the putt was never on the line," wrote Keeler, who had been watching Cruickshank since the sixth hole. The putt finished two feet to the left of the hole, and Cruickshank missed that little one, making a double bogey. Now he needed to play the last two holes, both par fours, in one-under to tie.

Keeler walked to the nearby clubhouse to give Jones the news and ran into 1913 champion Francis Ouimet, who was rooming with Jones for the week and finished T29. Asked if Jones was safe, Ouimet replied, "No man on earth could play those two holes in seven shots under these circumstances."

A USGA official asked Jones to come to the 18th green to be ready to receive the championship trophy.

"Not me," Jones responded. "I'll wait until the last putt is down."

Cruickshank parred 17 and hit a 250-yard drive into the fairway on 18. Needing an unlikely birdie, he pulled out an iron and sent the ball soaring toward the green 175 yards away. It cleared the water and, right on target, came to a stop six feet behind the hole. He had to make his way through an excited gallery to reach the green, the spectators eventually settling down when Cruickshank prepared to putt. He knocked the pressure-packed putt into the hole for a final-round 73, setting up an 18-hole playoff with Jones the next day.

"A cheer went up, hats went into the air, and there was a mad rush to shake the hand of the little player who had accomplished the seemingly impossible," the Associated Press reported.

In the *Brooklyn Daily Eagle*, Trevor wrote of Cruickshank's shot to the 18th that "...we will always consider [it] the greatest shot we ever saw. Personally we doubt, considering that a championship depended on this single shot, whether a better one has ever been made by anyone."

Sizing up the playoff prospects, Trevor would report (after the playoff's conclusion) that one expert put it this way: "Never has Jones come through when victory hinged on his efforts. He'll break down this time, sure as you live. Just watch and see for yourself. The boy lacks grit."

For his part, a distraught Jones said, "I never can forgive myself for that disgraceful exhibition on the last few holes. All I ask now is a chance to show my friends and my enemies that I'm no quitter."

Cruickshank was a 10-to-7 favorite in the playoff, not so much because of a distinguished record on his part—he was still early in what would become a successful career with 17 tour wins—but rather as a reflection of Jones's track record of coming up short in championships and his poor finish in the fourth round.

The playoff drew a crowd estimated at nearly 10,000, whom Keeler described "insane golf fans." It was near pandemonium, with that many people following a twosome at a time when there were no gallery ropes. They witnessed a thrilling battle in which the two Bobbys carded the same score on only three holes. They remained within one stroke of each other or tied for all but three holes (where one of them was just two ahead). "It is impossible in cold type to depict the strain and tension of that round," Keeler wrote in his book, *The Bobby Jones Story*.

Cruickshank fell behind on the first hole when he drove left into a ditch leaving him with a nearly sideways pitch to get in the fairway. He bogeyed, while Jones missed a chance to go ahead by two as a six-foot birdie putt didn't drop. The Scotsman quickly squared it with a birdie on the par-four second from seven feet.

The consecutive trio of par fives played similarly on the first two shots, with Cruickshank about 10 yards short of the green in two, while Jones reached either a greenside bunker or greenside rough on each. Jones got up and down for a birdie on the fourth but missed birdie attempts of 10 feet or less on Nos. 3 and 5. Cruickshank parred the fourth and birdied the third from 10 feet and the fifth from 18 feet, giving him a one-stroke lead though five holes at two-under with three birdies. He went ahead by two at the sixth when Jones bogeyed, missing a three-foot putt.

The seventh hole brought the first of two bold decisions that would pay off for Jones. No. 7 was a brutal par three: 223 yards with out of bounds on both sides. It had taken a heavy toll on players during the week, with many double and triple bogeys, including doubles by Jones in the third and fourth rounds. Cruickshank elected to play short of the green with an iron while Jones decided to chance the O.B. trouble by hitting a fairway wood. The Atlanta amateur executed it beautifully by hitting the green just 20 feet from the hole. He pulled back within one stroke by making a par while Cruickshank pitched to eight feet and two-putted for a bogey.

Finally, on the eighth hole, both carded the same score for the first time, coming away with pars. Cruickshank bogeyed the par-four ninth, going over the green in two, chipping nicely to four feet, and missing the putt. Each player finished the front nine with an even-par 37.

Up to that point, the golf had been very good, but both players were shakier on the back nine, especially at the beginning. On the short par-four 10th, which should have provided a birdie chance, Cruickshank drove into the rough, hit his second shot over the green, and then chipped through the green, chipped again, and two-putted for a double bogey. Jones hit his drive into a fairway bunker, clipped a tree with his second, and made a bogey, gaining a stroke. Both bogeyed the par-four 11th, hitting into the same bunker to the left of the green on the approach.

The 12th was a par three of just 108 yards and Jones hit his tee shot to two feet. When his opponent managed only a two-putt par, Jones had his first two-stroke lead of the day.

Cruickshank avoided falling three behind when he saved par out of a bunker on 13, making a 12-foot putt. He pulled back to within one with a birdie on the par-five 14th. Both were on the green in two, but Jones three-putted from 50 feet for a par.

With tension tightening by the minute, both players faltered on the par-four 15th. Cruickshank found a bunker and bogeyed, yet gained a stroke when Jones missed the green, flubbed a chip, and made a double bogey. Now both were three-over for the round.

They went four-over through 17 after trading bogeys, Cruickshank on 16 and Jones on 17, both from bunkers. A fine bunker shot to two feet on 17 enabled Cruickshank to make a par and send the duo to the 18th tee tied.

The Scotsman was up first, and the pressure seemed to get to him. He half-topped and hooked his drive, which traveled only 150 yards and finished in the left rough behind a tree. He would have no chance to reach the green in two. Jones's drive was better, but not great, finishing 190 yards from the green in the rough, sitting in a dirt patch.

Cruickshank punched out to the fairway short of the water front-ing the green. Now Jones had a decision. He could play safe and leave himself in the same position as his rival. Or he could go for the green, risking that even a slight mishit would send the shot into the water and quite possibly lose the championship.

Though it seemed like a tough choice, Jones showed no hesitation whatsoever in grabbing his mid iron. In those days, when clubs were named instead of numbered, the club called the mid iron was actually the longest iron in the bag, with loft equivalent to a modern two-iron and probably as hard to hit as the notoriously challenging modern one-iron. Jones's caddie, Luke Ross, and teacher Stewart Maiden, who was in the gallery, both said they had never seen Jones play a shot more quickly or decisively.

The ball flew off the clubface "as perfectly hit and as bold a shot as ever came off a golf club," wrote Keeler, straight at the flag, carrying the moat, bouncing on the green, and rolling to six feet from the hole as the spectators roared.

Cruickshank pulled his pitch shot into the same bunker that Jones visited the previous day, came out to 20 feet, two-putted for a double bogey, and shook Jones's hand. All that remained was for Jones to cozy his six-footer close to the hole, tap in for par, and claim the first of his eventual four U.S. Open titles. He was carried to the clubhouse on the shoulders of a rapturous gallery.

Trevor had to take back what he had written in his report on the final round. "On Sunday we wrote that Cruickshank's iron shot to this home green was the greatest shot we had ever seen, but that was before we saw Bobby Jones come through with his super-stroke. This mid-iron clout of Jones will go thundering through the ages! ... Into that shot, Bobby put all the pent-up energy of four long years of ceaseless striving."

For Jones, Cruickshank's birdie on the 72nd hole to tie was per-haps a blessing in disguise. Instead of winning the U.S. Open despite staggering down the stretch, he won with a spectacular shot, deliver-ing in the tensest of moments.

As Keeler would write, "They said Bobby Jones could not win because he didn't have the punch. They said he was the greatest golfer in the world but he lacked the punch. We had heard it a thousand times, but we never had to hear it again. One stroke settled that little matter forever and ever."

TOP-10 FINISHERS		
1	Bobby Jones	71-73-76-76—296*
2	Bobby Cruickshank	73-72-78-73—296
3	Jock Hutchison	70-72-80-78—302
4	Jack Forrester	75-73-77-78—303
T5	Johnny Farrell	76-77-75-76—304
T5	Francis Gallett	76-72-77-79—304
T5	W.M. Reekie	80-74-75-75—304
T8	Leo Diegel	77-77-76-76—306
T8	William Mehlhorn	73-79-75-79—306
T8	Al Watrous	74-75-76-81—306

*Jones won playoff, 76-78

1930

JONES IS GRAND

B obby Jones entered the U.S. Open fresh off a trip to the UK that had netted him titles at the British Amateur and British Open. The prospect of adding victories at the U.S. Open and U.S. Amateur for a Grand Slam year was tantalizing and thus made the U.S. Open perhaps golf's most highly anticipated event to date. And, certainly, the one most focused on a single player.

"It is the field against one man—Bobby Jones. Nothing like this has ever happened in golf, from the days of Vardon and Taylor and Braid to the present moment. It is almost unbelievable, but it is true," asserted Walter Hagen in a pre-tournament radio interview. And this from a man who won the U.S. Open in 1914 and 1919 and, in the 1920s, captured five PGA Championships and four British Opens. The last of those major titles had come as recently as 1929. Despite still being a crowd-pleasing showman, the Haig—at least as this U.S. Open neared—was simply an afterthought.

The British double wasn't the only reason all eyes were fixed on Jones. He was on a remarkable run in the U.S. Open, having finished first or second in seven of the last eight years. He was second in 1922, scored his breakthrough victory in 1923 at Inwood, second in 1924, lost a playoff in 1925, won in 1926, lost a playoff in 1928, and won a playoff in 1929.

If there were any hope for the field, it was in Jones's preparation for the championship, which wasn't ideal. He was coming off a nearly two-month trip to Britain (including ship travel) where he led the

U.S. team in the Walker Cup before his British Amateur and Open triumphs. His return to the U.S. was marked by a ticker-tape parade in New York City. From there, he hopped on a train for Minneapolis, arriving at 8:50 a.m. on the Saturday before the U.S. Open at Interlachen Country Club.

"With only three or four days of practice available, my clubs had a strange feel, and I was finding it difficult to get back into the habit of thinking about golf," Jones wrote in his book *Golf Is My Game.* "I was not playing really badly in practice, but I was very aware that the keenness was not present."

In an informal poll of the field, Jones wasn't universally picked to win. It was felt that the strain of vying for the Slam, along with the effects of travel, might be too much. However, it may also have been a matter of wishful thinking among some professionals who were tired of an amateur stealing the show. Hagen was tabbed by many as the favorite, with Horton Smith also getting some mentions.

Smith was a 22-year-old who had come out of Missouri to take the tour by storm. He won seven times on the 1928-29 winter tour that was then a feature of the PGA schedule and five times in 1929-30 to stamp himself as the top professional of the moment. Notably, he had beaten Jones in the Savannah Open in February, one of two open events that Bobby had played in his native Georgia that winter. Of course, it should be noted that Jones won the Southeastern Open in Augusta in the following week by 13 strokes over a field of top pros, including Smith, who was runner-up. They were Jones's only U.S. appearances before the U.S. Open.

Smith's overnight success had led to an exhibition tour with Hagen in 1929, which was how the very top pros made money in those days. Both were managed by Bob Harlow, later the PGA's tournament director. The *Atlanta Constitution* reported that Harlow had bet $2,000 that either Hagen or Smith would beat Jones at Interlachen. He didn't have much trouble finding someone to take the other side.

Jones played 36 holes at Interlachen on the Sunday before the Open, and in a Monday practice round he broke the course record with a 70. By Wednesday, he told his Atlanta chronicler and friend, O.B. Keeler, that for the first time since the Southeastern Open in

Augusta he felt his entire game had come together. He wasn't espe-cially sharp with his long game in the British events, while manag-ing to prevail in both, which had been noted by those who didn't favor him winning the U.S. Open.

A first-round 71 showed that his game was in fine shape. "All those rumors that have been going around concerning the strained rela-tionship between Bobby Jones and his golf clubs seem to have been greatly exaggerated," William D. Richardson wrote in the *New York Times*. The Associated Press called it, "as fine an exhibition off the tees and through the fairways as he has ever given."

Jones missed only three fairways, two of them by about a foot. He birdied the two par fives on the front nine, one of them on a two-putt, bogeyed the 10th, and parred the other 15 holes. He gave himself many birdie chances, leaving three of them on the front lip as he putted conservatively.

It was a fine round despite the intense heat, with temperatures reaching between 95 and 105 degrees (depending on the source of information). Jones wore a red tie that, by the end of the round, had bled into his white shirt. The necktie was so soaked with sweat that Keeler had to cut it off with a pocketknife.

On a day when ten spectators were treated by the Red Cross for heat prostration, 1927 U.S. Open champion Tommy Armour sent a messenger to the clubhouse for a bag of ice after playing four holes. The rest of the way, he rubbed the ice on his face and forehead before each shot. It worked, as he carded a 70 to earn a share of the lead. He managed to stay fresh all the way to the end, shooting a 33 on the back nine with an eagle on the par-five 11th and a birdie from six feet on the 18th.

Also shooting a 70 with a 33 on the back nine, despite bogeying 18, was 40-year-old Macdonald Smith. Way back in 1910, at the age of 20, Smith had lost the U.S. Open to his brother Alex in a three-way playoff. He played almost no tournament golf from 1915 to 1922, then from 1924 through 1929 scored multiple wins on tour every year except one and finished T2 to Jones at the 1930 British Open, his fourth top-five finish in that event.

Hagen and Horton Smith were in good shape with 72s. Hagen recovered with a 34 on the back nine after going out in 38 with a double bogey on the eighth hole. Smith, on the other hand, missed a shot at the lead as he bogeyed 17 and 18.

The strangest round belonged to 1928 U.S. Open champion Johnny Farrell. He started with a quadruple bogey eight on the first hole and bogeyed the par-five fourth yet escaped the front nine with a 36 thanks to five birdies, including four in a row on Nos. 6 to 9. A 38 on the back left him with a 74. Gene Sarazen, the 1922 champion, double bogeyed the 18th hole for a 76 and would never be a factor.

It wasn't quite as oppressive on Friday, but it was still quite warm, and Jones wore a shirt designed with an untucked tail. He was followed by a large gallery, but as the day developed word spread that Horton Smith, in the twosome ahead, was making a strong move. Many fans started running back and forth to catch the action of both Smith and Jones, who were reprising their battles at the two Georgia events earlier that year.

Smith took the lead with a 70, a round especially impressive for its ball-striking. "It was as fine a round of golf as anyone has seen in an Open championship," wrote Grantland Rice, who went on to credit Smith for the "unique idea" of continually hitting his drives in the middle of the fairway and his iron shots six to eight feet from the pin.

Many of those birdie putts didn't find the cup, but he made up for it by holing from 20 feet for an eagle on the par-five ninth after a two-iron approach. Combined with a birdie at the second and a string of effortless pars, it gave Smith a 33 on the front nine and the lead.

Jones gave the fans a different kind of thrill on the 485-yard ninth. He hit a decent drive down the right side of the fairway and pulled out a fairway wood for his second shot. A pond intervened between him and the green, but it shouldn't have been in play, because the water stopped some 40 yards before the putting surface. At the top of his backswing, he noticed movement in the gallery just ahead of him; someone had leapt onto the fairway. There were no ropes to constrain the galleries in those days, though, at Interlachen, marshals attempted to corral the throngs with long bamboo poles. Distracted,

Jones half-topped the shot. The ball dived into the pond, then took two skips long skips across the water, climbed the bank on the other side, and ended up in the fairway. He pitched within two feet of the hole and walked away with a birdie.

The shot became known as the Lily Pad Shot since some believed the ball stayed above the water because it hit a lily pad. In fact, no lily pad was necessary. A low shot with topspin will skip across water much like a thrown stone will, as seen these days at Augusta National where Masters competitors have fun in practice rounds skipping balls across the water on the 16th hole.

The birdie gave Jones a 34 on the front nine and tied him for the lead. He had bogeyed the first hole before rebounding with birdies on the fourth (up-and-down from just short of the green in two) and fifth (25-foot putt).

Jones cooled off on the back nine, failing to birdie either of the par-five 11th and 12th and playing the last six holes in three-over. He went over the green and bogeyed No. 13. He doubled bogeyed the par-four 15th with a drive into deep rough, a hack out to well short of the green, a pitch over the green, a chip to four feet, and two putts. A birdie on the 16th from 20 feet was followed by a bogey on 17 with a missed par attempt from eight feet. A bogey on 17 was almost routine; at 262 yards, it was the longest par three to date in the U.S. Open (and retained that distinction for many years), requiring a driver or very strong fairway wood off the tee. It was the double bogey on the 15th that Jones said really bothered him after a back-nine 39 left him with a 73, adding, "For some reason I can't figure out I haven't played that last nine any too well...And yet it is the type of nine I usually like to play."

Smith had tap-in birdies on both back-nine par fives, but with bogeys on 10, 14, and 17 settled for a 37 on the back nine and a 70 that was good for a 142 total and a two-stroke lead.

Jones was joined in second place at 144 by 1927 runner-up Harry Cooper with a second straight 72 and 23-year-old Charles Lacey, playing in his first U.S. Open, who matched Horton Smith for the best round of the day with a 70 despite a bogey on 18. The 18-hole leaders fell back, Macdonald Smith with a 75 for 145 and Armour carding a

76 for 146. Farrell was still hanging in there at 146, making it a group of formidable challengers heading into the 36-hole final day.

The amateur from Atlanta nearly blew away all of those professional challengers in a brilliant third-round 68. It could have been even better, considering Jones bogeyed 17 and 18. Still, he walked away from the third round with a five-stroke lead.

Bobby had six birdies on the first 16 holes, all on putts of six feet or less. The longest putt he made was a 10-footer for a par on the long par-four first. He took advantage of the par fives, where he made three birdies, and the shorter of the par fours, where he made three more. The first birdie came at the 506-yard fourth where he was left of the green in two and pitched to six feet. Short-iron shots to two and five feet netted birdies on Nos. 6 and 7. The ninth was an opportunity lost, as he reached a greenside bunker in two and barely got out onto the green before two-putting for a 33 on the front nine.

Jones birdied both par fives on the back nine, Nos. 11 and 12, the first on a greenside chip to two feet and the second on a longer pitch to four feet after a lay-up second shot. The final birdie came at the 315-yard 16th, where he cut the corner of the dogleg with his drive and pitched within a foot of the hole.

Of his play as the round developed, Jones later wrote, "This was my one time that I played at my very best in a championship. I felt as I think a good halfback must feel when he bursts through a line of scrimmage and finds the safety man pulled out of position, sees an open field ahead of him, and feels confident he has the speed to reach the goal."

A bogey on the 17th was not unexpected, as the hole effectively played as a par three-and-a-half or more. His bogey on the 18th was more worrisome. There, he drove into the right trees, punched out, and knocked his third over the green before chipping on and one-putting.

Jones's 54-hole total of four-under 212 was the best in a U.S. Open to date. Cooper was the closest pursuer at 217 after a wild 73 that included five birdies and six bogeys. Horton Smith was in good shape after a 36 on the front nine before slipping with a 40 on the back. He double bogeyed the 17th after a tee shot into a clump of trees and was six strokes behind along with Johnny Golden, who had a 71. Farrell and Macdonald Smith could cling only to small hopes, seven strokes in arrears with a 73 and 74, respectively.

The final round also ushered in a sports broadcasting milestone. CBS radio announcer Ted Husing was equipped with a portable transmitter and a microphone, enabling him to describe the action from the course, which was a first. Unfortunately, it turned out to be a missed opportunity.

The nationwide broadcast was scheduled for 5 p.m. to 7 p.m. local time. In those days, the USGA spread the leaders throughout the field instead of clustering them in the final tee times. Failing to take advantage of the potential for media exposure, the USGA had Jones go off first among the contenders—so early that he finished before CBS went on the air. The broadcast also started 10 minutes late to accommodate coverage of a big horse race. In any case Jones had already walked off the final green before the scheduled 5 p.m. start. Husing ended up reporting only from the 18th green, with runners relaying news to him of action on the course. The broadcast was spiced with interviews of players after they finished, conducted in a studio in the clubhouse, but Jones wasn't among the interviewees after shooting a 75 that opened the door to challengers.

In his writings, Jones often stated that he played better when coming from behind and was less comfortable when protecting a lead. That proved to be true on this afternoon, when Jones made three double bogeys, all on par-three holes.

Following up on his third-round football analogy, Jones wrote of the final round: "But now, if I had been that halfback in the open field, I stumbled so many times before I got to the goal line that I am sure my coach would have made me turn in my uniform before taking himself off to the hospital to recover from a heart attack."

The first small hiccup was a three-putt bogey on the second hole. That was followed by a double bogey on the 180-yard third, where his tee shot found a bunker and his escape failed to reach the green. Jones got one stroke back with a birdie at the fourth, giving him four birdies in as many rounds on the vulnerable par five.

Jones didn't birdie any of the three remaining par fives. He mis-judged the wind on the ninth, sending his fairway wood second shot so far over the green that it finished on the practice putting green, from where he pitched onto the real green and two-putted. A drive in the rough left him well short of the 11th in two, leading to another two-putt par, and on the longer 12th he missed a 10-foot birdie try. With pars on Nos. 6 to 12, Jones was two-over for the round.

Macdonald Smith was three twosomes behind on the course, and he became the longshot pursuer with the best chance. A 34 on the front nine with birdies on Nos. 3 and 9 moved the veteran cam-paigner from seven strokes back at the start of the round to within hailing distance at three behind.

Jones received word of this at the 13th tee, and promptly double bogeyed the 194-yard hole. He hit his tee shot into a bunker, very close to the face, and was unable to get out on his first attempt. Sud-denly, the lead was now down to one stroke.

Bobby displayed his resilience with a birdie on the tough, 444-yard 14th, hitting his approach to 10 feet and sinking the putt. Smith matched him with a birdie on the 12th, staying within one.

Macdonald, however, bogeyed the 13th. When Jones birdied 16, driving around the corner and pitching to four feet, he was back up by three again. He still had the formidable 17th to play.

Jones aimed his two-wood tee shot at the right side of the green, hoping to draw it in. Instead, he blocked it to the right, and the wind carried it even farther to the right, some 50 yards off line. The ball then apparently caught a branch of a tree and was deflected some-where. No one was quite sure exactly where, but it was believed to have headed toward the marshy remnants of a pond.

A crowd of people tramped through the long, dense marsh grass searching for the ball, but to no avail. The ruling of how to proceed was left to USGA official Prescott Bush, a future USGA president whose son, George H.W. Bush, would become president of the United States. Bush announced that the marsh area was a parallel water hazard, which meant Jones could drop with a one-stroke penalty in the fairway next to the hazard some 50 yards short of the green. If it had been considered a lost-ball situation, Jones would have had to return to the tee under a stroke-and-distance penalty.

The decision generated some controversy. The first problem was the status of the marshy area. Bush stated that the area of the dried-out water body had been designated a parallel water hazard by the rules committee before the start of the tournament and that players had been advised. Nobody seemed to be aware of this, however, and it didn't help that, in that era, hazards were not marked by stakes or lines. Another point of confusion was that there was no separate lateral hazard rule at that time. The standard of the water hazard rule was a penalty drop behind the hazard, with an exception made for instances where that wasn't possible.

Further muddling deliberations on the ruling was the uncertainty surrounding where the ball had actually rested. Could it be reliably considered to have been in the hazard and not have deflected elsewhere? Bush accepted the testimony of spectators that it had gone into the marsh.

Jones pitched onto the green and two-putted for a double bogey. Given the difficulty of hitting the green from the tee on the 262-yard hole, it's very likely that the ruling saved Jones a stroke compared with a stroke-and-distance penalty (in less likely scenarios, he might have made the same score with a lost-ball ruling or done two strokes worse).

Sarazen was among those feeling that Jones, whom the USGA held in high esteem, had received a questionably favorable ruling. In a newspaper column shortly after the championship, he wrote, "It seems to me that Jones, who in the eyes of the public is a good sport, should have gone back to the tee and made another drive. There is no doubt in the minds of many who witnessed the unfortunate incident that the ball was lost. The rules of golf weren't made to be interpreted on presumption."

It should be noted, however, that Sarazen didn't really know what was in the minds of the many who had witnessed the shot, whereas Bush was on the scene to hear directly from those witnesses.

Whether or not he had been given a break, Jones was now in a precarious situation, with a one-stroke lead heading to the 18th hole and Smith on the course behind him.

Jones didn't catch his approach shot to the finishing hole quite solidly, and it finished on the front of the green 40 feet short of the pin. The hole was located on a back shelf, leaving a putt that would roll up one rise, cross a plateau, and then up another rise.

A three-putt could be disastrous, and Jones would tell Keeler that he was "quivering with every muscle" as he prepared to putt, hoping just to get it close enough to not leave himself with a tough putt for a par. Instead, the ball climbed both ridges with perfect speed, took a small break on the back shelf and tumbled into the hole for a birdie. The large crowd around the 18th green went "stark mad," reported the *Minneapolis Star-Tribune.* "The marshals had to muster all their might and main to fend [Jones] from his friends. Friends gone into a delirium."

So many hats were tossed into the air that it took a while to tidy things up and restore order so Jones's fellow competitor, Joe Turnesa, could putt.

Macdonald Smith heard the roar on the 15th fairway. Now two strokes behind, he missed birdie putts in the 15-to-20-foot range on 15 and 16. He did well to par the brutal 17th, coming up short of the green and chipping to four feet. That left him needing an eagle on the 402-yard 18th and, when he didn't pull off that miracle, Jones clinched his fourth U.S. Open title.

Players remained on the course, but none had a chance. Horton Smith, with a 36 on the front nine, and Cooper, with a 37, had retained faint hopes at the turn, but they would have needed great back nines—and some degree of a collapse by Jones—to pull it off. As it turned out, Horton Smith shot a 74 to finish third, five strokes back at 292, and Cooper a 76 for fourth at 293. Macdonald Smith's 70 was an outstanding final round on an afternoon when nobody else shot better than 73, but he had started too far back.

Jones's 75 wasn't pretty, but it was good enough, especially when combined with his 68 in the morning that put him in the driver's seat. He showed his grit by bouncing back from all three of his double bogeys with birdies on the next hole. Jones's 287 total was only one stroke over the then-existing U.S. Open record set by Chick Evans in 1916.

"All I can say is I'm thankful the long two months campaign is over," Jones said afterward. "It has been more of a strain than most people believe and no one will ever know how I felt when that last long putt rolled into the cup."

There would be a two-month break before the final act of the Grand Slam quest at the U.S. Amateur. Jones won that event to sweep the Open and Amateur championships on both sides of the Atlantic, an unprecedented feat and, as it turned out, a final statement.

Tired of the grind of competitive golf, the game's greatest amateur announced his retirement at the age of 28. His U.S. Open record of four titles and four runner-up finishes in a nine-year span is perhaps his greatest legacy.

TOP-10 FINISHERS		
1	Bobby Jones	71-73-68-75—287
2	Macdonald Smith	70-75-74-70—289
3	Horton Smith	72-70-76-74—292
4	Harry Cooper	72-72-73-76—293
5	Johnny Golden	74-73-71-76—294
6	Tommy Armour	70-76-75-76—297
7	Charles Lacey	74-70-77-77—298
8	Johnny Farrell	74-72-73-80—299
T9	William Mehlhorn	76-74-75-75—300
T9	Craig Wood	73-75-72-80—300

1932

SARAZEN'S SIZZLING FINISH

G ene Sarazen became the head professional at Fresh Meadow Country Club on Long Island in 1925, and still served in that role when the PGA Championship came to the course in 1930. He went all the way to the final of that match-play event, losing 1-up to Tommy Armour in a 36-hole match when Armour won the final hole with a par.

Soon after, the A.W. Tillinghast-designed Fresh Meadow course was named the site of the 1932 U.S. Open. Sarazen, feeling that the "home-pro jinx" might have cost him the PGA Championship, promptly started looking for another job, and landed at the Lakeville Club just 10 miles away.

Sarazen had won the U.S. Open in 1922 at the age of 20, and went on to win the PGA Championship later that year and again in 1923. Since then, however, he had been frustrated in his efforts at those two events and had also failed to win the British Open. American pros didn't routinely make the trip to Britain in those days. Only the very top pros typically made the effort. Sarazen had been playing the British Open since 1928, finishing second in 1929 and third in 1931 before breaking through to win by five strokes in 1932 with a record score of 283.

The son of Italian immigrants, Sarazen learned the game as a caddie at clubs in Westchester County north of New York City. After falling short in major events for nearly a decade, he was determined to make 1932 a good year. He went on a special diet, practiced more, and built a driver twice as heavy as his regular one, figuring that swinging it would strengthen his hands. His primary motivation was to win the U.S. Open.

Then again, perhaps the British Open would be enough. "I am not a choosy man. I'll settle for either of the Opens in any year," Sarazen would write in his book, *Thirty Years of Championship Golf.*

His problem, as far as the U.S. Open was concerned, was that he had only one week to prepare after returning from England. "The British Open had left me worn-out and nervously tired. The last thing I wanted to do was subject myself to the strain of another championship," Sarazen wrote.

He then encountered the added onus of rising expectations of matching Bobby Jones's feat of winning both Opens, achieved in 1926 and 1930. "I dragged myself out to Fresh Meadow, feeling like a businessman who had slaved for weeks so that he could take off on a short vacation and then had been called back to his office from the Maine woods. My golf game was listless. A week was too short a period, anyhow, for it to regain the sharp edge it had in England."

It happened that Jones, now retired from the game, was on hand to watch the U.S. Open. He even joined Gene's practice rounds on the Monday and Wednesday of championship week (and would play with Sarazen, Armour, and 1931 U.S. Open champion Billy Burke in a charity exhibition the day after the championship).

During the practice rounds, Sarazen told Jones that he planned a conservative strategy, playing for the more open front of the greens rather than firing at pins and bringing into play the severe bunkers flanking most of the putting surfaces. This was not only due to his local knowledge of the course from his days as home pro, but also because he felt his game wasn't sharp.

Sarazen felt that at that point in his career, he "had a tighter rein on my impetuousness" and avoided the risky, ultra-aggressive play that had gotten him in trouble at times. However, he probably went too far as the U.S. Open got underway at Fresh Meadow. He was not playing the type of game that came naturally to him. Opening rounds of 74 and 76 left him five strokes off the lead, and he fell further back by playing the first eight holes of the third round in four-over.

The first-round 74 wasn't the problem; it was actually a good round on a day with strong winds that affected the flight of the ball and dried out the greens, making downhill putts particularly treacherous. Only 45 of the 141 finishers broke 80, and the average score was 81.4. Several pre-tournament favorites failed to break 80—Armour with an 82 and Horton Smith, Macdonald Smith, and Johnny Farrell with 80s.

In those conditions, Olin Dutra's one-under 69 was an exceptional round. It gave him a four-stroke lead, the largest first-round margin in a U.S. Open to date. Dutra, a burly 31-year-old Californian, traced his ancestry back to the early Spanish settlers of the Monterey Peninsula. His tour play was mostly limited to West Coast events, but he ventured east for the U.S. Open, which he would win in 1934 at Merion outside Philadelphia (he would also capture the 1932 PGA Championship in Minnesota).

The lone blemish on Dutra's card was a bogey on the first hole. He made birdies on the 11th and 15th, and parred the rest, finishing with an impressive, low one-iron into the wind to 12 feet on the 18th before missing the birdie effort.

"The big boy simply couldn't miss," said 1921 champion Jim Barnes, who played with Dutra. "He hit his drives where we both wanted to be. He approached so well that he almost never had more than two easy putts to make."

Dutra was playing with a bandage on a sprained right wrist. Jones, playing the role of an interested observer at this Open, speculated it might have helped Dutra by preventing his right hand from being overactive in the swing.

Jones spent much of his day watching the twosome of Sarazen and defending champion Burke, who was tied for fifth at 75, noting he was impressed with their low shots in the wind and that both were still "big factors."

Sarazen had five bogeys against a lone birdie on the 17th, where he holed a 35-foot putt. The *New York Times* observed that he drove well but left himself long putts, an indication of his conservative strategy. The *Daily News*, on the other hand, reported that he "topped a spoon [fairway wood] on a wild gamble from the rough" on the fifth hole, ultimately making a bogey on the par five. Perhaps he hadn't completely suppressed his impetuous nature.

Well-known sportswriter Paul Gallico, who wrote a nationally syndicated column, chatted with Sarazen after the round and called him "as cocky and colorful as ever," and very proud of his long driving.

Leo Diegel held the competitive course record of 68 at Fresh Meadow, accomplished in one of the qualifying rounds for the 1930 PGA Championship (and shooting 69 in the other). He was a formidable competitor, having won the PGA Championship in 1928 and 1929 and finished T2 in the 1920 U.S. Open at age 21. He got off to a blazing start with birdies on the first and third before going five-over the rest of the way while missing three short putts. Still, his 73 was good for second place.

Sarazen was joined at 74 by Argentina's José Jurado, one of two international players entered in the championship. The other was Japan's Tomekichi Miyamoto, who made a 10 on the fifth hole and shot the first of a pair of 82s to miss the cut.

The 32-year-old Jurado was playing in the only U.S. Open he would ever enter, but he was a legitimate threat. The previous year, he led the British Open until the final three holes and finished second. The Prince of Wales took a liking to him, and invited Jurado to play golf with him. They ended up playing together for 20 days after the British Open.

Now Jurado had "caught the fancy of the galleries" on Long Island, according to the *New York Times*, as he was making a strong bid for the U.S. Open title. His 71 gave him a 145 total for two rounds and a share of the lead with Philip Perkins.

Perkins, 27, was also foreign-born, hailing from England. He won the British Amateur in 1928 and was runner-up to Jones in the U.S. Amateur that same year. Perkins moved to the U.S. in 1931, now listing New York City as his residence. He turned pro just a couple of weeks before the U.S. Open, though unaffiliated with a club, so he could play for prize money at tournaments. He had finished T7 at the 1931 U.S. Open as an amateur.

Perkins would only play the tour part-time, and only for a few years. His pro debut was perhaps his highlight, though he did end up with one tour victory in 1937. He shot the best round of the day on Friday with a 69. He had five birdies in his one-under round, including the 16th and 17th, the latter on an ultra-slick downhill, sidehill 15-foot putt. He gave that stroke back with a bogey on 18, hitting his second shot into a bunker.

That anybody but Dutra would end up leading through 36 holes didn't seem likely for a long portion of the second round. The first-round leader birdied the first and third holes and lipped out a birdie try on the second. He offset a bogey at the fourth with a birdie at the fifth. Bogeys on Nos. 7 and 8 didn't seem too alarming, considering that a 35 on the front nine enabled him to build on his four-stroke lead entering the day. Dutra's game abandoned him on the back nine, however, with three double bogeys leading to a 42. The last of them came on the 18th, giving him a 77 for a 146 total that put him one stroke off the lead at the end of the day.

Diegel was next at 147 after a 74, followed by Walter Hagen at 148. The Haig could have been better if not for a double bogey on the par-five 16th, where his third shot hit the roof of an adjacent barn and rolled off to finish next to a tree, forcing him to play the next shot left-handed.

Overall, Hagen's biggest problem was putting. The two-time U.S. Open champion was 39 now and, just as many players before and since, he struggled on the greens in the descending arc of his career. In the first round, he missed three two-foot putts.

"If only he had the old Hagen putting touch, he would be four strokes ahead of the field," Grantland Rice wrote after the second round. "The hands and wrists no longer function as they did 10 years ago."

Hagen went on to shoot himself out of it with a 79 in the third round, a closing 71 merely enabling him to squeak into the top 10.

Sarazen had no birdies in the second round, hanging around with a 36 on the front nine, but five bogeys on the back nine left him limping to a 40. Looking back on it, Sarazen said his play was shabby and that he had to putt well just for a 76. It wasn't great, but at five strokes back he couldn't be dismissed.

"Plucky little Gene isn't out of the running by a long shot," Ralph Trost wrote in the *Brooklyn Daily Eagle.*

With 36 holes to play on Saturday, Sarazen entered the third round sticking to his conservative strategy, figuring that with all the trouble at Fresh Meadow, the leaders might come back to him. It wasn't working, though. Sarazen was four-over through eight holes, all four bogeys coming on missed greens. He was putting well, but as he later wrote, the rest of his game "had degenerated from cagey conservatism to downright timidity."

On the ninth tee, he made a couple of impulsive decisions. He told two policemen who had appointed themselves as his private body-guards to go away, telling them that they were a jinx. "And there and then I made up my mind to chuck my dainty safety tactics. Maybe they paid dividends for other golfers, but I'd given them a fair trial and they suited me like a cage does a robin."

Sarazen hit a seven-iron to 12 feet on the par-three ninth and holed the birdie putt. "From that hole, I threw caution to the winds. I belted my drives harder. The harder I hit them, the straighter they went. I rifled my irons right for the flags—to blazes with the bunkers."

The unleashed Sarazen was hitting the ball well enough to avoid the sand and close enough to the hole to run off a string of three bird-ies on 14, 15, and 16. Along with six pars, that gave him a 32 on the back nine for a round of 70.

Since all the leaders had earlier tee times, Sarazen knew when he finished that he was now within one stroke of the lead with a 220 total. Perkins could have led by more than that, but he played the last eight holes in three-over for a 74 and 219.

Jurado and Diegel joined Sarazen in a tie for second. Jurado blew a chance to lead by bogeying 15, 16, and 17 for a 75. Diegel had a 73 with only one birdie, which he scored on the first hole. Dutra was another to let a potential lead slip through his fingers. He was at 221 after a 75 that included a quadruple bogey on the 15th, where he drove out of bounds and, following the stroke-and-distance penalty, hit his second drive next to a tree, compounding his trouble.

Bobby Cruickshank came from seven behind to pull within two of the lead at 221 with a 69. The 37-year-old Scotsman had finished second to Jones in the U.S. Open nine years earlier not far away at Inwood. He had accumulated 12 tour wins so far, ultimately finishing with 17, but none were a major. After opening with rounds of 78 and 74, Cruickshank birdied Nos. 7, 8, and 9 in the third round for a 32 on the front nine before bogeys on 10 and 12 led to a 37 on the back.

Sarazen's 32 had come on the back nine of the third round, followed by a quick lunch with Jones in the clubhouse. Stunningly, he added another 32 on the front nine of the final round, covering 18 consecutive holes in 64 strokes, an extraordinary feat for that era and on a day when the average score was around 76 (76.2 in the third round and 75.7 in the fourth).

Gene started with a routine par and then bogeyed the second hole after an approach shot into a bunker. Undaunted, he kept firing at pins with his new strategy of aggression. It paid off with birdies on the third (12 feet), fourth (10 feet), and a particularly satisfying one on the tough sixth (10 feet after a two-iron approach).

Sarazen hit his tee shot 18 feet from the hole on the 143-yard ninth. It left a downhill putt, but he felt confident enough to hit it firmly—he had spent many hours practicing his putting on this green near the pro shop during his time as professional at Fresh Meadow. His line was perfect, and the birdie was his fourth in seven holes.

Meanwhile, Perkins, an early starter, had recently finished with a fine round of 70. He was one-under through 15 holes, with two birdies and one bogey, before an eventful final three holes. The Englishman bogeyed the par-five 16th where he three-putted from above the hole. He had to scramble for a bogey on 17 after dumping a pitch shot from right of the green into a bunker, blasting out to two feet to avoid a double bogey.

Perkins hit an excellent approach shot to 18, leaving a six-foot birdie putt. As he was about to hit it, the whirring of a movie camera for a newsreel outlet distracted him. He asked the cameraman to turn off the machine so he could recover his concentration and promised to replay the shot for the camera. Perkins knocked the ball into the hole to complete his round, then repeated the putt for the benefit of the cameraman, making it a second time.

Many around the green hailed Perkins as the champion with a fine total of nine-over 289. They were unaware that Sarazen's exploits on the front nine would soon bring him to the turn at seven-over, positioning him to win outright with a one-over 36 or better on the back nine.

Sarazen received word from a friend at the 10th tee. He knew what he had to do. He decided to play the back nine a bit more carefully, without reverting to the timid conservatism he felt had hindered him for the first two-and-a-half rounds.

A key moment came on the par-three 12th hole, where his worst iron shot of the day left him with a pitch over a bunker. He needed to land not far past the bunker to get close to the pin, but decided the gamble was worth it and pulled off the shot perfectly, finishing two feet from the hole to save par.

Sarazen felt fortunate to get a couple of breaks on the 15th hole, his drive landing softly on the right side of the fairway instead of bouncing into the rough behind a tree, and his seven-iron approach landing short but bounding onto the green 10 feet from the hole. He made that for a birdie to get to six-over. Now he could play the last three holes in two-over to beat Perkins.

There was still a wild card in Cruickshank, who was playing two twosomes ahead of Sarazen. Bobby nearly matched Sarazen's 32 on the front nine, ending up with a 33. He birdied Nos. 3-5 for his second three-birdie streak on the front nine that day. Two bogeys tarnished his otherwise fine effort, though he did add another birdie on the ninth.

Cruickshank was solid on the back nine with a birdie on 15 making up for a bogey on 13. He rifled his approach shot to the 18th to seven feet from the hole, reminiscent of his brilliant fourth-round approach shot at Inwood in 1923, which got him into a playoff. This one might have been even better, because it came from the rough. However, unlike at Inwood, he failed to convert the birdie putt. Cruickshank's round of 68 gave him a tie with Perkins at 289. His total of 137 for the final 36 holes was a U.S. Open record—but it only lasted for a few minutes.

The top three had pulled dramatically away from the rest of the field. Jurado and Dutra closed with 76s, while Diegel claimed fourth place with a 74 for a 294 total. It was a full five strokes behind the Perkins/Cruickshank duo, who each could feel they played well enough to win. When Sarazen made drama-free pars on 16 and 17, it was clear they wouldn't even make a playoff, as Gene needed only a double bogey at 18 to win outright.

Sarazen bombed the longest drive he could remember ever hitting on 18. His seven-iron approach was a brief misstep, finishing in a bunker to the right of the green. Sarazen had to fight his way through spectators to get to the bunker, not unusual in the days of galleries unrestrained by ropes. Worse, fans completely ignored marshals and swarmed onto the green as Sarazen was in the bunker preparing to play.

Gallico wrote that the gallery "became an unruly and uncontrollable rabble, something dreadful to look upon, sweating, pushing, squabbling, screaming and fighting, completely overpowering the marshals and the lone policeman who had somehow found himself inside the circle of the last green." They were even stomping around the vicinity of the ball of Willie Klein, Sarazen's fellow competitor, just 12 feet from the hole.

"Helpless marshals [were] leaping up and down, waving their hats and their hands and hissing 'Shhhhh! Shhhhhhh!' After which they would scream 'Quiet! Quiet! Keep quiet!' at the top of their lungs," is how Gallico described the scene.

Sarazen waited only long enough for his line of play to be clear, hitting his bunker shot while the commotion persisted. He got it to within eight feet of the hole.

The crowd control issues continued unabated. The gallery inexorably seeped onto the green, and ultimately formed a circle of some 20 feet around Sarazen. After a wait of a few minutes for some degree of order to be restored, during which Sarazen lay down on the green next to Gallico, Gene finally was able to hit the putt. He rolled it into the hole for a 66 and a three-stroke victory, at which "10,000 throats burst forth with applause so tremendous that the idling blimp which hovered above, turned tail and fled," according to the *Brooklyn Daily Eagle*.

While waiting to putt, Sarazen admitted to Gallico that he was afraid of what would happen when he tried to make his way through the teeming masses to the clubhouse. Fortunately, the two policemen Sarazen had sent away that morning returned to the course as he was playing the 18th, having heard what was happening on the radio after leaving the course. They escorted the conquering hero to safety.

Sports writers spared no superlatives in describing Sarazen's final 28 holes, which he had played in 100 strokes.

Rice called it "the most remarkable finish any golf open ever knew."

William D. Richardson of the *New York Times*: "two smashing finishing rounds, unquestionably the greatest ever played in any golf championship."

Alan Gould of the Associated Press: "the greatest finish in all the history of the game."

Sarazen's 66 set a new U.S. Open record for 18 holes. In hundreds of rounds at Fresh Meadow during his time as a professional, Sarazen had never shot better than a 67, even in casual rounds or exhibitions. His greatest round came in the ultimate crucible, the final round of the U.S. Open with the title on the line.

Perhaps most impressive, considering the overall scoring trends in golf through the years, his 136 total for the final 36 holes remained the U.S. Open record for 51 years.

TOP-10 FINISHERS		
1	Gene Sarazen	74-76-70-66—286
T2	Bobby Cruickshank	78-74-69-68—289
T2	Philip Perkins	76-69-74-70—289
4	Leo Diegel	73-74-73-74—294
5	Wiffy Cox	80-73-70-72—295
6	Jose Jurado	74-71-75-76—296
T7	Billy Burke	75-77-74-71—297
T7	Harry Cooper	77-73-73-74—297
T7	Olin Dutra	69-77-75-76—297
10	Walter Hagen	75-73-79-71—298

1939

NELSON
PREVAILS IN
DOUBLE OVERTIME

Ralph Guldahl was the clear favorite going into the 1939 U.S. Open at Philadelphia Country Club's Spring Mill course. The 27-year-old had claimed the title in 1937 and 1938, and continued to prove his big-tournament mettle by adding a victory at the Masters in 1939. Two weeks before the Open, Guldahl said, "I can't see why I shouldn't win it again."

After his first practice round, the straight-hitting Guldahl said he didn't like that the rough had been trimmed since his earlier visit to the course. Still, he was reported as looking and sounding confident as the tournament neared. "The others were hoping, Ralph was sure—sure that he would at least put a roaring fight in defense of the title," Fred Byrod wrote in the *Philadelphia Inquirer*. Guldahl was a unanimous choice as the favorite in a poll of players, with two other 27-year-olds, Byron Nelson and Sam Snead, most often mentioned as the next strongest contenders.

Nelson claimed a Masters title of his own in 1937, one of six victories in his first four years on tour. The tall Texan added two more wins in early 1939, including a stunning performance at the Pheonix Open, where he won by 12 strokes in a tournament shortened to 54 holes by rain, shooting 68-65-65.

Snead emerged from the hills of West Virginia to win five times in his first year on tour in 1937, and was the sensation of 1938 with eight victories, becoming the most talked about player in the game. His naturally smooth swing impressed observers, and he also quickly became known for his folksy, down-home demeanor.

Snead's pace slowed during the winter of 1938-39 in what was termed a slump, but he was back on track with two wins, one second (at the Masters), and three thirds in his last seven events heading into the U.S. Open. He had finished second in his U.S. Open debut in 1937, but some skeptics pointed to his T35 Open finish in 1938 with no score better than 76 in his otherwise spectacular year as a sign that this might not be his best event.

The first round revealed Snead to be a true contender, as he grabbed the lead with a one-under 68. He was three-over on the first 11 holes, but the key was a hole-out from the bunker for a birdie on the 480-yard 12th hole, one of two holes that the USGA decided to play as a par four instead of a par five, making the course play to a par of 69 instead of 71. The other was the 479-yard eighth. The only par five on the layout as it played for the Open was the 558-yard 18th.

Snead was a changed man after that fortunate 12th, adding birdies on 13, 14, and 16 to make it four birdies in five holes and ultimately the one-under round. After the bunker hole-out, he said, "I just knew whatever I did would end up alright. I got up on that 13th tee and whanged the best one-iron I ever hit in my life... It just goes to show what a difference one shot can make."

Lawson Little, who swept the U.S. and British Amateurs in 1934 and again in 1935 before turning professional, headed three players at 69. He was joined by Bud Ward, a 26-year-old amateur from the state of Washington, and local Philadelphia pro Matt Kowal. Five players followed at 70, while Guldahl wasn't unhappy with a 71, saying, "I'm not worried a bit."

While scoring relative to par was typically tough for a U.S. Open, the Spring Mill course was more vulnerable down the stretch than most courses that hosted the championship, with 16 and 17 relatively short par fours and 18 a par five that some players could reach in two in the right conditions. Little finished with a flourish, scoring birdies on 15 and 16 and holing a 45-foot putt for an eagle on 18. It was quite an ending for a man who started the round by topping his tee shot on the first hole. Olin Dutra, the 1934 champion, was five-over through 12 after starting the back nine bogey-bogey-double bogey, then bird-ieing 13, 14, 15, and 18, lipping out a 15-foot eagle attempt on the closing hole.

Nelson got off to an even worse start, going five over through eight holes with five bogeys. On the eighth tee, he sat under a tree while waiting for the twosome in front to clear and realized what he was doing wrong in his swing. "I got it now," he told a writer from the *Reading Times*, the newspaper from the town that was now his base and where he was pro at Reading Country Club. "If I can get it straightened out before it's too late, I'll be right there."

It took one more hole for the fix to click—Nelson bogeyed the tough eighth—but he birdied the ninth with an approach to eight feet and added another birdie on the 11th. He made up for a bogey on the 12th with a birdie on the 16th to post a respectable 72 before making the 45-mile drive back to Reading.

Syndicated columnist Joe Williams wrote, "Lord Byron's 72 was a scrambled round that might so well have been an 82 that the finger of destiny might be pointing straight at his blond, square bean—he's got a frightful round out of his system, and still is up there near the front."

Snead's 71 in the second round was good enough to keep him in the lead with a 139 total. As in the first round, he needed a strong finish to end the day in front. The action on No. 12, however, was the antithesis of the previous day. On the same hole where he sank a bunker shot for a birdie, Snead this time hit the green in regulation—and proceeded to four-putt from 30 feet for a double bogey. His first putt went eight feet past, his next stopped 18 inches past the hole, and he missed that short one.

Having made three bogeys and one birdie on the first 11 holes, Sam was four-over for the round after his putting gaffe. Snead later said that, while steam had blown from his ears after the four-putt, he reminded himself of his hole-out the day before and figured the good and bad breaks had evened out: "So why worry?" Snead saved par from a bunker on the 13th and birdied 16 and 17 to escape with a two-over round. The birdies were greeted with boisterous cheers, as Snead emerged as "the people's choice," according to the *Inquirer*, and drew the largest gallery.

Horton Smith scored the day's only subpar round, a 68, to move into second place, one stroke behind at 140. At age 32, he had accumulated 28 tour wins (he would add only two more), but his third-place U.S. Open finish in 1930 was his only top-five in the event to date. He lived up to his reputation as one of the game's best putters, needing only 29 putts on a day when most players struggled on the hard, slick greens.

Guldahl, by contrast, said he missed 10 putts of under 10 feet in shooting a 73. "I played the best golf I've ever played from tee to green in any championship, but the greens seem to be too slick for the way I putt," he said.

Nelson's putting was perhaps even more futile. He three-putted five times, including taking three to get down from 15 feet on the 18th after reaching the par five in two. The other three-putts accounted for four of his five bogeys, and he managed only one birdie in the round, when he sunk a 15-footer on the 14th. It added up to a 73 for a 145 total, six strokes back and tied for 16th heading into Saturday's 36-hole finale. In the *New York Times*, William D. Richardson wrote that it looked like Nelson and everyone else at 145 and higher were out of the running given the caliber of the 15 players ahead of them.

Nelson didn't agree. "I figure I am still in the running. I can take all kinds of chances tomorrow while the others are playing cautiously to protect their margin. It's a good position to be in. I hope my irons hold up and that the putter gets hot for one day."

Players in front of Nelson included three-time major runner-up Craig Wood at 141, three-time major champion Denny Shute at 142, four-time major runner-up Harry Cooper at 143, and three-time major champion Guldahl and major winners Henry Picard and Dutra at 144. The long-hitting Wood had a chance for the lead before slipping up with bogeys on 14 and 15 to end up two behind despite a strong start to his round.

Snead was sharing a hotel room with 1922 and 1932 champion Gene Sarazen, who had taken the younger player under his wing.

Sarazen, who finished T-47, was surprised when Snead was doing calisthenics just before going to bed. "I asked him if he didn't get enough exercise out there under the hot sun and he said he wasn't doing the bending for exercise; it was to relax his nerves before going to sleep," Sarazen told the *New York Times*.

In his book, *The Education of a Golfer*, Snead wrote of the night before the final two rounds, "I finished my sit-ups in the dark [after Sarazen went to bed] and then slept like a possum in his mother's pouch. I felt another 68 or 69 score coming on when I woke up. Couldn't wait to go out there and win me that $100,000 Open," referring to amount that some felt an Open winner could earn in exhibition fees and endorsements (first prize was only $1,000).

Saturday morning's third round was instead a setback for Snead. He was four-over through six holes with bogeys on Nos. 2, 4, 5, and 6, and added another bogey on 13 before his lone birdie of the round on 17. His 73 dropped him out of the lead with a 212 total, but only one stroke back.

The surprising 54-hole leader was Johnny Bulla, a 25-year-old without a lot of tour experience who made the field as an alternate from the Chicago sectional qualifier. He followed opening rounds of 72-71 with a 68 that was built on two birdies, one bogey, and 15 pars. He couldn't be comfortable in his position, though, with four players just a stroke behind. Joining Snead at 212 were Shute (70), Wood (71 with birdies on three of the last six holes), and Clayton Heafner (66, tying the U.S. Open 18-hole record). Heafner was another surprise, a 24-year-old playing in just his 10th tour event, described in a United Press International report as "a raw public links pro playing with borrowed clubs and virtually no money in his pocket."

Heafner had finished second in the Greater Greensboro Open in his native North Carolina in March and would go on to win four tour events in his career. Here, though, he disappeared with an 80 in the final round. Bulla would go on to be a frequent contender in major championships, where he had five top-four finishes, though he claimed only one tour victory. In this event, he finished sixth with a closing 76.

Amateur Ward continued to hang tough with a 71 to stand two back at 213. Former U.S. Open champions Tommy Armour (with a 69) and Dutra (70) headed a group of four players at 214 and Smith struggled to a third-round 75 to fall to 215. Nelson, Guldahl, and Picard were accomplished players at 216, in hailing distance at five strokes off the lead but in need of heroics to have a chance of passing the 11 players in front of them.

Nelson's third round was an erratic 71. He started with a flourish, holing his second shot for an eagle on the 384-yard third hole—then quickly gave those strokes back with bogeys on the fourth and sixth. Byron went birdie-bogey on Nos. 7 and 8 before meeting disaster on the ninth. His approach shot momentarily stopped on the green, then trickled down into a bunker. He blasted onto the green and three-putted for a double bogey and a two-over front nine. Bogeys on the 12th and 14th threatened to knock him out of contention. Birdies on 16 and 17 gave him at least a fighting chance going into the final round.

Before heading back out to the course, Nelson had lunch in the clubhouse with playing partner Dutra and a friend, J.K. Wadley. Dutra ordered a big lunch, and Nelson told the waiter he wanted the same. "No, you won't," said Wadley, who ordered a lighter fare for Byron. Dutra went on to shoot a 78 on the hot and muggy afternoon, while Nelson made a run at the title. "It taught me a good lesson, not to eat too heavy a meal before going out to play," Nelson wrote in his book, *How I Played the Game*.

Armour plummeted with an 80 in the final round to drop out of the top 20, Smith had a 76 to finish 15th, and Picard also made no headway with a 74 for a T12. Guldahl's 72 netted him a T7 finish that wasn't what he had in mind. "If I'd done any putting at all I'd be on top again," he said afterward.

In contrast to his third round, Nelson was steady in the fourth, hitting every green in regulation. He birdied the first hole, made his lone bogey on the third, and parred all the way until the 17th, which he birdied after narrowly missing several birdie putts along the way. A par on the 18th gave him a 68. It wasn't a thrill-packed round, but under U.S. Open pressure on a course where subpar scores were rare it was good enough to at least give him a chance.

His 284 total was one better than Ward, who had the earliest tee time among the contenders and shot a 72 for 285. Ward's strong bid to join Bobby Jones (1930) and Johnny Goodman (1933) as an amateur to win in the 1930s was spoiled by double bogeys on both back-nine par threes. He blasted too strongly out of a bunker on the 11th, going over the green and taking three more to get down. He got a bad break on the 13th, where his tee shot deflected off a spectator standing close to the green and ended up in a bad lie on the back edge of a bunker. From there he couldn't do much except knock it into the bunker, leading to a frustrating double. Ward had four birdies in the final round, but too many slips—three bogeys and the two double bogeys.

Now Nelson sat in the clubhouse waiting to see if his 284 total would hold up. He wasn't optimistic. "That score won't win for me. Maybe I'll finish second," he said at the time.

The first challenger was right behind him in the following twosome. Snead wasn't setting the world on fire, but with Bulla dropping back and Nelson coming from so far behind, he didn't have to be. Sam was one-over through 16 holes with bogeys on Nos. 4 and 8 and a birdie on 11. He missed a three-foot birdie putt on the third hole but made a long one on the 11th. He then caught a break on the 12th when, according to reporting in the *Inquirer*, a spectator kicked his drive that was bounding into the woods, and redirected it into the fairway. At six-over for the tournament with two holes remaining, he was in good shape to beat Nelson's eight-over total.

Snead dropped a shot on the 17th when his short-iron approach took a hard bounce and went over the green. He chipped on to five feet but missed the putt. Still, he could beat Nelson with a par five on the last hole.

The 18th got off to a bad start. Snead hooked his drive into the left rough. He then committed a fateful error that would be compounded by a string of blunders and misfortunes on subsequent strokes. From a lie in tangled, trampled rough, he decided to hit a brassie (two-wood) to try to get close to the green and give him a better chance at a birdie instead of going with a safer iron. He half-topped the wood shot, with the ball taking a low, ugly dive and ultimately coming to rest in a bunker 110 yards short of the green.

Although the ball was close to a high lip, Snead chose an eight-iron to try for the green instead of grabbing a wedge to be sure to get out of the bunker. The shot didn't carry the lip and the ball partially embedded in the grass bank above the sand. From there he could do nothing except hack it out as far as he could manage, which turned out to be into a bunker 40 yards short of the green.

With a stance outside the bunker, Snead's fifth shot was a very difficult one, and he did well just to get it on the green 40 feet from the hole. He needed to make that long bogey putt to tie Nelson, but it was too much to ask. Dispirited, Sam missed a four-foot second putt and made a triple bogey for a final-round 74 and 286 total.

In later writings, Snead lamented not being told on the tee that a par would beat Nelson's total. If only he had known that, he said, he wouldn't have gambled trying for a birdie. He recalled that a spectator told him after his fourth shot that a bogey would tie Nelson, at which point Snead said he blew up and yelled, "Why didn't someone tell me that, so I could have played it safe!"

That analysis, though, uses the benefit of hindsight. Nelson was in the twosome immediately in front of Snead, so Nelson's total wouldn't have been known when Snead was just starting the hole. Also, Wood and Shute were playing behind Snead. He didn't know where they stood, and he had no way of knowing what their ultimate total would be. Shute, in fact, at that point, had a very good chance to finish at 283 or better.

In truth, it was understandable for Snead to think that he *might* need a birdie. But it wasn't wise to recklessly gamble to try for a birdie that he might or might not need, considering that a safe iron second shot still would have left him with a chance to hit a third shot close and make a birdie.

The greatest likelihood is that Snead's aggressive nature simply got the better of him when he decided to go for broke on the second shot. That's essentially what he said after the round. "I guess I blew up when I took a wood instead of an iron after I had hooked into the rough. I had a feeling it was the wrong club, and it was," he said. "A fellow should know better than that... Oh, what a sap I was."

It was a sad scene when Snead trudged off the 18th green to consoling applause from the gallery. "Some women were crying and men were patting me on the back as I walked to the locker room," Snead wrote. "It was worse in there. There was dead silence. The other pros avoided looking at me, to spare me embarrassment."

This was only Snead's third U.S. Open and he would go on to have a very long career and accumulate a record 82 victories, a total matched only by Tiger Woods. None of those wins, however, was a U.S. Open, a spot of tarnish on an otherwise sterling record. For that reason, his eight on the 18th hole at Philadelphia Country Club would have even greater resonance through the years and be woven into the fabric of golf lore. "If I'd murdered someone, I would have lived it down sooner than the '39 Open," he wrote.

Wood was the next player with a chance. He was one-under through five holes, then went in the wrong direction with a bogey on the sixth, a double bogey on the eighth, and bogeys on the 12th and 14th. That left him needing a birdie on the 18th to tie Nelson.

One of the longest hitters on the tour, Wood's drive accounted for about half the distance of the 558-yard 18th hole. He then pounded a brassie that took off on a line for the green, bounced in front of the putting surface, and rolled onto it, a brilliant 280-yard shot that finished 20 feet from the hole. Two putts later, Wood finished with a 284 total to tie Nelson.

That left Shute. The 34-year-old was a formidable player who had won the 1933 British Open and 1936 and 1937 PGA Championships. But he was a quiet sort, only a semi-regular tour player, and not a very long hitter, so he didn't stir the masses. He drew the smallest gallery of the contenders.

In the locker room, Nelson learned that Shute needed just to play the last four holes in one-over to win. "Denny's in, then," Byron said.

Through the first 14 holes, Shute had two birdies (Nos. 9 and 11) and three bogeys (Nos. 2, 5, and 10) when all he needed was a two-over round to win outright—a situation he said he knew as he played the 15th. The closing stretch had been the most forgiving part of the course all week, but trying to close out a victory on that stretch was another matter. Shute's second shot to the 421-yard 15th found a bunker, he came out poorly, and made a bogey.

Pars to the clubhouse would still earn him the title, but he bogeyed the seemingly benign 363-yard 17th, where he drove into a fairway bunker and missed the green.

Now Shute needed a birdie on 18 to win. He hit two good shots to get reasonably close to the green and then a so-so pitch shot to 25 feet. His putt looked good as it rolled toward the hole. His caddie screamed, "Get in!" but at the last moment the ball veered off and slid by the lip of the cup. Shute tapped in for a par, a 72, and a 284 total that set up an intriguing three-way playoff scheduled for 18 holes the following day.

Wood had a hard-luck record in major playoffs. He lost the British Open—to Shute—in a playoff in 1933. He fell to Paul Runyan in the 1934 PGA Championship in a match-play final that was determined in extra holes. And he lost a playoff to Gene Sarazen at the 1935 Masters, an event Wood would have won outright if Sarazen hadn't made a double eagle on the 15th hole of the final round. In addition, Wood lost a playoff in the 1933 North and South Open, a premier event in that era.

"This tying business is getting to be a habit with me," he said after the fourth round. "No, I never won a single one of those playoffs, but I'll certainly be out there tomorrow. I'm 38 years old now [he actually would turn 38 later that year] and if I'm ever going to win it, tomorrow should be the time."

Wood, who hailed from upstate New York, was one of the few pros who had been to college, and his marriage to a New York socialite had made the *New York Times* society pages. Jimmy Thomson, a pro who wrote a daily column in the *Inquirer* during tournament week, described him as "big, blond, handsome, the Park Avenue dandy type." A multiple winner on tour in every year but one from 1929 to 1934, Wood's career had hit a skid. He was winless in 1937 and didn't even qualify for the U.S. Open or PGA Championship in 1938. A victory in December of 1938 helped get him back on track. While Wood didn't play much on tour in early 1939, he was in good form when he did, finishing in the top six in all five of the events he entered before the U.S. Open. One of those was a runner-up finish at the Goodall Palm Beach Round Robin the week before the Open.

Shute was looking to add to his legacy and become only the sixth player to win the PGA Championship, British Open, and U.S. Open. Nelson was the relative newcomer among the three, though he had been around long enough to become well established and a Masters winner. Already recognized as one of the best players in the game, a victory in the Open would move him a step closer to being *the* best. A Texas native who had grown up in the same caddie yard as Ben Hogan in Fort Worth, Nelson had a friendly, homespun manner and was well-liked by the members at Reading Country Club. Although Byron had recently lined up a job at Inverness Club in Toledo, Ohio starting in November, dozens of Reading members were nevertheless on hand each day to cheer their pro on.

Thomson wrote that all three were even money in the playoff, while *Inquirer* reporter Cy Peterman wrote that Nelson in the final round was playing "with a confidence that makes him favored in today's playoff."

The playoff turned into an epic two-man battle between Nelson and Wood, with Shute merely along for the ride, shooting a 76. Nelson and Wood were separated by more than one shot after only one hole, Wood going two ahead on the sixth. Both shot one-under 68s on a course where only four subpar rounds had been posted all week, and on a day when brisk winds presented a challenge.

Wood, not known as a great putter, was rock solid on the greens this day. He kept himself alive by scrambling, saving par five times on putts of between five and 10 feet. Those saves resulted in a scorecard with only one bogey against two birdies. Nelson, on the other hand, had five birdies and four bogeys, two of them on three-putts.

Three of Wood's par saves came on the first five holes. Both parred the first four, Nelson hitting all of the greens. On the par-four fifth, both found greenside bunkers and came out to eight feet. Wood holed his putt; Nelson missed. Wood briefly went two ahead with a birdie at the sixth, hitting a seven-iron to 10 feet.

Nelson struck back immediately with a birdie from 18 feet on the par-five seventh. Both parred the eighth and then Byron evened things by sinking a sidehill 25-foot putt for a birdie on the ninth. Both finished the front nine one-under.

Wood ran into trouble on the par-four 10th with a drive into a deep bunker. His second shot caught the lip, leaving a full third shot and resulting in a bogey. Nelson had to scramble for a bogey on the 11th. He had a half-buried lie in a greenside bunker, knocked his next shot over the green, then chipped close for a tap-in. Now both were even par.

The 12th and 13th were tough: a long par four and a long par three. Wood's approaches with a three-iron and four-wood both found bunkers, and he got up and down both times, holing putts of six and 10 feet. Nelson also chose a three-iron and a four-wood, hitting a pair of excellent approaches. The first left a 10-foot birdie putt, which he made. He had a 20-foot chance for a birdie on No. 13 but walked away with a bogey after missing a second putt of two-and-a-half feet.

They stayed even with par and with each other as both two-putted from long distance on the 14th and missed the fairway but hit the green on the 15th. Nelson hit his tee shot into the rough on the 328-yard 16th, leaving a very difficult pitch to a tightly guarded green. Downwind, he realized it would be challenging to pull off a shot that would hold the green. It took "one of the greatest shots I've ever played" to stop the ball six feet from the hole. Nelson made the putt to go one ahead with two to play.

The 17th hole brought a reversal, a two-stroke swing in Wood's favor. Nelson overhit his 30-foot birdie putt, sending it eight feet past. Wood holed a 20-footer for a birdie and Nelson missed his second putt and made a bogey.

Wood was one ahead going to the 18th hole, where he had a good chance to reach in two and had made a crucial birdie a day earlier. Nelson was also relatively long off the tee, and, after a good drive, he hit his fairway wood just a yard short of the green. Wood outdrove Nelson by about 10 yards and clearly was in range of the green with a four-wood.

Unfortunately, he hit a pull-hook to the left, sending the ball flying toward the gallery gathered around the green. Marshals screamed, "Watch it!" but the ball hit a man's head with a sickening thud. The ball caromed back into the fairway instead of bouncing toward an area occupied by movie trucks and concession stands around the adjacent ninth green.

A commotion ensued as the stricken man, bleeding from the side of his head, fell to the ground unconscious. He was placed on a stretcher and carried across the green.

Back to the golf, Wood hit his pitch shot six feet from the hole. Nelson's relatively easy chip rolled seven feet past, so he was putting first. "I remembered the times as a caddie at Glen Garden [in Fort Worth] when I would say, 'This putt is for the U.S. Open.' It steadied me enough that I made the putt," Nelson wrote in *How I Played the Game*. Now it was Wood's turn with a six-foot putt for the U.S. Open title. He had been making putts from this range all day. Not this one; it was such a weak effort that it stopped six inches short of the hole.

In the press tent, Nelson's wife, Louise, fainted when Wood's putt missed and ended the 18 holes in a tie. She quickly recovered—as did the concussed spectator who had been whisked away in an ambulance to a nearby hospital. As it turned out the man, Robert Mossman, was the owner of a local driving range. Wood visited him in the hospital that evening. Mossman said to him, "Craig, if you open the face of your club, you'll cure that hook."

As they played the closing holes, Wood and Nelson had been asked whether, if the 18-hole playoff were to end in a tie, they preferred to go to sudden death or to play another 18 holes the next day. They both favored the extra 18, so Monday brought a sixth round.

The big blow of the second playoff round was struck by Nelson. On the 453-yard fourth hole, he hit a one-iron that cut through a crosswind, landed 15 feet short of the hole, rolled directly toward the cup, and lodged against the flagstick. When Nelson reached the green, he pulled out the flagstick and the ball fell to the bottom of the cup, making it officially an eagle.

Two holes earlier, Wood had pulled off nearly as magnificent a shot, a brassie to the 234-yard second hole to one foot for a tap-in birdie. He bogeyed the first and third holes, however, and Nelson birdied the third with an approach to two feet. It was the same hole where he had holed out for an eagle in the third round. Already known as one of the best iron players in the game, this week he was especially dangerous with that part of his game.

Nelson was three-under and four strokes ahead through four holes. It wasn't quite over at that point, especially with Byron bogeying the next two holes. On each, Nelson drove into the left rough and missed the green to the right in a tough spot where getting up and down was a dicey proposition.

Both players parred Nos. 7 and 8, and Nelson's margin went back up to three strokes when Wood bogeyed the par-four ninth after driving against the lip of a bunker. Poor driving would cloud his round. On two other par fours, Nos. 10 and 12, he drove into places where reaching the green was impossible. On the par-three 11th, his tee shot rested on a creek's grassy bank. Standing in the water, he escaped nicely with a shot to six feet, but failed to convert the putt.

Nelson wasn't quite able to put Wood away, as he bogeyed Nos. 10, 12, and 13, with his iron game mysteriously abandoning him for a while. He also missed the 14th green, hitting into a bunker. Coincidentally, Wood's approach landed in the same bunker within about a foot of Nelson's ball.

Nelson would later point to this as a pivotal hole. They each hit their bunker shots to about 10 feet from the hole. Former U.S. Amateur champion Jess Sweetser, a USGA official in this match, measured with the flagstick to determine who was away. Nelson was a couple inches farther, so he went first and knocked it into the hole. Wood missed his to fall four behind. If the scores had swung the other way, Nelson's lead would have been down to just two.

"My confidence might not have been so good if something had gone wrong on that 14th," Nelson said after the round. As it was, both birdied the 15th with putts of around 10 feet. Wood added another birdie on 17, but it was too little, too late. Pars on the finishing hole gave Nelson a 70 and the trophy, leaving Wood as a runner-up with a 73.

Wood now had second-place finishes in each of the four major championships, all on the losing side of playoffs. It was a litany of frustration that would later be matched by Greg Norman. It wasn't just the losing. It was the *way* Wood lost that tagged him as a hard-luck golfer. He had now been victimized by Sarazen holing a four-wood shot and Nelson holing a one-iron. In this U.S. Open, he had shot a 68 in the first playoff round, only to have Nelson also shoot a 68.

Happily for Wood, he was wrong about this being his last chance. He finally captured an elusive major at the 1941 Masters, and, later in the same year, he added a U.S. Open title. Snead would earn no such redemption—at least not in the U.S. Open.

As for Nelson, he would retire early at age 34, after the 1946 season. With the U.S. Open suspended from 1943 to 1945 because of World War II, he had limited opportunities in the event, so it was a good thing he was able to take advantage of this chance. He was in another three-man playoff in 1946, won by Lloyd Mangrum.

TOP-10 FINISHERS		
1	Byron Nelson	72-73-71-68—284*
2	Craig Wood	70-71-71-72—284
3	Denny Shute	70-72-70-72—284
4	Bud Ward	69-73-71-72—285
5	Sam Snead	68-71-73-74—286
6	Johnny Bulla	72-71-68-76—287
T7	Ralph Guldahl	71-73-72-72—288
T7	Dick Metz	76-72-71-69—288
T9	Ky Laffoon	76-70-73-70—289
T9	Harold McSpaden	70-73-71-75—289
T9	Paul Runyan	76-70-71-72—289

*Nelson won playoff, 68-70; Wood, 68-73; Shute, 76

1950

HOGAN'S STIRRING COMEBACK

I n February 1949, Ben Hogan was severely injured in an automobile accident in West Texas as he was driving home from the Phoenix Open. A Greyhound bus, passing a truck on a two-lane highway in the fog, smashed head-on into Hogan's car, leaving Ben with a fractured pelvis, a broken collarbone, and a broken ankle.

While those injuries were bad enough, they were compounded by blood clots developing after nearly two months in the hospital. Concerned that a large clot could move into a lung and be fatal, an operation was performed to tie off the vena cava, the largest vein that returns blood from the legs to the lungs and heart. The surgery was successful, but Hogan would feel the aftereffects for a lifetime with poor blood circulation in his legs.

Hogan finally left the hospital after a three-month stay. It was likely that he would be able to play golf again after a long rehabilitation, but unknown whether he could play well enough or be able to walk well enough to play the pro tour at all, let alone resume the torrid pace he had shown in the three years after World War II. The Fort Worth, Texas native had gotten off to a sluggish start on the tour in the 1930s, but his indefatigable work ethic turned his fortunes around by the early 1940s. Hogan really took off in the post-war years to become the game's dominant player, winning 13 events in 1946, seven in 1947, 10 in 1948, and two of the three he entered in 1949 before the crash. He even landed on the cover of *Time* magazine in January 1949.

Hogan couldn't even hit balls until November, 10 months after the accident, and didn't play his first round until a month after that. He surprised everyone by playing in the Los Angeles Open the first week of January after announcing he would attend some of the West Coast events, though he wasn't sure he would play. Shockingly, he reached a playoff with Sam Snead, and would have won outright if Snead hadn't birdied the last two holes. Hogan lost the playoff but won adoration and respect with his performance.

Ben struggled in two other West Coast events, largely because of his legs, and thus decided it prudent to pare down his schedule. In three other tournaments before the U.S. Open, he finished T4 at the Masters with a final-round 76, won the Greenbrier Pro-Am (not an official tour event but one that drew a strong field), and was T3 at the Colonial Invitational in his hometown of Fort Worth.

The biggest question mark for Hogan entering the U.S. Open at Merion outside Philadelphia was whether his legs would hold up on the 36-hole final day. "If they were going to play without walking—just hitting the shots—I would pick Ben without a moment's hesitation," said two-time champion Gene Sarazen, who was still competing at age 48. "But, unfortunately, he will have to walk."

Snead was an overwhelming favorite, picked to win by 21 of the 25 competitors and local pros polled by the *Philadelphia Bulletin*. It made sense, considering that Sam had won seven tournaments already in 1950 (he would win 11 on the year) and had 12 top-three finishes in 15 starts. On the other hand, there was his winless U.S. Open record, and he was returning to the vicinity of his worst Open collapse, his triple bogey on the 72nd hole at Philadelphia Country Club in 1939. "Why don't you forget that awful round?" Snead asked a group of reporters.

Jimmy Demaret, who won the Masters in April, was next on the list of touted players. Cary Middlecoff received surprisingly little attention, considering he was the defending champion and had eight victories since the start of 1949. Some felt that he didn't putt well enough to handle Merion's greens; others opined that defending an Open title might prove too difficult a task.

Also getting surprisingly little notice was Lloyd Mangrum. He had recovered from being wounded in World War II combat in Europe to win the 1946 U.S. Open and went on to score 11 victories in 1948-49. The hardscrabble Mangrum had missed the first three months of the 1950 season due to another injury, but one far less heroic: a fractured shoulder bone from a scuffle with a neighbor. However, he did manage to win the Fort Wayne Open the week before the U.S. Open.

The favorites took a back seat in the first round to one of the most obscure players ever to lead a U.S. Open—with a record 18-hole score, no less. Lee Mackey was an unemployed 26-year-old pro from Birmingham, Alabama, who had made it through sectional qualifying and, up to that point, had played in only four tour events.

Mackey shot a six-under 64 to break the U.S. Open mark of 65 set in 1947 by James McHale. It was the lowest score Mackey had ever shot anywhere—he had never done better than 65, even in casual rounds. The only tournaments he had ever won were the Birmingham city amateur and the Michigan assistant pros' championship. He had moved to Michigan to be an assistant to his Birmingham mentor, Sam Byrd, at Plum Hollow Country Club for three years. He moved back to Alabama in 1950 and, as the *Bulletin* reported, "teaches on a driving range when he gets work."

For one day in his life, Mackey played like Hogan with his woods and irons and like renowned putter Mangrum on the greens. He was three-under on the front nine with birdies on Nos. 4, 7, and 8 and a pair of bunker saves preserving his score. His gallery grew from non-existent to a curious crowd of onlookers as word spread early on the back nine, then swelled to an enthusiastic throng as he continued his assault on par on the back nine.

The day's unlikely hero birdied the 11th with a 30-foot putt, birdied the short par-three 13th with a tee shot to two feet, and added another birdie on the 15th with a 40-foot putt. Now he was six-under, and he nearly birdied the 16th, his six-foot putt catching the edge of the hole but staying out.

The 17th brought Mackey his only bogey of the day, on a three-putt from 50 feet. He didn't catch his drive cleanly on 18, and it barely made the 210-yard carry over the old quarry that crosses the last three holes at Merion. That left a three-wood to the green, which Mackey struck solidly and watched as it rolled up to 10 feet from the hole. He sank that to ink his name in the record book.

After showing no signs of nerves on the course, Mackey became flustered when he had to talk to a group of reporters looking for background on the unknown leader. He at first told them he was 28 years old before correcting himself, saying, "I plumb forgot my right age."

There were six subpar scores in the first round, none by established players. Part-time tour pro Al Brosch was second at 67, followed by Skip Alexander and Julius Boros at 68. Boros would go on to win two U.S. Opens, but, at Merion in 1950, he was a 29-year-old who had just turned pro in November after working as an accountant in Connecticut. At the time, there was a six-month probation period before a pro could accept prize money in a tournament. Boros bided his time during those months as an assistant professional at Mid Pines Resort in Pinehurst, North Carolina, playing in only one tournament. With the probation period now up, Boros was eligible to be paid, making this U.S. Open essentially his pro debut.

Boros made his own threat to the 18-hole record with a four-under 32 on the front nine and a birdie on the 11th to go five-under. He stayed five-under through 15 before making a bogey on 15 and a double bogey on 18, where his drive ended up next to a tree on the right side.

The smart money said that the winner would come from among the players who shot between 71 and 73, including defending champion Middlecoff and Masters runner-up Jim Ferrier at 71, Hogan, Demaret, and Mangrum at 72, and Snead at 73.

Middlecoff somehow missed an eight-inch putt on the second hole and made a double bogey. "That shocked me back into concentration," he said, and he rescued his round with a one-under 33 on the back nine.

Hogan also had a 33 on the back nine after a lackluster 39 on the front. He didn't get many approaches within short range, making only two birdies, one of them on a 35-foot putt. That might have been by design, though, as he would say after the tournament that his strategy for the week was to aim at the center of greens and not fire at the flags. It left him slightly adrift on this day of relatively low scoring, but not out of it by any means.

Snead only had one birdie and was a stroke further back, lamenting afterwards, "Ah putted like mah arms was broke." (Newspapers liked to quote him in his hillbilly style.)

Temperatures for Friday's second round reached 95 degrees in the afternoon. Mackey wilted in the dual heat of the weather and the pressure of leading. He had a bogey and a double bogey on the two front-nine par fives to make the turn in 40, then a string of five straight bogeys followed by a double bogey on Nos. 11-16 to shoot an 81.

"Yesterday, I couldn't get off the fairway. Today, I couldn't get on," said Mackey, who admitted to a mostly sleepless night after his first-round heroics. He would shoot 75-77 on Saturday to finish T25. Mackey would never play the tour and in the two other U.S. Opens he qualified for, in 1951 and 1958, shot 84-WD and 86-WD. He was truly a one-day wonder.

Dutch Harrison surged into the 36-hole lead with a 67. The 40-year-old from Arkansas was a steady performer, having finished in the top 10 money winners on tour in each of the last seven seasons with victories in all but two of those years. So far in 1950, he had won the Wilmington (N.C.) Open and ranked sixth in earnings.

One-over through eight holes, Harrison birdied the ninth and shot a three-under 31 on the back nine with birdies on 10, 13, and 16, and a par save from deep greenside rough on the closing hole. His birdie putts were all from 12 feet or less. "I shot me some golf today," said the man called the Arkansas Traveler, who was known to earn perhaps as much money in gambling games as he did in those days of relatively small purses on tour.

Johnny Bulla had the day's low round, a 66 to stand one stroke back at 140. The 36-year-old had an unconventional background, representing Walgreens and promoting the drug store's discount golf ball, and later signing a contract with Sears, instead of being affiliated with a club. He was also a pilot who co-founded Arizona Airways to serve the then small but growing Phoenix area, where he had settled. The nascent airline was struggling financially, which was perhaps why Bulla took his first club pro job in 1949. Now based in the Pittsburgh area, he didn't have an arrangement with the club that would enable him to play much on tour, and the U.S. Open was only his fourth event of 1950.

Bulla was better known now than when he was an unheralded 54-hole leader in 1939. His only tour win came in the 1941 Los Angeles Open, but he was second in the British Open in 1939 and 1946 (one of the few Americans to annually make the overseas trip in that era) and in the 1949 Masters. Bulla matched Harrison's 31 on the back nine with birdies on Nos. 11, 13, and 14, and a par save from a bunker on 18. Known more for his ball-striking, Bulla had an excellent day on the greens with 29 putts.

Joining Bulla at 140 were Ferrier and Boros. Ferrier was a 35-year-old born in Australia who moved to the U.S. in 1940 and turned pro. He had won the 1947 PGA Championship, added three wins in 1949, and was third on the 1950 money list entering the U.S. Open. Still, he was trying to erase the memory of his meltdown at the Masters that April, where he bogeyed five of the last six holes to finish two behind Demaret. The long-hitting, six-foot three Ferrier struck the ball beautifully in a second-round 69, missing only one fairway. Three-putt bogeys on the 15th and 16th cost him the lead. Boros also had a chance at the lead, finishing with bogeys on 16, 17, and 18 for a 72.

Perhaps more noteworthy was Hogan's 69, pulling him within two strokes at 141. He got to three-under on the round with birdies on Nos. 2, 6, 8, and 10 and a bogey on No. 7. Ben made putts of eight and 20 feet for his first two birdies, but his putting was substandard the rest of the way. The birdies on Nos. 8 and 10 came from four feet and one-and-a-half feet. He three-putted the seventh, missed birdie putts of just inside 10 feet on the 12th and 13th, three-putted the 16th for a bogey, and missed a six-foot par putt on the 17th. Hogan gathered himself to sink a five-foot putt for a par on 18 to avoid a third straight bogey.

Mangrum (72) and Middlecoff (71) were the most formidable players in the group which stood at 142. Snead, on the other hand, essentially shot himself out of it with a 75 to stand nine strokes behind at 148. He seemed to have no touch on the slick greens, so spooked that he left a three-foot putt short and then overcompensated by knocking some putts well past the hole. He had 38 putts, didn't make a single birdie, and double bogeyed the 15th. Demaret was also adrift at 149.

The biggest question looming over the 36-hole Saturday was whether Hogan would be able to manage it. On Friday, he had cramped up while walking from the 11th green to the 12th tee. His legs were swollen, and he soaked them in a tub of water and Epsom salts for an hour after returning to his Philadelphia hotel room. At dinner, he told friend and Merion member Frank Sullivan that he dreaded the double round. Later, he told his wife Valerie that he wasn't sure he would even be able to finish.

Hogan's morning routine each day included an hour-long soaking of his legs, followed by wrapping each leg in elastic bandages to minimize swelling. His third-round tee time of 9:30 was among the later ones of the contenders, though it still necessitated an early wake-up call.

Hogan didn't play like himself in the third round, hitting into the rough seven times, out of bounds once, and finding three bunkers instead of his usual tee-to-fairway-to-green game. Fortunately, he was able to stay in contention thanks to some very good scrambling that enabled him to escape with a 72.

Ben birdied the third hole to get to one-under, then drove into the rough on the par-five fourth. That eventually led to a long third shot and a three-putt bogey from 50 feet. He scrambled for pars after missing the sixth and seventh greens but couldn't save par from a bunker on the ninth, leaving him one-over on the front.

Promising birdies on 10 and 11 were followed by bogeys on 12 and 13. His drive on the 15th was out of bounds, three inches outside the stakes that lined the road bordering the left side of the hole. He was able to emerge with a bogey under the distance-only penalty for out-of-bounds then in force. Pars on the last three holes got him in at one-over for the round, remaining two strokes off the lead.

The morning round didn't leave the impression that Hogan should be the pick as the man to emerge with the title. He wasn't yet showing any visible signs of leg problems, but a second round on the same day would be sure to take its toll. Could he be expected to regain his swing form if his legs started aching more, as they surely would?

Merion's East Course was stiffening as a challenge on this Saturday, with the greens firming up considerably. There were six subpar scores in the first round and seven in the second, but only one in the third. That was turned in by Mangrum, a one-under 69 that gave him the 54-hole lead at 211. He had been two-over for the round through 10 holes before heating up with birdies on 11, 15, and 16, all of them thanks to approach shots within six feet.

Harrison, while compiling a fairly strong record on tour, had never distinguished himself in majors. His best showings were a semifinals loss in the 1939 PGA Championship and ties for seventh in the 1941 U.S. Open and 1942 Masters. His third round got off to a terrible start with a double bogey on the first hole, where his approach found a bunker and he three-putted. The rest of the front nine was also a struggle, as he shot a four-over 40. He got it together with a one-birdie, eight-par back nine for a 33 and a 73 for a 212 total, just one stroke off the lead.

Middlecoff was paired with Hogan in the featured twosome and shot a third straight 71 to tie his playing partner at 213. It could have been better. The defending champion was one-under through 16 holes with two birdies and a lone bogey, playing with Hogan-like precision, while Ben was more wayward. Middlecoff's tee shot on the tough par-three 17th went way to the right, leading to a bogey. He thinned his approach shot to the 18th, but the ball managed to roll up onto the front of the green 60 feet from the hole. Middlecoff told an official that he would replace the ball, which had been dented when he bladed it on the approach. The official refused the substitution, assessing that the damage to the ball was merely a "slight abrasion." A highly displeased Middlecoff then three-putted for a bogey.

Joining Hogan and Middlecoff in a tie for third was 31-year-old North Carolinian Johnny Palmer, who had won the biggest first-place check of 1949 ($10,000) at the World Championship of Golf. He shot the only even-par round of 70, helped by saving par from three of the four greenside bunkers he hit into.

Boros held the lead midway through the round thanks to pars on the first 10 holes. He coughed it up with four straight fives starting on the 11th hole, a five-over stretch, compounded with bogeys on 17 and 18 for a 77 to leave him at 217. Ferrier coincidentally also had four straight fives starting on the 11th. He at least recovered to birdie the 18th where he nearly holed a four-wood to shoot a 74 and stay in hailing distance at 214.

Bulla came crashing down in the closing stretch. He was even with playing partner Mangrum through 14 holes before a triple bogey on 15 led to playing the last four holes in five-over. He lost seven strokes to Mangrum on those four holes, leaving him seven off the lead after a 78.

The front nine of the final round turned into a massive retreat by the entire top of the 54-hole leaderboard. The nine-hole scores of the top six entering the last round were: Mangrum, 41; Harrison, 40; Hogan, 37; Middlecoff, 39; Palmer, 41; Ferrier, 40. Granted, the course was playing tough, but it was also due to players failing to rise to the occasion. Arthur Daley wrote in the *New York Times* that the championship had "all the characteristics of a cake of soap in a bathtub, being slippery, elusive, and then tantalizingly lost altogether."

Mangrum "led" the backwards movement with bogeys on six of the first seven holes, with a lone birdie providing little solace. Ferrier triple bogeyed the first hole, rocketing his second shot from the rough out of bounds over the green and hitting his next approach under a tree. Harrison double bogeyed the third and fourth. Middlecoff bogeyed both par fives, the second and fourth, and added a double bogey on the fifth after driving into a creek.

Hogan could see Middlecoff's troubles with his own eyes, and he also was informed at some point on the front nine that others were blowing up. "His expression did not change," wrote Lincoln Werden in the *New York Times*. "It seemed a bit grim and determined as he holed par after par."

Hogan's ball-striking acumen had returned. He hit every green in regulation on the front nine. A three-putt cost him a bogey at the third and he missed a six-foot birdie putt at the fourth; otherwise, he two-putted for pars from mostly medium range under his aim-for-the-center-of-the-green strategy.

The collective struggles of the others enabled Hogan to move into the lead. They also opened the door for players who started further back, including George Fazio, who was in the first twosome off the tee.

Fazio grew up nearby in Norristown, Pennsylvania, one of eight children in a working-class family of Italian immigrants. He got into golf as a caddie, with an additional teenage job of repairing golf clubs. His gregarious personality and golf skills eventually helped him land pro jobs at such prestigious clubs as Pine Valley in New Jersey and Hillcrest in Los Angeles. He didn't make a full-fledged run at the tour until age 33 in 1946, when Hillcrest's former pro returned from the service and Fazio landed a deal, along with Demaret, to promote Schenley rum on the pro tour (a Hillcrest member ran the Schenley company). An entrepreneurial sort, Fazio started a scrap metal business in Conshohocken, Pennsylvania with his five brothers in 1949. Later, he would become a golf course designer, and bring his nephew Tom into the business. On tour, he posted victories in the 1946 Canadian Open and 1947 Bing Crosby Pro-Am.

At Merion, he opened with 73-72-72, six strokes off the lead. He started the afternoon round with all pars on the front nine except for a three-putt bogey from seven feet on the seventh hole. The front-nine 37 hardly counted as a charge, yet it did move him closer to the lead as Mangrum and others were faltering behind him.

Fazio birdied the 13th from four feet, bogeyed the 14th, and birdied the 15th from nine feet. Sensing he might have a chance, he gambled on hitting a four-iron over the quarry from a lie in a divot hole in the rough on the 16th. The shot finished four feet from the hole, but he missed the birdie putt. Pars on the difficult 17th and 18th holes gave him an even-par 70.

"It seemed ridiculous at the time that 287 would not be bettered," wrote Al Laney in the *New York Herald Tribune*, "but as Fazio sat in the clubhouse hour after hour, he began to see that he might win with it."

Another early starter was Joe Kirkwood Jr. Two years earlier, he and his father, Joe Sr., had become the first father-son duo to make the cut in the same U.S. Open. Joe Jr. was a part-time tour player who doubled as an actor, playing the boxer Joe Palooka in a series of movies (and later television show). Kirkwood was eight strokes back after rounds of 71-74-74, but he was the hottest player on the course in the afternoon. He followed a two-under 34 on the front nine with a birdie on the 10th to get to six-over on the tournament. If he had been able to play even par from there, he would have beaten Fazio's total. It was too much to ask on Merion's tough finishing stretch. Bogeys on 14, 15, and 16 left Kirkwood with a 70 for a 289 total. The even-par 70s shot by Fazio and Kirkwood were the best rounds of the difficult afternoon.

Not far behind in the pairings was Mangrum. He steadied himself after his terrible start and had eight pars and a bogey on the back nine for a 35 and a 76. His 287 total tied Fazio, but he didn't think it would be good enough.

"I really thought I was going to win today, but it looks like it's just [Hogan's] turn," he said while waiting in the locker room. "I was always a strong finisher. That was my game. But the way I played today—embarrassing."

Next came Harrison. Like Mangrum, he had eight pars and a bogey on the back nine to shoot a matching round of 41-35—76. He started one behind Mangrum, however, so he finished at 288.

It seemed likely the winner would come from the twosome of Hogan and Middlecoff, who drew the lion's share of the gallery as they made the turn at four-over and six-over, respectively, after the front nine. Cary made it hard on himself with his second double bogey of the round on the 10th hole. His tee shot landed in a bunker on the short par four, 60 yards from the hole, and his second shot caught the lip of the trap and fell back into the sand. His next attempt didn't reach the green, and after a pitch and two putts he was eight-over. Hogan's tee shot found the same bunker, but he hit the green with his second and made a par.

Both parred the 11th, Hogan missing a 10-foot birdie try. The effect of the marathon walking day was taking its toll on Hogan's legs, which had become swollen and painful. Middlecoff, noting Ben's hobbling, had begun marking Ben's ball on the greens and taking it out of the hole. "By now, every step had become agony," said Jim Finegan, a college student in the gallery who later became an acclaimed golf writer. "Here, obviously, was a man whose legs were near to buckling under him."

On the 12th tee, Hogan's legs *did* buckle on the follow-through of his drive, causing him to stagger and nearly fall. He grabbed onto a friend nearby in the gallery, Harry Radix, who donated the Radix Trophy to the pro with the lowest scoring average on the year. "Let me hang onto you for a bit," Hogan said to him. "My God, I don't think I can finish."

Hogan gathered himself and managed to walk gingerly up the fairway. He hit his approach to the back fringe, used a putter to knock a delicate downhiller six feet past, and missed from there. The bogey put him at five-over and needing to play the rest of the round in one-over or better to beat Mangrum (who had just finished) and Fazio.

If Hogan was worn out physically, Middlecoff was spent mentally. On the way to the 13th hole, he confided to the USGA's Joe Dey, "I just can't do it, Joe. I just can't. I can't play my game for thinking about Ben. Did you see him on that last hole? He almost fell off the tee. Gee, he's making a great go of it. I can't concentrate."

Hogan's legs cramped on the 13th tee, and he rubbed them while his caddie teed up his ball for him. Finegan remembers that Hogan's "mouth was set in a tight line suggesting a permanent grimace."

He got through the short par-three hole with a par, then nearly doubled over in pain when he walked off the green, which is next to the clubhouse. He told his caddie to bring his clubs to the clubhouse because he was finished, an oft-told story of Merion lore that Hogan later confirmed was true. The caddie, a Merion veteran named Whitey Williams, didn't go along. Certain that Hogan could will his way around the course with an Open title on the line, Williams reportedly replied, "I'll see you on the 14th tee, sir."

Hogan limped to the 14th tee and made a two-putt par on that hole. He hit his second shot safely to 25 feet on the par-four 15th, left his first putt two feet short, went to tap in for a par—and missed it. His swing was holding up alright, so to give a stroke away with a putting gaffe was highly frustrating, especially since it removed his last margin for error. Hogan now needed to play the last three holes in even par to win outright, which was no easy feat on that gauntlet.

Ben got a break on the 16th when his errant second shot hit a spectator and was deflected into a relatively benign position just off the green. He chipped to four feet and made the nerve-wracking putt.

The opposite occurred on the par-three 17th, where he thought he hit his long-iron tee shot well. Instead of fading toward the back right pin, however, it stayed straight, landed on the left side of the green, and took a big hop into the back left bunker. He blasted out to six feet from the hole. Hogan surveyed the putt carefully, took two practice strokes, and left the putt just short, on the lip of the hole.

Now he needed a birdie on the 458-yard par four 18th to win outright. Nobody had birdied the hole in this round in any of the twosomes before Hogan, nor would anybody after. There was only one birdie in the morning's third round. More to the point, Ben needed a par on this brute of a hole to tie Mangrum and Fazio.

Hogan didn't know the scoring situation, and after hitting his drive into the fairway, he wanted to find out what he needed. He asked a USGA official if anybody had finished at 286. The official said he wasn't sure. Jimmy Hines, a fellow pro who had come out to watch, told Hogan that there was a score of 286 in the clubhouse. Fred Corcoran, former PGA tournament manager and a well-known figure on the golf scene, also had worked his way nearby. Hearing the exchange, Corcoran offered a correction. "No," he said. "Two-eighty-seven is low." Hogan glared at Corcoran, wanting to be sure. "Two-eighty-seven is low," Corcoran repeated.

Now trusting that a par would get him a tie, Hogan drew a long iron out of the bag rather than trying to get at the back pin with a four-wood. He hit a good one, bouncing up to the green 45 feet from the hole and avoiding the bunkers left and right of the putting surface. Various sources and stories say that the shot was hit with a one-iron; others that it was a two-iron. The definitive truth is lost to history; in any case, the shot was immortalized in a photo taken by

Life magazine photographer Hy Peskin, showing Hogan in a classic follow-through.

Under the circumstances, it was a fine shot. But Hogan's work was by no means done. His ball was now 45 feet from the hole, and he needed to two-putt to stay alive. He struck the first putt a little too hard, and misread it, sending the ball past the hole to the left, and leaving a four-footer for a par. How much could a man's nerves take? Hogan, having gone one-for-three on putts in the two-to-six-foot range on the last three holes, didn't wait long to find out. He stepped up to the putt quickly, drew the putter back, and knocked the ball into the hole.

There were still 20 players on the course, but only one with a chance, and a remote one at that. Henry Ransom came through the 16th hole at eight-over par, needing to play the last two holes one-under to join the tie. Instead, he bogeyed the 17th and finished two strokes back.

Hogan's fourth-round score was a 74 that didn't include a single birdie. He let a lead slip away with three bogeys on the last seven holes. Nonetheless, it was a worthy accomplishment, a round to be inspired by. It came on a testing course where the top six players through 54 holes averaged 76.5 in the final round, with Hogan's 74 the best. Even more so, it was a test of endurance, the second act of a two-round day which many close observers didn't think Hogan would even be able to complete on his bandage-wrapped, weakened legs.

The USGA's Dey called it the most memorable of all the Opens he witnessed. "I thought Ben was going to pass out on the 12th hole. It was the greatest physical accomplishment I've ever seen. Hogan pushed himself beyond the limits of endurance that day."

And now there was another day to play. Ben's legs swelled so much, and he was so exhausted, that his wife, Valerie, later said that she "had given up on his being able to tee off in the playoff, but I couldn't tell him that." But when he woke up the next morning, she said, he was "fresh as a daisy."

The playoff didn't start until 2 p.m. because of Pennsylvania's blue laws governing events on Sundays. That was fortunate for Hogan. It gave him more time to recover.

That morning a group of reporters gathered in the lobby of Hogan's hotel, probably to check if he was going to be able to play in the play-off, or at least to gauge his condition. They were surprised by Hogan's freshness, and after chatting for a couple of minutes, they applauded him as he left the hotel.

Hogan was a heavy favorite of the large gallery that followed the playoff. His remarkable comeback from his injuries had turned him into a sentimental favorite. The public reaction after the accident— telegrams to the hospital during his recovery and cheers after his return to the tour—also made Hogan more appreciative of the fans.

"Hogan was the least tense of the three men in the playoff," wrote Shirley Povich in the *Washington Post*. "He was gallery-conscious, and they liked it. For the first time in his career, he was probably trying to win for the gallery as well as for Hogan."

The playoff was tight nearly all the way. All three were even par through five holes. Hogan's precision game was decidedly on, as he churned out routine pars, while Fazio went bogey-birdie on the first two holes and Mangrum birdie-bogey on the second and third.

Fazio bogeyed the sixth with a long approach and the seventh with an out-of-bounds drive, then got one stroke back with a birdie at the eighth. Hogan missed a four-foot birdie putt on the sixth but holed from a similar length for a birdie on the seventh. He then bogeyed the eighth after a one-iron tee shot found a bunker, and he missed the green from there.

It was Hogan's only missed green of the front nine. Mangrum was nearly as solid, missing only two greens. All three parred the ninth, leaving Hogan and Mangrum at even par and Fazio one over. Fazio, who later said he was too keyed up, overshot several greens with approaches and hit only three greens on the front nine, but kept himself in it with chipping and putting.

Hogan's relentlessly steady play carried over to the back nine. Mangrum, by contrast, had a volatile nine marked by erratic play and two very costly mental errors. Fazio slowly faded out of it midway through the closing nine.

Mangrum drove into a fairway bunker on the 10th and made a

bogey, then drew back even with Hogan when he birdied the 11th after an approach to five feet. Lloyd's first blunder came on the 12th hole, where he badly mis-clubbed on his approach, the ball sailing over the gallery and bouncing across the road that cut through course. USGA official Ike Grainger had to make a ruling because the road was out of bounds but the ball came to rest on course property near the 13th hole. Grainger ruled the ball was out of bounds, which wasn't bad for Mangrum under the distance-only out of bounds rule, as a pitch from across the road to a downhill green would have been very difficult. Using the proper club this time, Mangrum found the green and made bogey.

All three parred the 13th, so Hogan was even par and one ahead of the other two. With his machine-like precision, Hogan posted routine pars on 14 and 15. Fazio three-putted both to fall three behind. Mangrum bogeyed 14 from a greenside bunker and continued his back-and-forth act with a birdie on 15 from 12 feet to get back within a stroke of Hogan.

Hogan had yet to miss a fairway or green on the back nine, and he again hit both on the 16th. Mangrum drove into the right rough, had to lay up short of the quarry, and hit his third shot to 15 feet. He addressed the putt, saw a bug on the ball, lifted the ball while keeping his putter down to mark the spot, and blew the bug off. Lloyd then holed the pressure putt to (apparently) stay within one of Hogan, who missed a 10-foot birdie try. But, no, Mangrum had incurred a two-stroke penalty for lifting and cleaning his ball on the green, which was then not allowed by the rules (a player could mark his ball only if it interfered with the play of another player, and even then, was not allowed to clean it). Blowing away a bug was no exception.

Nobody seemed aware of the violation, however, until Grainger made his way through the crowd to the 17th tee and informed Mangrum of the penalty. Instead of being one stroke behind with two holes to play, he was three behind with a double bogey on his scorecard for the 16th.

Had Mangrum lost by two strokes or less, it would have been an awful way to lose. Fortunately, Hogan finished in style, holing a 50-foot birdie putt on the 17th, eliciting a roar that could be heard at the clubhouse. He hit the fairway on 18, missed the green with his approach for the first time on the back nine, chipped to seven feet, and holed the putt for a par. He conquered Merion's East Course with a 69 in the playoff and vanquished his opponents as Mangrum recorded a 73 and Fazio a 75.

A year earlier, Hogan had been physically unable to defend the U.S. Open title he claimed in 1948. A day earlier, he had barely been able to make his way around the course. Now he had his second U.S. Open title and would add two more in 1951 and 1953.

Columnist Red Smith summed up Hogan's Merion triumph in the *New York Herald Tribune*: "Maybe once in the lifetime of any of us it is possible to say with accuracy and without mawkishness, 'This was a spiritual victory, an absolute triumph of will!' This is that one time."

TOP-10 FINISHERS		
1	Ben Hogan	72-69-72-74—287*
2	Lloyd Mangrum	72-70-69-76—287
3	George Fazio	73-72-72-70—287
4	Dutch Harrison	72-67-73-76—288
T5	Jim Ferrier	71-69-74-75—289
T5	Joe Kirkwood Jr.	71-74-74-70—289
T5	Henry Ransom	72-71-73-73—289
8	Bill Nary	73-70-74-73—290
9	Julius Boros	68-72-77-74—291
T10	Cary Middlecoff	71-71-71-79—292
T10	Johnny Palmer	73-70-70-79—292

*Hogan won playoff, 69; Mangrum, 73; Fazio, 75

1955

OLYMPIC UPSET

B en Hogan followed his 1948 and 1950 U.S. Open victories with two more in 1951 and 1953, matching Willie Anderson and Bobby Jones for the most titles with four (later joined by Jack Nicklaus). At age 42 in 1955, the blood-circulation condition in his legs wasn't improving. Hogan wasn't entering many events, but the quest for a fifth Open drove him to grind hard when the national championship came around in June.

The Olympic Club in San Francisco would host its first Open that year. Architect Robert Trent Jones was called in to update and toughen up the club's Lake Course, which opened in 1924, in preparation for the championship, just as he did at Oakland Hills in Michigan for the 1951 Open, resulting in a course that was described as a "monster."

At Oakland Hills, Jones tightened the course by pinching in fairway bunkers in the landing areas. Olympic had no fairway bunkers, and Jones added them on just two holes; one on the sixth hole, positioned in the landing area for tee shots and two on the first hole, placed in play for the second shot on that par five. More significantly, new tee placements added about 350 yards to stretch the course to 6,727 yards, and some fairways were narrowed.

The course ended up being a fearsome challenge and produced a higher scoring average than Oakland Hills—78.72 versus 77.23— with both playing to par 70. The extreme difficulty wasn't necessarily a result of Jones's alterations, though. It was perhaps more due to the work carried out by the Olympic Club itself.

The club overseeded and fertilized the rough that spring and let it grow and grow. Not only did it grow long, it also grew thick. The U.S. Open was typically known for heavy rough, but this was the heaviest ever. The week before the championship, the USGA ordered it to be cut to four-and-a-half inches, but it was still severely punishing. When asked about the rough, Sam Snead responded, "If I told you what I think you couldn't publish it. The strongest man in the world can't hit the thing 10 feet out of some of that grass."

Architect Jones predicted that the winning score would be 282. Hogan, arriving as usual nine days before the start of the championship to scope out the course, predicted after a few practice rounds that 287 would do it. The key to winning, he felt, would be to keep the ball in the fairway. For that reason, he cut down on his swing to favor accuracy over distance.

Gene Littler, the runner-up the year before at Baltusrol as a tour rookie (and later the 1961 U.S. Open champion), also arrived early and said the course was eight times harder than Baltusrol. After the rough was cut, he assessed it as four times harder.

The first round served as proof that the Lake Course was a West Coast monster. The average score was 79.8, and 82 of the field of 162 didn't break 80. There were five scores in the 90s, including a 96 by host pro John Battini. The only subpar round was turned in by Tommy Bolt, who took a three-stroke lead with a 67.

The 39-year-old Bolt, only in his sixth year on tour, had already accumulated nine of his eventual total of 15 victories (he would win the U.S. Open in 1958). He was just as well known for his volatile temper and club-throwing antics as for those victories.

Bolt didn't have much to get mad about that Thursday, especially not on the greens, where he needed only 25 putts and holed six putts of 10 feet or longer. He knew he couldn't keep up that pace. "I still think something between 286 and 290 will win the Open," Bolt told the press.

The guy who lost his cool that day was Snead in his endlessly futile quest to capture the U.S. Open. He missed a couple of short putts early and became frustrated. Swinging from his heels, trying to pound out long drives, he hit into the rough on every hole from Nos. 5 to 12, a recipe for disaster at the Lake Course. The result was a 79, and he needed a 12-foot par putt on 18 to do it. Along the way, he occasionally paused to glower at photographers, once barking at them that they were lousing him up. At the end of the day, he hustled out to his car still wearing his spikes to dodge interviews. "Only one reporter had the fleetness of foot to stay within hollering distance and the answer he got was a growl," reported the *San Francisco Examiner.*

The only even-par round was shot by little-known Walker Inman, while Jack Burke Jr. had a 71 with a bogey on 18. Next came Hogan, the only player at 72, a score he was very satisfied with.

Hogan said he played "darn good" in hitting 15 greens, and that he was "exactly even par—72." Hogan explained that he felt par was realistically 72 instead of the 70 on the scorecard, because the par-four fifth and 11th holes were essentially par four-and-half and the 17th, which had been converted from a par five to a 461-yard par four, still played like a par five. He made only one birdie and left several putts on the lip of the hole. "I haven't figured out whether these greens are slow or fast," he said. "Maybe I'll know more after tomorrow."

Cary Middlecoff, one of the best players of the 1950s and the winner of the Masters two months before the Open, had a promising start with a 35 on the front nine only to shoot a 41 on the back. He took four from the fringe to double bogey the 10th, afterward saying, "I couldn't shake out of it." Ed Furgol and Littler, who finished 1-2 in the 1954 Open, both shot 76, with Furgol losing a ball in the rough on the first hole. Also at 76, and receiving absolutely no attention, was Jack Fleck.

Fleck began to attract a degree of notice when his second-round 69 matched the low score of the day on Friday, giving him a 145 total that moved him within one stroke of the lead shared by Bolt and amateur Harvie Ward. Referred to by the *Examiner* as a "little known Davenport, Ia., professional," the 33-year-old Fleck had a flimsy resume on the tour.

Fleck knew nothing about golf until the tour made a one-year stop in Davenport for the Western Open when he was 15. Quickly hooked, he became a caddie, started to play, and by the time he finished high school, was determined to somehow make a living at the game. At the time, he couldn't regularly break 80, but he managed to land an assistant pro job at a Davenport course, one that involved mainly menial tasks such as cleaning clubs. He soon moved to Des Moines Country Club before joining the Navy in World War II and serving on a warship during D-Day at Normandy.

After the war, he returned to a pro position in Des Moines and worked on his game. He began to be intrigued by the idea of playing some on the pro tour, especially after he finished fifth when the tour came to Iowa for the 1949 Cedar Rapids Open. By then, he had been hired to manage two municipal courses in Davenport.

Fleck played a few events on the winter tour each year from 1950-53. In the summer of 1953, his wife Lynn encouraged him to take some time to play the tour while she managed the courses in Davenport. It wasn't exactly a way to make a living. The purses were paltry in those days. Fleck earned $1,020 in 12 events in 1953 and $3,613 in 16 events in 1954.

He was making his most extended effort yet in 1955, playing in 14 events before the U.S. Open with earnings totaling $2,752. He had compiled an interesting record, with 11 top-25 finishes in those 14 tournaments but none in the top 10. While Fleck was becoming a consistently decent player, he couldn't quite get over the hump. He had only one top-10 each in 1953 and 1954, with a best of T8.

Fleck qualified for the Open in a sectional qualifier outside of Chicago and made a two-and-a-half day drive to the West Coast. This would be his third U.S. Open, having missed the cut in 1950 and finished T52 in 1953. Nobody practiced harder at Olympic. He played 44 holes each day on Saturday through Tuesday before the event (the eighth hole on the Lake Course comes back to the clubhouse) and 36 on Wednesday. His goal was a top-10 finish to avoid sectional qualifying the next year. Early in the week, Fleck sent a letter to the sports editor of the *Davenport Democrat*. "Will play this one for keeps, not that I don't do it in all tournaments, but the Open is the big one,"

Fleck wrote. After expressing that Olympic would earn recognition as one of the great courses, Fleck predicted that the old guard would win and offered his picks for the top-10 finishers, concluding, "and yours truly might sneak in there."

He advanced toward that goal on Friday with a four-birdie, three-bogey round. Fleck would later recount that on the fifth green something changed with his putting. He didn't adjust his grip or stance, but "I had some kind of wonderful feeling in my hands over the ball." He made a 15-foot birdie putt there and needed only 26 putts on the round, a welcome change for a player who often struggled on the greens. Straight driving was Fleck's strong suit, and that was particularly beneficial at the Lake Course. Nearly holing a seven-iron at the eighth hole—it popped out of the cup and stopped a couple inches away—also helped.

Still, Fleck received little more than a token mention in reports of the second round. The other 69s were turned in by Snead and 1952 U.S. Open champion Julius Boros. Other players at 145 alongside Fleck included Boros and Hogan.

Snead's turnaround 69, bringing him within four strokes after his opening 79, was the story of the day. A day after running away from the press, he was "all affability" according to the *Examiner*, as he strode into the press tent to recount the details of his round. There was still a tinge of annoyance, however, as he missed six putts of eight feet or less in a superb ball-striking round. After a one-over front nine, he had a two-under 33 on the back with a putt for a birdie on every hole.

Hogan, meanwhile, had gotten off to a poor start, missing a two-foot birdie putt on the par-five first hole and bogeying Nos. 3, 4, and 5. He recovered with three birdies the rest of the way, though he also made three more bogeys in an uncharacteristically erratic round. On the 16th, his drive hit a tree and ricocheted sideways into the fairway merely 150 yards from the tee on the 610-yard par five. He got out of it with a birdie after a two-iron third shot to 25 feet and a great putt.

The Associated Press reported that Hogan "brooded as he finished his round. He studied his card intently but had little to say." The scorecard added up to a 73, leaving Hogan in a good position, one stroke off the lead.

That was enough for Middlecoff, in the daily column he was penning for the *Examiner*, to assert, "I don't see any way—not any way—they're going to beat Ben Hogan ... He drives better than anybody in contention. That driving is going to pay off—driving and patience. And he's always had more patience than anybody in the game."

Boros's straight driving paid off in the second round. He didn't miss a fairway in his 69. He had a two-under 33 on the back nine that could have been even better had he not taken three from the back fringe to bogey the 18th. That left him one stroke off the lead, along with Hogan, Fleck, and Inman, who bogeyed the last three in a 75.

Bolt, like Snead, had a 10-stroke difference in his first and second rounds, but in the opposite direction as he hobbled to a 77. Tommy's putting magic eluded him during the round, and, to make matters worse, he double bogeyed the 18th after his drive finished unplayable in a shrub, forcing him to walk back to the tee. He initially refused to talk to reporters, perhaps peeved by the double bogey, though his stated reason was discontent over how the press treated him after the first round, with articles focusing more on his hot temper than on his cool 67. Eventually, he agreed to be interviewed.

Bolt was tied for first at 144 with Harvie Ward, who had won the 1952 British Amateur and was about to firmly establish himself as the best amateur in the nation with victories in the 1955 and 1956 U.S. Amateur. At Olympic, he started with rounds of 74 and 70 and was trying to become the first amateur to win the Open since Johnny Goodman in 1933. The 29-year-old Ward was a native of North Carolina, but now lived in San Francisco, so he was able to commute to the Open from his house.

Ward sold cars at a dealership owned by Eddie Lowery, who, after caddying for Francis Ouimet in his victory at the 1913 U.S. Open outside Boston perhaps improbably went on to own a major car dealership in San Francisco and to eventually serve on the USGA's executive committee. Lowery allowed Ward plenty of time to work on his game and play in tournaments. The boss had the same arrangement with another employee, Ken Venturi, who would later turn pro and win the 1964 U.S. Open.

Ward had been able to play the Lake Course a number of times, so he had an advantage in local knowledge. He made one of the few birdies recorded all week on the brutal 17th hole, hitting a four-wood to two feet in the second round.

Another player with even greater local knowledge made the biggest noise in Saturday morning's third round. Bob Rosburg grew up playing Olympic Club and, at age 12, defeated baseball legend Ty Cobb to win the first flight of the club championship. Cobb would not live that down, receiving such a harsh ribbing that, afterwards, he hardly ever showed up at the club. Now 28 years old, Rosburg shot a 67 in the third round to pull within two strokes of the lead.

Rosburg—called "Bobby" in many accounts—was in only his second year on tour, with one win so far. He would go on to claim a total of six victories, becoming perhaps more well known after his playing career as a roving on-course reporter for ABC at U.S. Opens and other events.

Hogan was the leader through 54 holes, shooting a 72 while others faltered. Hogan himself stumbled at the finish, bogeying the last three holes to lead by one at 217 instead of by a wider margin. He had been steady on the first 15 holes with a lone bogey at the third and birdies on the 10th and 15th. Hogan, walking slowly and often with a limp, was observed falling further behind than usual from the twosome ahead. A photo in the next day's *Examiner* showed him grabbing his thigh while walking. Perhaps he tired down the stretch, though his problems on the last three holes were more on and around the greens than with his long game.

Ben three-putted the 16th from 25 feet, missing a four-foot second putt. He didn't quite reach the tough 17th in two, chipped on, and missed another four-footer. His approach on the 337-yard 18th bounced onto the fringe, only about 18 feet from the hole. He deliberated, changed clubs, and shockingly stubbed the shot, leaving it 12 feet short, barely onto the green, and he couldn't hole the putt.

That opened the door for others, including Snead and Boros,

playing together, who ended up just one stroke out of first at 218. Snead again struck the ball very well in shooting a 70 but was overheard at lunch grumbling about his putting. Boros had a 73.

Bolt bogeyed the last two holes for a 75 and joined Rosburg at 219. Ward suffered the indignity of his tee shot at the par-three eighth taking up permanent residence in a tree, leading to a double bogey. He shot a 76 and was tied at 220 with Burke and Fleck, who didn't have a single birdie in a round of 75.

In the final round, Boros double bogeyed the third hole on the way to a 77 and Rosburg also fell back early with bogeys on two of the first three holes, ultimately shooting a 76. Ward and Burke shot themselves out of it with 40s on the front nine, finishing with 76 and 77. Bolt hung reasonably tough until a double bogey on the 14th.

Snead was two-over on the front nine, still striving for that elusive first Open title. Alas, he missed birdie putts of nine, five, and seven feet on holes 12-14. Bogeys on 16 and 17 ended his bid.

While others were falling, Hogan was grinding out a round that, as it unfolded, appeared to be enough for his fifth Open title. He traded birdies and bogeys early in the round, not a bad thing on a course where an even-par score was a worthy accomplishment. He birdied the first after a pitch to three feet, bogeyed the third with a three-putt from the fringe, birdied the fourth on a 20-foot putt, and bogeyed the fifth when he drove behind some trees and had no shot at the green.

A steadying string of pars followed. On the ninth fairway, Hogan asked a USGA official how other players were doing. When he learned that Snead and Boros, playing a few holes ahead of him, were over par, he gave a trace of a grin and then went about his business.

Hogan had chances for birdies on Nos. 10-12, missing putts in the 8-to-10-foot range on each of them. The par-three 13th was trouble. He hit a two-iron tee shot into a bunker, then failed to catch enough sand on his explosion shot, sailing the ball over the green. A chip to within a foot of the hole enabled him to escape with a bogey.

A drive into the rough looked like more trouble on the 14th. The area had been largely trampled down by the gallery, but it was still a surprise—and a risk—when Hogan chose to hit a four-wood. He pulled it off beautifully, the shot bouncing in front of the green and rolling up to 20 feet from the hole for a two-putt par.

Ben got back to even par for the round with a 30-foot birdie putt on the 15th. It appeared to be hit too hard, but it caught the back center of the cup and dropped. The birdie put Hogan in such a good mood that he uncharacteristically chatted with a reporter while walking down the 16th fairway instead of maintaining his usual steely focus.

A routine par on 16 brought Hogan to the challenge of the 17th. He missed the green just to the right with a three-wood, and chipped within a foot for a par. It was the first time he managed to par the hole, including practice rounds.

At 337 yards, the 18th wasn't such a stern test. Hogan hit his second shot to 15 feet. He didn't make the putt but was plenty satisfied with an even-par round of 70, breaking into a big smile as he acknowledged the applause from the gallery.

NBC was televising the event nationally for only the second time, enlisting two-time champion Gene Sarazen as its commentator. It was the first U.S. Open Sarazen hadn't played in since his 1920 debut. Sarazen rushed over to Hogan and, on the air, congratulated him for winning his fifth Open championship. Hogan demurred only slightly, and shortly thereafter was persuaded to hold up five fingers for a posed news photograph. He also gave his ball to the USGA's Joe Dey for the organization's museum.

A Hogan victory was almost assured—the operative word being "almost." Of the players still on the course, there was one who still had a chance. Fleck was two-under for the round and eight-over for the championship through 12 holes. Hogan had finished at seven-over 287.

A marshal named George Tompkins had befriended Fleck during the week. When Hogan finished, Tompkins set out to inform Fleck of the target score, reaching him on the 14th tee after Fleck parred the 13th, where he got up and down from a bunker. Tompkins told Fleck that he needed one birdie to tie. Overhearing the exchange, Littler, who was playing with Fleck, said, "He'll need some pars, too." (Littler had begun the final round five strokes off the lead and was in the process of shooting a 78.)

Ironically, the unlikely challenger Fleck had been heavily influenced by Hogan. He perhaps even idolized him. When the two were playing in the same event, Fleck would carefully observe Hogan on the range. Fleck admired and adopted Hogan's meticulous preparation for tournaments, his intense focus on the course, and, to a certain extent, his swing. He even wore the same type of cap, though at six-foot-one, he cut a much taller figure.

He also was the only man in the field—other than Hogan—to be playing Ben Hogan golf clubs. Hogan started an equipment company in 1953 and produced its first run of clubs in 1954. In the spring of 1955, while playing the winter tour, Fleck spotted a set in a pro shop in Florida. He wrote to the Ben Hogan Company, requesting a set, and received a letter from Hogan himself, who obliged and added that the company would be happy to fit the clubs to Fleck's specs.

An unexpected bonus was that Hogan saw to it that Fleck received an invitation to the Colonial tournament in May in Fort Worth, Texas where Hogan lived and where the company was based, to pick up his clubs. The Monday before the Colonial was the first time Fleck met Hogan face-to-face, Ben greeting him warmly, and conveying how pleased he was that Fleck would use his clubs, and that the set was complimentary. There had been production problems in the latest run of clubs, so the irons weren't ready until Wednesday. The woods were delivered to Fleck at a tournament two weeks later, and Hogan hand delivered the wedges during practice rounds for the U.S. Open. It might seem odd that an obscure pro was the only one playing Hogan clubs, but it made sense given that most established pros already had equipment contracts with other companies.

Fleck started the final round three strokes back, and it began unpromisingly with a three-putt bogey at the second hole, followed by leaving himself a 35-foot putt for a par on the third. Fortunately, he made that one. He stamped himself as a contender with consecutive birdies on Nos. 6-8. He hit a six-iron to five feet on the sixth and took advantage of the short par-four seventh and short par-three eighth with birdies from eight and 15 feet. Fleck gave one back with a bogey on the ninth, where he drove into deep rough and had to play out short, but it was still a one-under 34 on the front nine.

Fleck's approach to the 417-yard 10th was spectacular, finishing inches from the hole for a birdie. Three holes later, he got the word from Tompkins—and promptly bogeyed the 14th. He hit a big drive, but his six-iron second shot dove into a bunker. Now he somehow needed to play the last four holes in two-under to tie.

Meanwhile, Hogan was lounging in the clubhouse nursing a Scotch and water, surrounded by a gaggle of sportswriters. He seemed relaxed and relieved it was almost certainly over—the tournament and, he said, his career. "I'm through. Tournament golf is too much of a physical and mental strain on me, and I've had enough. I've had to work too hard. I doggone near killed myself preparing for this one." The comments echoed statements he'd made earlier in the week.

Periodically, runners would interrupt with reports on the progress of Fleck's longshot bid. When Fleck birdied the 15th hole—now needing to go one-under on the last three to tie—Hogan excused himself to take a shower.

The Fleck birdie on 15 came on a six-iron tee shot to eight feet. He hit a longer-than-usual drive on the par-five 16th and, on his third shot, approached with a shorter iron. He pulled it into the left fringe rough, however, and ultimately made a par thanks to a deft chip.

He still needed a birdie, but, apropos to Littler's comment, he would need a par, too. That was no mean feat on the 461-yard 17th hole that played to a left-to-right sidehill on the tee shot and uphill on the second. A drive in the fairway was a must, and Fleck accomplished it. He still needed a three-wood to reach the green, and struck a good one—hitting it so solidly that it reached the back of the green, leaving a downhill putt from 40 feet. Fleck, still with the good feeling in his hands, nearly holed it, the ball catching the lip and stopping six inches away.

NBC, which had cameras only on 17 and 18, now signed off the air. The USGA had not set up its tee times to fully utilize the one-hour television window. They had come on the air only in time for Hogan's second shot on 18. Now they weren't able to show Fleck's bid to tie.

Onsite, a huge throng of people would witness that bid. The Lake Course has perhaps the world's best natural amphitheater for an 18th hole, with a tall hillside to the left of the green affording a view for thousands. Fleck, of course, had never performed before an audience that large.

He hit a three-wood off the tee on the short par four to try to stay in the fairway. It was pulled ever so slightly into the rough—not the deep stuff but rather the intermediate cut just a few inches off the fairway. Fleck selected a seven-iron for the uphill shot to the green. He was up to the enormity of the situation, swinging smoothly, judging the distance properly, and sending the ball to rest just seven feet from the hole.

Hogan by then had emerged from the shower and was preparing for the award ceremony. A runner informed the Hogan gathering that Fleck had a putt to tie. Soon after, they heard a huge roar, and knew that Fleck had sunk the pressure putt to force a playoff the next day. Hogan dropped his head and cursed softly. Raising his head, he said, "I was wishing he'd make either a two or a four. I was wishing it was over—all over."

Turning to a locker attendant, he said, "Well, we might as well get these things [clubs] back in the locker. Gotta play tomorrow, looks like."

It was an extraordinary turn of events. An unknown pro from Iowa, who had never finished better than fifth in a tour event, played the round of his life to tie a living legend. Fleck's 67 was the best fourth round by three strokes, and Hogan's 70 was the only even-par round. They were five strokes ahead of the rest of the field over 72 holes.

Could Fleck outscore Hogan again in the playoff? Hogan's record in playoffs wasn't very good—he had seven wins and 10 losses to date (and would finish his career with an 8-12 record). But still, the accomplishments and status in the game were so lopsided in Hogan's favor that a Fleck victory would have to be considered a major upset.

Hogan later said that he never saw anyone as nervous as Fleck was on the first tee. Visibly shaking, the underdog didn't catch his drive solidly and was well short of Hogan's. Fleck didn't hit his second shot especially well, either, leaving a nine-iron third shot to the 530-yard par five. He hit the green and equaled Hogan's par.

Fleck drove into the left rough on the second hole with a lie so bad, it was impossible to reach the green. He escaped with a par on a five-foot putt. He settled down after that, matching two-putt pars with Hogan on the next two holes. The third hole was a missed opportunity for Ben, when he failed to convert a four-foot birdie putt after a brilliant two-iron tee shot on the par three.

Hogan fell one stroke behind with a bogey on the fifth. His normally reliable driver betrayed him with a tee shot into trees on the right side, forcing a lay-up second. Fleck also had a bit of tree trouble on the left side after an errant tee shot, but rebounded by hooking the ball around a tree in front of him, and managed to hit the green for a two-putt par.

Fleck's newfound putting prowess manifested itself on the sixth hole, where he holed a 25-foot putt for a par to stay one ahead. Both parred the seventh, and then, for the second consecutive day, Fleck reeled off a three-birdie streak around the middle of the round.

Both birdied the eighth, Hogan draining a 35-foot putt and Fleck an eight-footer. Both were about 20 feet from the hole on the ninth, requiring the USGA's Dey to judge who was away. Fleck went first and holed it; Hogan couldn't match. Fleck went ahead by three by sinking a 15-foot, left-to-right sidehill birdie putt on the 10th.

The margin went back down to two when Fleck bogeyed the 11th after a drive into Olympic's punishing rough left him with a lay-up second. Hogan got up and down from a bunker for his par, making a five-foot putt. Ben quickly fell three behind again on the next hole. He recovered well enough from a drive in the rough to hit the green, then three-putted from 40 feet, missing a two-footer for his second putt, drawing a groan from the crowd.

Hogan made up for it at the 13th with his second bunker save in three holes, this time with a blast to six feet. On the 14th hole, it was Fleck's turn for bunker wizardry. His approach shot plunged into a half-buried lie in the sand, and it appeared he might have little chance to get close to the hole. Miraculously, Fleck thumped it out and somehow got the ball to check up quickly enough to stop three feet from the hole. It was a good thing he saved par; it enabled him to lose only one stroke of his lead as Hogan birdied from 20 feet. The 15th and 16th were relatively drama free, with all two-putt pars in the 15-to-25-foot range.

After both found the fairway on the 17th, it turned into a battle of three-wood second shots on the brute of a par four. Hogan hit a wonderful one to 14 feet and a chance for a birdie. Fleck's drifted to the right, leaving a pitch over a bunker, which he executed nicely to six feet. Both missed their putts, with Hogan's par pulling him within one stroke. Heading to the finishing hole, Fleck was one-under for the round, and Hogan was even par.

Hogan now had the honor of hitting first. The 18th was a hole where many, including Hogan, had been hitting three-woods off the tee. For some reason, this time he chose driver. Unfortunately, during his swing, his right foot slipped on a teeing ground that had been top-dressed with sand, and he hit a vicious pull to the left into some of the deepest, thickest rough on the course—an area from which the gallery had been cordoned off. The ball was so deep in the long grass that Hogan's attempt to hack out of it moved the ball only a few feet. His second effort moved it only a few feet more. Finally, he hit a shot out onto the fairway, now lying four. It was a stunning scene for a player known for his accuracy off the tee.

Hogan's chances were gone. Fleck hit the fairway with a three-wood off the tee and followed with an eight-iron to 12 feet. Hogan hit his fifth shot onto the green and holed a 30-foot putt that helped his score but not the outcome. The double bogey gave Ben a 72. Remarkably, Fleck broke 70 for the second straight round, finishing with a 69. His first tour victory was a U.S. Open. Hogan's run at a fifth U.S. Open was thwarted.

At the award ceremony, Hogan became choked with emotion as he announced to the crowd that he was through with competitive golf. "From now on, I'm a weekend golfer," he said.

Hogan indeed didn't play in another tournament in 1955. On further reflection, though, he continued to play in three to five tournaments a year into his 50s, continuing what would be a fruitless hunt for a fifth U.S. Open title.

Fleck, in a radio interview after claiming the title, seemed shocked. "I can't believe it. I guess it's the truth, but right now I just don't know how I feel or what to think. I just keep pinching myself."

Olympic would remain by far Fleck's finest hour. He won two more events on the tour and made one more run at a U.S. Open. Later in life, Fleck bristled at the common perception that his Open win was a fluke. In the context of the two protagonists' careers, it could perhaps be called that. But the way Fleck played on the course at Olympic, especially given the final-round and playoff pressure, certainly left no question that his victory was very well-deserved.

TOP-10 FINISHERS		
1	Jack Fleck	76-69-75-67—287*
2	Ben Hogan	72-73-72-70—287
T3	Tommy Bolt	67-77-75-73—292
T3	Sam Snead	79-69-70-74—292
T5	Julius Boros	76-69-73-77—295
T5	Bob Rosburg	78-74-67-76—295
T7	Doug Ford	74-77-74-71—296
T7	Bud Holscher	77-75-71-73—296
T7	Harvie Ward	74-70-76-76—296
T10	Jack Burke	71-77-72-77—297
T10	Mike Souchak	73-79-72-73—297

*Fleck won playoff, 69-72

1960

CHARGE!

A RNOLD PALMER strode to the first tee at Cherry Hills Country Club determined to try to drive the green on the 346-yard, downhill opening hole. But his tee shot went awry, and his ball wound up in a creek to the right and short of the green. After a penalty drop, Palmer's next shot hit a tree, and his fourth went over the green. He ultimately salvaged a double bogey with a chip and a six-foot putt.

This was the first round of a U.S. Open where Palmer entered as a heavy favorite after winning the Masters and four other tournaments in the first five months of the year. At the age of 30, the dynamic son of a club professional from western Pennsylvania had clearly hit his prime. The week before the U.S. Open, the *Saturday Evening Post* published a first-person article by Palmer titled "I Want That Grand Slam," in which he plotted out his quest to win all four major championships in one year.

In fact, Palmer was essentially inventing the modern Grand Slam (as opposed to Bobby Jones's sweep of the U.S. and British Open and Amateurs in 1930) by planning to travel across the Atlantic shortly after the U.S. Open to shoot for a title at the British Open, an event that, until then, had been skipped by most U.S. professionals.

His bid to earn the second leg of the Slam to add to his Masters title was off to a decidedly bad start. "You could have fried an egg on my head in that moment," Palmer wrote in his autobiography *A Golfer's Life* of how he felt after his double bogey. To make matters worse,

Palmer got into a spat with his caddie as they played the second hole. Fellow competitor Jack Fleck approached him as they walked down the second fairway and inquired, "Arnie, what the heck are you fighting with your caddie for? You've got a long way to go."

Palmer settled down and birdied the second and fifth holes. But he bogeyed the ninth, and, after offsetting a pair of back-nine birdies with two bogeys, he finished with a one-over 72.

When asked after the round if he would continue to hit driver on No. 1, a hole where most of the field was laying up, he asserted he would. "You never can tell when you hit for a green. You might get a hole-in-one."

Palmer, however, had by no means taken himself out of contention. He was four strokes behind the leader, Mike Souchak, who had a four-under 31 on the front nine before cooling off with a one-over 37 on the back for his 68. There were a pair of 69s and eight 70s—not quite the salvo of subpar scoring that had been anticipated by many.

Cherry Hills measured 7,004 yards, a reasonably robust number for that era, but it effectively played much shorter due to the increased distance the ball travels at a mile-high altitude. The front nine was particularly vulnerable, with the first six par fours playing no more than 426 yards and all essentially a drive and a wedge for most pros.

"There are so many holes where you can get birdies," said two-time major champion Doug Ford.

During the practice rounds, USGA official Joe Dey said, "A player actually came up to me today and complained that he thought it played too easy. What a switch!"

The course's main defenses were small greens that were firm and hard to hold, and a formidable finishing stretch of holes. That proved to be enough to prevent an all-out onslaught, though scoring was lower than the typical U.S. Open of the time.

Among the tough holes was the 468-yard, par-four 18th with a large pond that guarded the left side of the fairway. The hole was the scene of some odd action in the opening round.

Tommy Bolt, the 1958 U.S. Open champion known for his terrible temper, came to the finishing hole already steaming from a triple bogey on the 12th. He proceeded to hit two tee shots into the water (the pond fronted the championship tee, so a ball in the water required another shot from the tee after a penalty stroke), and then flung his club in after it with a mighty two-handed heave. With a quadruple bogey, Bolt shot 35-45—80, and promptly withdrew after the round.

Bolt was distracted on his first drive when a carp jumped out of the water and splashed during his backswing. The same thing happened to Doug Sanders in a more consequential situation. Three-under at the time, Sanders was startled by a splash he later described as sounding like "somebody unloading a truck of empty beer cans." He drove into the water and made a double bogey for a 70.

The jumpy fish weren't the only distractions created by animals. The local sheriff had set up a horse patrol around the border of the course for traffic and pedestrian control, and players complained about the horses' whinnying.

There were mechanical disturbances, too. During the final round, Ben Hogan would complain about a helicopter flying overhead. Officials radioed the pilot to direct him away from the course.

Hogan would play a major role in the final round, which was quite a turnaround from the 75 he shot in Round 1. At the age of 47, he was still a force in the game despite his reduced schedule. He won at Colonial in 1959, trailed by one stroke through 54 holes of the 1960 Masters before a 76 dropped him to T6, and lost in a playoff in Memphis two weeks before the U.S. Open. Before the tournament, Hogan was listed as the second favorite, at 6-to-1 odds, just behind Palmer at 5-to-1.

At that stage of his career, Hogan's main problem was putting, but in the opening round a string of four straight bogeys on Nos. 7-10 was punctuated by a wild drive that hit a spectator in the stomach on the ninth. A double bogey on 18 after a missed green and a poor chip ended his day on a bad note.

Before the second round, Hogan told some friends, "I've got to go today." Determined to get back into the picture, the Hawk birdied four of the first seven holes and shot a 32 on the front nine. Even par on the back nine through the 17th, he hit a beautiful three-iron to two feet on 18 for his sixth birdie of the round and a 67.

In the locker room, Hogan was in an expansive mood as he chatted with a group of writers. He expressed confidence in his ability to handle the 36-hole final day, but little confidence in his putting. While he didn't have a three-putt in the second round, he did miss three short birdie chances. Hogan was well aware of how long he was standing over putts before pulling the trigger.

"I cannot, for the life of me, bring the putter back. And I don't know why. Short putts or long putts—it doesn't matter. I can't bring the putter back," he said.

Hogan then related the story of when Bill Mehlhorn, a notable pro of the 1920s and 30s, putted into a bunker, saying that's the kind of thing that can happen. Hardly an encouraging note heading into the final day.

Souchak matched Hogan for the low round of the day with a 67 for a 36-hole total of 135. That was a U.S. Open record by three strokes and gave him a three-stroke lead. Souchak was a burly 33-year-old who had played college football at Duke, where he was a defensive end, before embarking on a successful golf career that so far had netted him 11 tour victories. None of them was a major championship, however.

Once known as the longest hitter in the game, Souchak said he had dialed it back a bit in favor of accuracy once George Bayer came along to claim honors as the top bomber. At Cherry Hills, Souchak used driver only six times in the second round but still had just wedges into many of the greens. His putter remained hot for a second straight day, and his chipping and bunker play were also on point as he saved par several times to go along with five birdies. His only bogey was on 18 where he hit a three-wood off the tee and a four-iron approach that went into the gallery and ended up next to a paper cup.

Palmer shot a 71 that left him more frustrated than his opening 72. Two-under par through 11 holes, he bogeyed Nos. 12 and 14 to fall eight strokes back of the leader at 143. The 14th could have been worse. He drove out of bounds, which was then a distance-only penalty, and hit his third shot onto the bank of a creek before making a 30-foot bogey putt. His frustration was further piqued by his pairing with slow players Cary Middlecoff and Fleck. "I figure it cost me four shots in the pairings," Palmer said. "I could play three holes while those guys were playing one."

Fleck was looking like a better bet than Palmer at this point. With a pair of 70s, the 1955 U.S. Open champion trailed only Souchak and Sanders (70-68). Earlier in the year, Fleck had scored his first victory since that Open triumph, and he was looking very good from tee to green through two rounds.

Also at 140 were Dow Finsterwald and Jerry Barber. Finsterwald was a real threat, having won seven times in the past three years including the 1958 PGA Championship. He was in contention despite having his caddie quit on the 15th green after a heated argument that began on the previous hole. "Why should I tell you?" the caddie gibed when asked about club selection on the shot into the 14th. "You've asked me twice already and didn't use my advice."

Finsterwald was playing with Hogan, and a Hogan fan in the gallery offered to carry Dow's clubs for the last three holes. It all worked out, as Finsterwald birdied 16 and 17 to shoot a 69.

The cut came at an Open-record low 147. Souchak held the tournament in his hands, but if he came back to the field there were plenty of quality contenders. Defending champion Billy Casper was at 141 and so was Sam Snead, at age 48 still looking for the U.S. Open title that had always eluded him. Joining Hogan at 142 were 1952 champion Julius Boros, 1959 British Open champion 24-year-old Gary Player, and 20-year-old amateur Jack Nicklaus, winner of the 1959 U.S. Amateur who was attracting attention for his prodigious drives. Then came Palmer, heading a group tied for 15th at 143.

The USGA made a change in its pairings setup for the 36-hole final day. For the first time, all the leaders were bunched in the pairings instead of being spread out. Also, for the first time, the pairings were made according to scores, so Souchak and Sanders were paired together as the two leaders. But the field wasn't sent out in reverse order of scores. The first third of the pairings were players in the middle of the pack, the next third were the leaders, and the final third were the players at the bottom.

The leaders weren't in reverse order, either. First came five twosomes of players at 142 or 143, with the intriguing twosome of

Nicklaus and Hogan leading the way. After that came pacesetters Souchak (135) and Sanders (138), followed by Finsterwald and Fleck (140), Barber (140) and Bruce Crampton (141), Casper and Ted Kroll (141), and Snead and Don Cherry (141).

When Nicklaus found out he was paired with the legendary Hogan, the budding star was worried. "To say I would be a little nervous would be an understatement," Nicklaus wrote in his autobiography *My Story*. "I had not at that point met Mr. Hogan, and I was aware of how intimidating a presence he could be. It turned out to be a perfectly pleasant experience. Silence was fine, it helped me settle into my own little cocoon."

In the third round, Nicklaus observed a clinic by Hogan, who reportedly hit all 18 greens in regulation on the way to a 69. Young Jack kept pace, shooting a 69 of his own.

How much ground would they make up against Souchak? The leader had an up-and-down round with four birdies and four bogeys leaving him at even par through 17 holes. He was one-over on the easier front nine but appeared to have righted himself by playing the back nine in one-under so far despite a pair of bogeys.

His round unraveled on the 18th hole. A loud noise from a spectator's smuggled-in movie camera during his swing caused Souchak to flinch, and he pushed his tee shot out of bounds to the right. "You've ruined my shot!" exclaimed Souchak, while marshals pursued and caught the fleeing offender who was trying to hide the camera under his shirt. With the distance-only penalty, an OB drive wasn't as costly as one in the water to the left, but Souchak ended up missing the green with his approach and made a double bogey.

"I don't know what's the matter with me. I'm in a fog," said Souchak in the locker room between rounds. "I can't figure out what I'm trying to think about. Maybe that six on 18 will wake me up."

Souchak finished with a 73 for a 208 total, and what could have been a four-stroke lead entering the final round ended up at two. Boros, with the morning's best round (68), was at 210 along with Finsterwald and Barber, who both shot 70. Hogan and Nicklaus were next at 211.

Palmer was languishing back in a tie for 15th at 215, seven strokes behind, after a disappointing 72. Among other big names, Snead and Casper shot 73 and were at 214, Player a 71 for 213, and Sanders a 77 for 215. They wouldn't figure in the final round—but Palmer would.

Palmer's third round included five birdies but was soured by four bogeys and a double bogey at the ninth, where his chip ran across the green and off the other side. He bogeyed the first when his drive stopped in the strip of rough in front of the green, and he took four more to get down. It ended badly, too, when he went for broke on 16 and 18 and bogeyed both.

Arnie wasn't giving up. To a group of writers in the locker room, he remarked, "I've thought right along I could lick this course. It isn't too late to do it." Palmer then encountered a writer friend, Bob Drum of Pittsburgh, along with Dan Jenkins of Fort Worth. Trying to pump himself up about the final round, Palmer said, "What if I shoot 65? 280 always wins the Open. What would that do?"

"It won't do you a damn bit of good," Drum harrumphed.

"Oh, yeah? Watch and see!" Palmer snapped, then stormed out of the locker room and onto the practice range, teed up a ball, and slammed it with a driver to the back of the range.

Palmer swung with the same fury on the first tee. This time the ball took off straight and true, bounced through the rough in front of the green and stopped on the putting surface, 20 feet from the hole. "As I reached the green, all the anger melted away," Palmer told *Golf* magazine in 1985. "Then, as I waited to putt, I began to feel very, very nervous. To this day, I don't know why. It was as if I were anticipating something that I *wanted* to happen."

He surprisingly left the eagle putt short but made the second putt for a birdie. Most of the spectators stayed around the first green to wait for Souchak, due to begin his round in less than 15 minutes.

Palmer marched to the second hole where he landed another blow, this time at the green, chipping in from 30 feet for a birdie. The third hole was another short par four at 348 yards. Arnie nearly drove the green, finishing to the left, and pitched within a foot of the hole for a birdie. The charge was on, and it wasn't finished. On the fourth, another par four, he hit a wedge to the green and made a 10-footer for a fourth straight birdie.

People were now flocking to watch Palmer, including Drum and Jenkins. "I knew I'd get you guys out here some way," Arnie said to the writers.

The fifth hole was a par five reachable in two, but the rally temporarily stalled there as Palmer found a greenside bunker with his second shot, came out to 20 feet, and two-putted for a par. No worries, he made up for it by holing a curving 25-foot putt for a birdie on the sixth. The exclamation point came at the seventh where he made a six-footer for his sixth birdie in seven holes. The Open, known for its stiff defense of par, had never seen anything like this.

The gallery roars for Palmer were ringing in other players' ears. It had an early effect on Souchak, who heard the cheer on the first hole and was told that Palmer had driven the green. Long-hitting Mike had laid up with a four-wood in the first three rounds, but this time he went with a driver—and hit it into the same creek Palmer found in the opening round. The result was a bogey, but Souchak recovered with a birdie on the second hole and a string of pars left him at five-under while Palmer reached four-under with his birdie burst.

Meanwhile, Nicklaus was making a move of his own thanks to pure ball striking. He birdied the first and missed birdie putts inside 10 feet on Nos. 2 and 3. A three-putt bogey on the fourth was a setback, but it was followed by an eagle on the fifth where he launched a one-iron second shot to 20 feet and holed the putt. He was now two-under on the day and four-under on the tournament.

The next couple hours of action were almost impossible to follow, with seven players holding at least a share of the lead at one point or another. In *Sports Illustrated*, Herbert Warren Wind called it "the most unbelievable jam-up the Open has ever seen."

Finsterwald and Fleck, playing together four pairings behind Palmer, each made a run on the early holes. Finsterwald birdied the third and fifth to get to five-under and a share of the lead. He dropped back slightly with a bogey on No. 6. Worse, he double bogeyed the ninth, where he was stymied by a pine tree after his drive and followed with a bogey on the 10th. With so many players now in front of him and a tough back nine ahead, his chances were essentially extinguished. He was the first of many players to rise and then fall.

Fleck nearly matched Palmer's torrid start with birdies on five of the first six holes, though he bogeyed No. 2. Starting the final round at one-under, the grinder from Iowa reached five-under through six holes. If he could recall his magic of 1955 and pull off another comeback victory, it would give him a second U.S. Open title to go along with only one other tour win at age 38. Fleck missed a seven-foot birdie putt on the seventh that would have given him the outright lead—a precursor of putting woes to come—and bogeyed the tough par-three eighth, finishing the front nine with a 32 to stand at four-under.

The less challenging front nine also yielded 32s to Dutch Harrison and Ted Kroll. Early starter Harrison went from one-over to two-under, with a chance to post a number for others to look at if he could follow it up on the back nine. Kroll had fallen to three-over with a 75 in the third round before rallying with five birdies on the first seven holes in the afternoon, tempered by a pair of front-nine bogeys. At even-par for the tournament at the turn, though, Kroll trailed too many players to have much of a chance.

Meanwhile, Palmer had his sights on a 29 on the front nine, which he could accomplish with pars on Nos. 8 and 9. He bogeyed the eighth, however, bunkering his three-iron tee shot, blasting out nicely and then missing a three-foot putt. Now he needed a birdie on the ninth for a 29, but it was a difficult hole where he hadn't even managed a par in the first three rounds. He salvaged a par this time after missing the green, holing an eight-foot putt for a 30 that tied the U.S. Open record for nine holes and kept him at three-under for the championship.

Hogan and Boros were also three-under through nine holes. Hogan birdied the sixth and made routine pars on the rest of the front nine, while Boros birdied the third to each four-under before a bogey on the sixth.

A dark-horse contender was amateur Don Cherry, a 36-year-old more well-known as a singer with a string of 1950s hits, including "Band of Gold." He was a good enough golfer to make the U.S. Walker Cup team in 1953 and 1955. At Cherry Hills, he had held an even keel in the first three rounds with 70-71-71. In an unlikely bid for golf glory, Cherry birdied the fifth and seventh to get to three-under before a bogey on the ninth dropped him to two-under.

No amateur had won a U.S. Open since Johnny Goodman in 1933. While Cherry was a longshot, young Nicklaus had a more realistic chance, and he was looking the part of a potential Open winner. When a 22-foot birdie putt dropped on the ninth, Nicklaus had a 32 on the front nine and was tied for the lead with Souchak at five-under. When Souchak bogeyed the ninth after driving under a bush, the kid had the lead all by himself.

Ohio State football coach Woody Hayes was in Nicklaus's gallery— Jack played on the Buckeyes' golf team. Hayes, who had been at a coaching clinic in Colorado Springs just before the Open started, was insistently shooing spectators out of the way to give Jack's father, Charlie, a view. Also on hand was Nicklaus's Ohio State teammate Robin Obetz, who caught an early flight from Ohio to Denver with his father on Saturday morning because he had a feeling Jack was going to win.

The possibility of winning crept into Jack's mind, too, especially when he glanced at the leaderboard after the 12th hole. Despite missing birdie chances on 11 and 12, he saw that he had a one-stroke lead. "Looking at that board was my first mistake," Jack said in his autobiography.

Nicklaus gave himself another birdie opportunity on the 13th, hitting his approach shot to 12 feet. He missed the putt, the ball stopping 18 inches past the hole, with an imperfectly repaired pitch mark in his line. As a still-green amateur playing in the final round of a major championship paired with a golf legend, Jack's mind froze. He should have asked Hogan or called in a rules official to check that he could repair the pitch mark. Instead, he went ahead and putted. The mark deflected the ball, and Nicklaus bogeyed to drop into a four-way tie for the lead.

Palmer was part of that quartet at the top, recording a two-putt birdie at the par-five 11th after hitting the green with a four-iron second shot. Now six-under for the round, it had taken only 11 holes for him to make up the seven-stroke deficit.

One twosome ahead of Palmer, Boros had also birdied 11 to reach four-under. The fourth player at that figure was Fleck. Soon it was five. Souchak had bogeyed the 10th, missing a putt from inside two feet, to drop to three-under, but he got back to four-under with a birdie on 11.

Souchak, however, dunked his tee shot in the water on the par-three 12th and double bogeyed. It would prove to be a fatal blow for the 54-hole leader, who would ultimately finish at one-under after a 75. "There'll be another day, I suppose," said a disappointed Souchak after the round. He would win four more tour events to run his total to 15, but never had that other day in a major championship.

One by one, the co-leaders all fell by the wayside except for Palmer. Nicklaus three-putted the 14th from 40 feet for a bogey. Boros found a bunker on 14 and made a bogey; he would finish with bogeys on 17 and 18. Fleck's putter let him down in stunning fashion. He three-putted the 13th from seven feet and jabbed at and missed a one-footer on 16 for a pair of bogeys.

Two players who reached three-under on the back nine also turned in the wrong direction. Harrison got to three-under with a birdie at the 10th before making three bogeys down the stretch. Barber, who began the round three-under, got back to that figure with a birdie on 11, but promptly bogeyed 12 and dropped with a thud when he double bogeyed 15.

Suddenly, an old-fashioned U.S. Open of attrition had broken out. Bucking the trend was Hogan. Starting at two-under, he birdied the sixth to get to three-under and ground out a string of two-putt pars. He finally got a birdie putt to drop, holing a 15-footer on the 15th hole. Now he was tied for the lead with Palmer and Fleck, and then just Palmer after Fleck faltered.

A fifth U.S. Open title for Hogan, one that would make him the oldest champion as well as the most prolific, was in sight. The living legend hit his approach to 12 feet on the 16th but couldn't convert the birdie. The green at the par-five 17th at Cherry Hills was surrounded by water, one of the first greens anywhere to be located on an island. Hogan laid up with his second shot and surveyed his wedge approach.

The hazard short of the green was a moat attached to the large

pond that also lines the 18th hole. The hole was cut near the front
of the putting surface, bringing the moat very much into play for a
player trying to get the approach close. With a wedge in his hand,
Hogan was looking to make a birdie. He didn't have much confidence in making a 15-footer, considering that he had been missing
those all day.

The shot looked good in the air to most. "I thought it was going to
be perfect," Nicklaus later said. Not quite. The ball didn't quite clear
the top of the bank in front of the green. Instead of the ball landing
on the front of the green and hopping close to the hole, it caught the
bank and tumbled backwards into the water.

Shaken but not thoroughly daunted, Hogan surveyed the situation
and saw that he could play the ball out of the shallow water. He took
off his right shoe and sock, put the shoe back on, stepped into the
water with one foot, and blasted out to within 15 feet. A good escape,
but not good enough for Hogan, since he didn't make the putt.

The bogey dropped him to three-under. Hogan compounded the
error on the 18th when he again hit a shot that barely failed to clear
water, this time his tee shot. He finished with a triple bogey, a round
of 73 and an even-par 284 total that didn't reflect how close he had
come to winning the championship.

Hogan took the defeat hard. "Don't play golf," he told reporters in
the locker room afterward. "There are so many disappointments, you
want to cut your throat."

About the decision on 17, he said, "Maybe I should not have done
it, but I wasn't more than this far from finishing at 279 [holding his
hands about six inches apart]. I'm just a dumb guy, I guess."

Time didn't heal the wound. In a 1983 interview on CBS television
with Ken Venturi, Hogan admitted as much. "I find myself waking
up and thinking about that shot today. . . . It's been 23 years ago and
there isn't a month that goes by that that doesn't cut my guts out. I
didn't miss it. I just didn't hit it far enough."

Nicklaus, at three-under, came to the 17th more in need of a birdie
than Hogan. He laid up, though, in retrospect many years later, he
thought he should have gone for the green in two on the 548-yard

hole. He hit his third shot to the 15-foot range that Hogan didn't want, missed the putt, and settled for a par. Young Jack then bogeyed 18, later lamenting that a lapse in concentration contributed to a mediocre chip and missed a six-foot putt when a par and three-under finish would have exerted greater pressure on Palmer, who by then was the sole leader at four-under. Instead, Nicklaus shot a closing 71 for a two-under 282 total.

While the Nicklaus and Hogan pairing had provided a master-class in ball-striking, neither could quite finish the deal—either on individual holes with the putter or on the closing two-hole stretch. Nicklaus emerged practically in awe of Hogan's tee to green game. "He really hits the ball like it should be hit," he said in the aftermath. "I just scrape it."

Jack was undoubtedly being modest on the latter point. The 20-year-old who would go on to become perhaps the greatest player in the history of the game made a strong impression on the 47-year-old who was already established as one of the all-time greats. "I played 36 holes today with a kid who, if he had a brain in his head, should have won this thing by ten strokes," Hogan said.

Instead of being claimed by a past or future icon, this U.S. Open would belong to the player who was currently the best in the game. Palmer made pars on Nos. 12–16, four of them routine and a key save on the 15th, where he escaped from a bunker to within two feet. While playing the 17th, he was surprised to learn about his position on the leaderboard. "You mean I'm leading the tournament all alone? Well, now it's a different story," he said.

The man who boldly drove the first green now played the 17th safely and two-putted for par from 30 feet. Palmer's main task on the finishing hole was to keep his drive out of the water and in bounds. He did that successfully, missed the green, chipped to two-and-a-half feet, made the par putt for a 65, and flung his visor into the gallery.

At about the same time Palmer was finishing at four-under, Fleck made his putting gaffe at 16 to fall to two-under. It wasn't quite over, but it was trending that way. Souchak was two-under playing the 17th and finished par-bogey. Fleck also went par-bogey on the last two holes to join the group finishing at one-under comprising Harrison, Boros, Souchak, and Finsterwald, eventually joined by Kroll.

One player remained with an outside chance, the longshot Cherry, yet another who came to the 17th at two-under needing two birdies to tie Palmer. Or maybe an eagle at 17, thought Cherry, who went for the green in two. He struck his second shot so poorly that it bounced into the water in front of the green, leading to a double bogey.

Palmer won by doing exactly what he said he would do—shooting a final-round 65. The comeback from seven strokes behind entering the final round was a U.S. Open record. Go-for-broke Arnie's driving the green on the first hole and spectacular start of six birdies on the first seven holes would become the stuff of legend, representing perhaps the seminal example of Palmer's motto of "Charge!"

But the opening surge was only half the story. Just as important as the 30 on the front nine was the steady one-under 35 coming home, consisting of eight pars and one birdie, accomplished on the tougher back nine where all the other contenders succumbed to Open pressure. The only other top-10 finisher to shoot under par on the back nine was Kroll, with a 35 for a 67, but he started too far back. None of the others in the top 10 could even match par on the back nine. Their scores: Finsterwald and Harrison 37; Boros, Barber, and Cherry 38; Nicklaus, Hogan, Souchak, and Fleck 39. Seven players reached four- or five-under during the final round; only Palmer managed to finish at four-under.

The victory didn't lead to a Grand Slam—Palmer's bid ended with a runner-up finish at the British Open. It would remain the lone U.S. Open title for Arnie, but he certainly made it one to remember.

TOP-10 FINISHERS		
1	Arnold Palmer	72-71-72-65—280
2	Jack Nicklaus	71-71-69-71—282
T3	Julius Boros	73-69-68-73—283
T3	Dow Finsterwald	71-69-70-73—283
T3	Jack Fleck	70-70-72-71—283
T3	Dutch Harrison	74-70-70-69—283
T3	Ted Kroll	72-69-75-67—283
T3	Mike Souchak	68-67-73-75—283
T9	Jerry Barber	69-71-70-74—284
T9	Don Cherry	70-71-71-72—284
T9	Ben Hogan	75-67-69-73—284

1962

THE KID
AND THE KING

I n the early 1960s, Arnold Palmer was known as the King, and
he was ruling his realm with an iron hand over the first half of
1962. Arnie won six times from January through May, including a
12-stroke victory margin romp at the Phoenix Open, a playoff victory
at the Masters, and three wins in a row later in the spring.

Now he was headed to his home turf for the U.S. Open at Oakmont
Country Club just outside of Pittsburgh and 40 miles from Latrobe,
Pennsylvania, where he grew up and still lived. The event drew record
U.S. Open crowds as a sizable portion of the population of western
Pennsylvania turned out to cheer their native son on to an expected
victory that—just as in 1960—would furnish him the first two legs of
the Grand Slam.

There had been rumblings of a possible contender to the throne
when Jack Nicklaus turned pro for the 1962 season. The kid from
Ohio won the U.S. Amateur in 1959 and 1961 and had demonstrated
he could more than hold his own against the pros. He tied for second
at the 1960 U.S. Open and was T4 in 1961, the best cumulative performance in the Open over those two years (Palmer followed his 1960
victory with a T14 in 1961). Through his first 17 events in his rookie
PGA Tour season, Nicklaus had yet to notch a victory. He did have
three seconds and two thirds, so perhaps a breakthrough was only a
matter of time.

One of those runner-up finishes came the week before the Open at the Thunderbird Classic, the richest event on that year's tour. The $10,000 check left Nicklaus far from satisfied. "Although finishing runner-up was a pleasing measure of my form, it also made me angry at myself . . . I had never been hungrier," Nicklaus recounted in his autobiography *My Story*.

Palmer's lead-in to the championship was even more frustrating. After a T35 finish—his worst of the year—and a flight home to Latrobe, Palmer cut the ring finger on his right hand while loading luggage into the trunk of his car. It required three stitches, but he was able to practice on Monday. By tournament time, the stitches had been removed, and, while he altered his grip slightly because of his bandaged finger, Palmer said he was essentially unaffected.

With the sense of drama that the USGA sometimes injects into its first-and-second-round pairings, Nicklaus and Palmer were put together for the first 36 holes, which that year were played in twosomes. For Palmer, it was a chance to keep an eye on the player he considered his biggest challenger.

"Everybody says there's only one favorite, and that's me," Palmer said. "But you'd better watch the fat boy." Arnold would later note that he meant no disrespect with that description. Indeed, nearly every newspaper article referred to Nicklaus as "chunky," "hefty," or some such adjective. *Los Angeles Times* columnist Jim Murray went so far as to write, "If he gets tired of golf, [Nicklaus] can make a living as a department store Santa. . . . He gets any heavier, and he'll have to fly as freight."

It wasn't that the young Nicklaus—who weighed in at about 200 pounds before slimming down later in his career—was unathletic. He wowed everyone with his ability to hit drives a long way. But he was more like an offensive lineman compared to swashbuckling halfback Palmer.

In a way, the pairing seemed unfair to the rookie, who would have to deal with a gallery that was so rabidly pro-Palmer that they were also anti-Nicklaus. In addition to the distraction of fans moving as soon as Palmer hit but while Nicklaus was still to play, there were catcalls such as, "Miss it, Fat Guts!"

Fortunately, Nicklaus's ability to focus on the task at hand was unmatched, even at that early age. "It all washed over me like water over a duck's back," he later wrote. "So far as I was concerned the noise was just that—noise."

Nicklaus did his best to quiet the gallery on the first three holes of the opening round, starting with three straight birdies, including a chip-in from off the green on the par-four third, where he drove into the church pew bunkers. Stunningly, he was five strokes ahead of Palmer at that point. Arnie doubled bogeyed the second, a short par four where he knocked a 75-yard approach shot into a tough spot over the green, watched his downhill chip roll 20 feet past, and three-putted.

In a quick reversal, Palmer was one ahead of Jack by the end of the front nine. First, Arnie answered Nicklaus's early birdies with a pair of his own on Nos. 4 and 5. Nicklaus bogeyed both par-threes on the front nine, the sixth and eighth, then stumbled to a double bogey on the ninth, a 480-yard par five where the pros were typically shooting for birdies. He drove into a bunker, failed to get out, hit his third into a ditch, and was still short of the green in four.

Just when the crowd was getting fully charged up, their hero hit a lull with bogeys on the 10th, 11th, and 12th, two of them on three-putts. Now Palmer was two behind. No problem. Arnie put together a streak of five straight threes, three of them birdies on Nos. 14, 15, and 17, the latter a two-putt as he drove the green on the 292-yard par four (shades of Cherry Hills). Nicklaus, meanwhile, had an even-par back nine with another par-three bogey on 16 and a birdie on 17.

The scores ended up being rather pedestrian, with Palmer shooting an even-par 71 and Nicklaus a 72, masking what had been a rollercoaster round packed with excitement, each player mixing brilliant play with sloppy mistakes.

Despite his rally from the early deficit, Palmer lamented a round that he felt should have been better, as he three-putted three greens and missed some birdie opportunities. "When you drive the ball like I did today, you should shoot 66, not 71," he said. "I'd just like to go around again, playing the same tee shots."

Not that even par was a bad round at Oakmont, known as a stern test for its slick, undulating greens, fierce bunkering, and punishing rough. It wasn't quite as harsh as usual, thanks to rain on Tuesday and Wednesday that softened the greens and made them not quite as dangerously fast. Still, nobody managed better than a 69 in the first round.

That score was turned in by defending champion Gene Littler, and he needed to hole a 100-foot chip shot for an eagle on the ninth and sink three birdie putts in the 30-foot range to be able to do it. The only other players to break par were Bobby Nichols and Bob Rosburg with 70s; Palmer led a group of six at 71 that also included Gary Player.

Phil Rodgers could have been in the par-or-better group, having reached the dogleg 17th hole at one-under. He hooked his tee shot on that hole, and it came to rest in the branches of one of the small pine trees that had been planted there short and left of the green to discourage players from trying to drive the green (though some tried, anyway). It took Rodgers four whacks to dislodge the ball from the branches before carding a quadruple bogey eight.

On Friday, Arnie gave his Army of fans plenty to cheer about, shooting a 68 to move into a tie for the lead with Rosburg at 139. His driving wasn't as accurate as the first round, but he avoided three-putts and holed a 20-footer for a birdie at the seventh. He also got up and down from near the green for birdies on the ninth and 17th and hit a great iron shot to two feet for a birdie on the 470-yard first, while making only one bogey.

Nicklaus, who told reporters that he watched two days of "super golf" by Palmer, also had only one bogey, but only two birdies (on Nos. 1 and 4) in a solid round of 70 that included pars on the last 10 holes. At 142, he was three off the lead, trailing only Palmer, Rosburg, and Billy Maxwell (141).

Rosburg gained his share of the lead with birdies on 16 and 17, the former on a chip-in. Nichols missed his chance to be atop the leaderboard with bogeys on three of the last four holes for a 72 and joined Nicklaus and Player at 142. Littler couldn't find the putting magic of the previous day and had a birdie-less 74 to sit at 143.

Looking ahead to Saturday's 36 holes, 1955 champion Ed Furgol opined: "I think it's just a one-horse race—Palmer. I don't know what the rest of them are running for."

Nicklaus wouldn't be paired with Palmer in the third and fourth rounds, but he was in Arnold's sight in the twosome ahead, paired with Maxwell, while Palmer played with Rosburg.

After Saturday morning's third round, Palmer still held a share of the lead, this time with Nichols. But Arnie was anything but happy. It was a rough round on the greens, with four three-putts and a total of 38 strokes on the putting surfaces as he shot a 73. He had 20 putts on the front nine, including a third three-putt on the ninth for a par after reaching the par five in two.

The tournament favorite appeared to rescue his round by driving the 17th green and holing a 20-foot putt for an eagle. The whooping and hollering from the gallery was louder than ever and lasted four minutes.

The scene at the 18th green was the opposite—stunned silence after Palmer three-putted from 12 feet for a bogey, not only missing a birdie chance but missing from two feet coming back. It was his fourth miss of the round from inside four feet. He backed away from the second putt because of an airplane flying overhead. As he walked off the green, Palmer muttered, "Man, if I'd had a BB gun, I'd have shot down that plane."

The noted club tinkerer then proceeded to the caddie shop and hammered on the shaft of his putter. As he did in 1960, Palmer chatted with Bob Drum of the *Pittsburgh Press* while grabbing a quick lunch in the locker room before the final round. "I gave them a chance to catch me instead of getting a big lead. I should have had a good round, at least a 69, and then I could relax," he said in frustration. Instead of stalking off to the practice range as he did at Cherry Hills, this time Palmer headed to the practice green before the final round to see if he could iron anything out.

Nichols gained his share of the lead with a two-birdie, one-bogey 70. The 26-year-old was in his third year on tour and had scored his first two victories earlier in the season.

Rosburg had a 74 and was one shot back at 213, joined by Rodgers, who birdied 16 and 17 for a 69. Like Nichols, Rodgers, at 24, was a young player on the rise. In his second year on tour, he also had scored his first two victories in 1962. His spot near the top through 54 holes was remarkable, considering not only his quadruple bogey on 17 in the first round but also a four-putt double bogey in the second round when he recovered with birdies on the last three holes for a 70.

That other young player, 22-year-old Nicklaus, hoping to soon post his first tour victory, shot a 72 and was tied with Player at 214, two strokes out of the lead. "I wasn't playing sensational golf . . . but I was doing two important things very well: driving far and into most of the fairways and making the five- and six-footers whenever I fumbled a long approach putt," he later wrote. Not to mention making the two- and three-footers that Palmer was missing.

Nicklaus didn't have any three-putts over the first 54 holes. His first came on the opening hole of the final round, from 20 feet. Not a good start—but it would be his only bogey of the round.

Player and Nichols also had rough starts. Player double bogeyed the first hole and wasn't a factor as he shot a final-round 74. Nichols was shaken when, with only 30 minutes between the end of his third round and his tee time for the fourth, his caddie didn't show up with his clubs until the last minute. Unsurprisingly, he promptly bogeyed the first hole. Rodgers was yet another player to bogey the first hole, so Palmer gained a stroke or two on nearly all the other top contenders by making a routine par.

The local hero assumed control of the tournament with birdies on the second and fourth holes to take a three-stroke lead over Nichols and Rodgers. Rosburg was rapidly falling out of it and would never recover, shooting a 79. Nicklaus, at that point, was five shots adrift.

Young Jack put himself back in the mix with birdies at the seventh, with a 15-foot putt, and the ninth, where he missed an eight-footer for eagle. Rodgers pulled within two with a birdie on No. 9, while Nichols followed a bogey on the sixth with a birdie on the ninth to go three back along with Nicklaus. It wasn't over, but the other contenders probably needed some help from Palmer.

Troubles for the leader weren't out of the question at rugged Oak-mont. When those difficulties emerged, though, it was at an unlikely spot—the ninth, the easiest hole on the layout. Palmer was in fine shape in two on the par five, in the greenside rough 50 feet from the hole. He flubbed the chip, though, advancing it only a few feet, still in the rough. His next effort came up eight feet short, and he two-putted for a costly bogey. He was still in front, but he was pain-fully aware that his lead was thinner than it should have been.

When Rodgers, playing about 45 minutes ahead of Palmer, bird-ied the 12th, he grabbed a tie for the lead. Amazingly, he had a real chance to win the Open despite his tree-induced quadruple bogey in the first round. The window of opportunity soon closed, however, with bogeys on 13, 15, and 16.

Nichols was within one after a birdie-bogey-birdie stretch on 11, 12, and 13. He, too, fell away on the closing holes with bogeys on 15 and 18. The championship battle would be reduced to Palmer and Nicklaus, the King and the kid.

Nicklaus birdied the 11th with a 14-foot putt. When Palmer bogeyed the par-three 13th after a six-iron into a bunker, the two were tied at one-under for the championship. Both parred every hole down the stretch, but there was plenty of drama packed into those par figures.

Nicklaus missed a birdie chance from five feet on 14, then saved par with a four-foot putt on 16. There was little hesitation as to what he would attempt on the 292-yard 17th. "When you were young, strong, long, racing with adrenaline, and tied with your chief adversary, the only strategy was to drive the green," he later wrote.

His prodigious smash ended up in a greenside bunker, leaving a tricky shot with not much green to work with. The shot barely cleared the lip of the bunker and settled into the rough short of the green. From there, his chip went four feet past. Jack read the putt as having a double break, so he decided to straighten it out by hitting it at a good speed, despite risking having a long comebacker if he missed. Four-time U.S. Open champion Bobby Jones later told Nicklaus that he nearly fell out of his chair watching on television as the ball sped into the hole.

Nicklaus impressed observers with a drive of some 300 yards on the 462-yard, par-four 18th, a tough finishing hole. He hit a six-iron approach to 12 feet but couldn't sink the putt and signed for a 69 before waiting to see if his one-under 283 total would win, lose, or get him into a playoff.

At about the same time, Palmer was playing the 17th, where a go-ahead birdie was a realistic possibility. He tried to drive the green—of course—and went to the left but avoided tree trouble. A pitch to eight feet gave him a chance for a birdie. He stepped away after taking his stance, later telling the press that he did so because he had overheard a TV announcer describing the putt. "Did you agree with him?" Palmer was asked. "No," he answered. The putt missed.

Palmer gave himself another chance to claim the title when his four-iron approach to 18 landed just short of the green and bounced and rolled to 10 feet from the hole. Fellow competitor Rosburg said to Arnie, "If you were ever going to make a putt, make this one, will you?" A hush fell over the crowd, which was poised to erupt in a raucous celebration. Instead, there was a collective groan as the left-to-right putt missed on the high side, leaving Palmer with a closing 71.

The local hero hadn't won it, but he hadn't lost it. An 18-hole playoff loomed the next day against an ambitious and supremely talented 22-year-old, which Palmer himself admitted wasn't an enviable task.

With both players appearing before the assembled press after the round, Palmer said of his young challenger, "I thought I was through with him yesterday." When asked if he would rather be facing someone else in a playoff, he said, "I certainly would."

"You don't really mean that," said Nicklaus. "Oh, yes I do, you big strong dude, you!" Palmer replied.

Palmer's greatest lament was his putting. "Are there any good putters in the crowd?" he asked the writers. "I could use a lesson."

In the locker room, chatting with some fellow pros, Palmer again pointed to his putting as the reason he didn't have the U.S. Open trophy in his hands.

"Boy, if I could have only had some semblance of a putting stroke out there today, life would be beautiful. I'm not talking about making any long ones, just not missing those shorties. I felt like I was putting with a wet noodle," he said.

Letting his guard down, Palmer admitted: "I just wanted to win this one so bad, maybe that's why it seemed so hard."

The playoff wouldn't be any easier. Arnie had some 10,000 spectators on his side, but one formidable opponent on the other side. Nicklaus later wrote that he wasn't nervous on the morning of the playoff. "I was hitting the ball very well tee to green and putting very well. What was there to be nervous about?"

Well, just the chance to become the youngest U.S. Open champion since Bobby Jones did it at age 21 in 1923.

Nicklaus certainly showed no signs of nerves on the first hole, bombing a long drive down the fairway some 35 yards past Palmer, who was in the rough. Arnie missed the green, chipped to 16 feet, and two-putted for a bogey while Jack hit his approach to 15 feet and two-putted for a par.

Wearing the same white shirt and shiny green pants as he had for the final round, the chunky Nicklaus didn't cut nearly as dashing a figure as marquee idol Palmer. Jack's game, however, clearly had star potential.

Both missed birdie chances from inside seven feet at the second and made routine pars at No. 3. They each hit their second shots in the vicinity of the green on the par-five fourth, Nicklaus chipping to four feet and making a birdie while Palmer came out of a bunker to six feet and missed the birdie putt. The kid now led by two.

The margin doubled to four on the sixth hole, where Nicklaus birdied with a six-iron to six feet to go two-under and Palmer three-putted from 15 feet and bogeyed to go two-over. Nicklaus remained wary, realizing that there was plenty of time left for Palmer to make a charge, the way he had in the first round after Jack took an early lead.

Palmer didn't take advantage of a Nicklaus bogey on the eighth as he also made a bogey, both missing the green on the formidable 253-yard par three. Arnie did gain a stroke at the ninth, chipping to three feet for a birdie while Nicklaus missed a five-foot birdie putt.

Things started to get interesting at the 11th, where Palmer birdied from seven feet to pull within two. On No. 12, Arnie showed Jack that he could hit the ball a long way, too, bashing two shots to within 15 yards of the green on the 598-yard par five. He pitched to five feet and made the birdie putt, while Nicklaus settled for a par after driving into the rough. Palmer was within one stroke, and the crowd was in a frenzy.

"In the past, whenever I mounted a charge I could almost *feel* that the player I was chasing was going to collapse and give ground," Palmer wrote in his autobiography *A Golfer's Life*. "But Jack Nicklaus was a different animal altogether, completely unlike anybody I'd ever chased . . . I had never seen anyone who could stay focused the way he did—and I've never seen anyone with the same ability since...You just couldn't crack that concentration."

Instead, it was Palmer who made a critical mistake. Debating between a five-iron and four-iron at the par-three 13th, he decided to go with an easy four-iron. He struck it poorly, getting a fortunate bounce away from a bunker near the front of the green but leaving himself 60 feet from the hole. He three-putted from there, missing a six-footer on the second putt, losing a stroke to Nicklaus's regulation par.

The duo parred the next four holes in remarkably similar fashion. They each two-putted from between 10 and 15 feet on the 14th, from between 20 and 25 feet on the 15th, and from long range on the 16th, Nicklaus holing a crucial five-foot second putt.

Both drove to the left on the short par-four 17th and pitched to 10 feet—so close to the same distance that a measurement was needed to determine that Palmer was away. He missed, threw back his head in anguish, and walked over to sit on his golf bag. Nicklaus missed, too, leaving Palmer with at least a little life, two strokes behind with one to play.

Jack kept the door open when he hooked his tee shot on 18 into such a bad lie that he asked for a ruling, while Palmer found the fairway. Denied relief, Nicklaus hacked the ball out short of a cross bunker, leaving a nine-iron third shot. Needing a birdie, Palmer instead hit his worst shot of the week, a fat three-iron that came up short of the green in the right rough.

Nicklaus hit his third shot to 16 feet. Needing a chip-in birdie, Palmer's third shot raced past the flagstick onto the fringe 15 feet past the hole. After Nicklaus putted to two feet, Palmer sent his par putt three feet past. Disgusted, he made a sweeping, one-handed attempt at the three-footer, missed, and tapped in for a double bogey. He conceded defeat by picking up Nicklaus's ball-marking coin and congratulating him on the title. A USGA official rushed in to tell Jack that he needed to replace his ball and hole out, since it was stroke play, not a match that could be conceded. Nicklaus did so for a bogey, a round of 71, and a three-stroke margin over Palmer in an anticlimactic finish to what had been a well-played playoff through 17 holes.

The deciding factor that swung the championship was clear. Palmer had 10 three-putts in the five rounds, including three in the playoff, while Nicklaus had only one, none in the playoff, handling Oakmont's perilous greens with aplomb.

"Any kind of normal putting and nobody could have caught me," lamented Palmer in the immediate aftermath.

But, deep down, there was more to it. This was a primordial battle between the established best player in the game and the youngster who deeply wanted to claim that title for himself. The kid showed that he had what it took—the skills and also the character—to make that happen. This was a big step on the way to Nicklaus becoming not only the best player of his era, but the best the game had ever seen. As for Palmer, his winning days weren't over. But the King had lost his crown.

TOP-10 FINISHERS		
1	Jack Nicklaus	72-70-72-69—283*
2	Arnold Palmer	71-68-73-71—283
T3	Bobby Nichols	70-72-70-73—285
T3	Phil Rodgers	74-70-69-72—285
5	Gay Brewer	73-72-73-69—287
T6	Tommy Jacobs	74-71-73-70—288
T6	Gary Player	71-71-72-74—288
T8	Doug Ford	74-75-71-70—290
T8	Gene Littler	69-74-72-75—290
T8	Billy Maxwell	71-70-75-74—290

*Nicklaus won playoff, 71-74

1971

SHOWDOWN AT MERION

H eading into the 1971 U.S. Open, Jack Nicklaus and Lee Trevino were on top of the golf world. Nicklaus had three victories, including the PGA Championship, which was played in February that year, because it was held in Florida. He finished second in the Masters, had two wins and two seconds in his last four starts, and led the money list. Trevino had two victories and had five top-five finishes in his last six starts, including a playoff loss the week before at the Kemper Open, and was second in earnings.

Golf is an unpredictable sport, and golf tournaments have large fields, so they rarely play out as battles for victory between No. 1 and No. 2. This U.S. Open was a welcome exception, resulting in a playoff where an irresistible force met an immovable object with a major championship at stake.

Nicklaus practiced at Merion for four days during the week before the championship and was surprised he didn't see any other Open competitors arriving early, especially since it was a course they didn't know. "I've played it four times, and I'm still getting to know the course," he said on Monday of championship week when he returned to Merion after a weekend at home in Florida.

Nicklaus was actually one of few players with past experience of the course. And it was quite an experience. At the 1960 World Amateur Team Championship he led the U.S. to victory with a score of

11-under 269 for 72 holes. It wasn't a U.S. Open setup, but the performance was still considered extraordinary.

The U.S. Open had last been played at Merion in 1950 when Ben Hogan won with a 287 total. There was some concern, or at least speculation, surrounding how the relatively short course (6,544 yards) would hold up against the advances of modern equipment and players like Nicklaus and Trevino.

When rain softened the course on Monday and Wednesday, there was talk that the Open record of 275 was in jeopardy. Others felt that the punishing rough and small, demanding greens would make breaking par for 72 holes difficult, if not impossible.

Trevino was in both camps, depending on when during the week he was asked. "I remember seeing the golf course for the first time and thinking the players would rip it apart," he wrote in the USGA publication *Golf Journal* in 1981. On Monday, he called it "a nice little course." But by Wednesday the 1968 U.S. Open champion had changed his tune. "No way anybody's going to break 280 here. The rough's too high . . . You're going to have to drive the ball straight for 72 holes, and who can do that?"

The first round didn't do much to help settle the debate. Merion proved vulnerable to birdie runs but also quite capable of biting back. No one did more to demonstrate both than Larry Hinson, one of the tour's top young pros. He was a sizzling five-under through 13 holes, perhaps on the way to matching or beating the Open record of 64, first established by Lee Mackey in 1950 at Merion. Instead, he shot a one-over 71 with four bogeys and a double bogey on 17 in his last five holes. "I'm not really sure what happened," Hinson said. "I hit it a little bit in the rough on four of the last five holes."

Bob Goalby also had a chance to post a low number, as he was four-under through 16. But he pushed his tee shot way right on the par-three 17th and made a double bogey, finishing with a 68. Tom Shaw went the other direction in his scoring, following a 41 on the front nine with a 30 on the back. Ralph Johnston had a 70 with seven birdies, five bogeys, a double bogey, and only five pars.

The leader was Labron Harris Jr., who had four birdies and two bogeys on the back nine after a relatively calm start for a 67. The

1962 U.S. Amateur champion, the son of the highly successful golf coach at Oklahoma State, had yet to win on the PGA Tour, his closest brush with victory coming not far from Merion at the 1968 Philadelphia Classic.

He was closely followed by the reigning U.S. Amateur champion, brash 21-year-old Lanny Wadkins, who was at 68. "Why shouldn't an amateur win? There are just more pros around here than us, that's all," said the Wake Forest All-American. "The pressure doesn't bother me more than anyone else . . . .There's nobody out here that can awe me."

Doug Sanders joined Goalby and Wadkins at 68, while Nicklaus, Jim Colbert, and Bobby Nichols were at 69, making a total of seven subpar rounds. Nicklaus felt he let a better round slip away. "The greens just kept getting faster and faster, and I just kept putting worse and worse," he said after three-putting three times.

Trevino bucked the trend with a steady round of 16 pars, a bogey at the seventh, and a lone birdie finally coming at the 18th, the toughest hole on the course. He was one of 10 players at 70.

The surprise 36-hole leader was Bob Erickson, a 45-year-old who didn't turn pro until age 31 and didn't play the tour until 10 years after that, who shot a 67 for a 137 total. In his first three years on the circuit, Erickson's best finish on the money list was 114th and he was in a constant struggle to either find a sponsor or support himself. Currently without a sponsor, he was barely staying afloat thanks to $4,500 he won in his first start of the year by "begging, borrowing and doing everything except stealing," he said. "If I don't do anything here, I may just give the clubs away and forget golf."

Erickson would finish T37 after closing rounds of 73-79 to earn just $1,080. He didn't give his clubs away, but played only five events the rest of the year and continued his mostly fruitless off-and-on tour quest until 1977.

Colbert was at 138, Jerry McGee at 139, and Gay Brewer at 140, but the attention was mostly on Nicklaus and Arnold Palmer, who headed a group of six at 141. That attention was less on their scoring and more on their post-round interviews in the press tent.

Nicklaus was unhappy with the pin positions, and he didn't mince words. "Every hole was sitting on top of a knob. It's too great a course to trick it up like this. Let it play the way it was built to be played. To try to make players shoot the same score they shot 20 years ago by changing the course is wrong," were just some of the comments Nicklaus made in a lengthy rant. Asked which hole locations he didn't like, he responded, "1 through 18," and went on to describe nearly all of them. The worst, he said, was on the par-three 17th. "There was no way to play it. The pin was right behind a bunker. The only way to play it is to top a three-wood and have it bounce off the bunker and roll up."

Some players agreed with Nicklaus, but others didn't, including Palmer.

"Severe yes, but not unfair. You expect tough pin placements at the Open," countered Palmer, who added another dig at Nicklaus by saying that what was unfair was having to wait on every tee because of slow play. "I understand Jack was 20-25 minutes behind on his round. Now that really slows things down."

While the 20-25 minutes may have been an exaggeration, the threesome of Nicklaus, Ray Floyd, and Dave Stockton, playing a little ahead of Palmer on the course, was in fact told to speed up by officials.

As for their rounds, Nicklaus said he was "sloppy" on the first 11 holes. That was particularly true on the par-five fourth, where he hit two great shots to reach a normally unreachable green in two, but three-putted from 30 feet. The 11th was a different kind of sloppy, as he hit a succession of poor shots before ultimately one-putting from four feet for a double bogey that put him three-over on the round. One birdie coming home got him in with a 72.

Palmer started his round with a bang by holing a nine-iron from the rough for an eagle on the first hole and completed his two-under 68 by sinking a 25-foot par putt on 18. The 41-year-old couldn't summon the form of his prime on the weekend, shooting 73-74 to finish T24.

Trevino had an up-and-down 72 in contrast to his steady first round. He was three-under with birdies on Nos. 1, 2, and 4, then gave it all back and more with a bogey on 5 and a triple bogey on 6. On the latter hole, he hit the rough on his first two shots, pitched over the green, and flubbed a chip before finally reaching the putting surface. Lee birdied the eighth to get back to even, but bogeyed 10 and 11 after finding bunkers. A birdie on 15 was offset by a bogey on 18. As he walked off that final green, Trevino was heard to mutter, "I'm gonna get drunk and beat up somebody." He trailed by five strokes at the halfway point.

There was a controversy regarding an unusual situation involving Bob Rosburg on the 18th, where his drive hit a tree. He found a ball with his make and number where he felt his shot deflected to, but the USGA had placed a spotter near the tee-shot landing area, and that official pointed to a ball in a much worse position—with the same make and number. Rosburg and his playing partners argued that the deflection to that spot was very unlikely and that the ball looked older and more worn than the one he was playing. But the USGA's ruling sided with the spotter based on his closer location to the landing area. Rosburg made a double bogey to shoot a 72 for a 143 total. (Such incidents, though rare, are why it is now the norm for players to put an identifying mark on their ball to distinguish it from another ball of the same make and number.)

An amateur moved into the lead in the third round—and it wasn't Lanny Wadkins. Jim Simons, a teammate of Wadkins at Wake Forest, surged ahead with a stunning 65. Wadkins, meanwhile, followed his opening 68 with a pair of 75s; he went on to close with a 68 for a T13 finish.

"I play a lot of golf with Lanny at school, and he usually beats me. He's much further along in the game than I am," said the 54-hole leader, who grew up just outside of Pittsburgh.

Simons was no slouch. He qualified for the 1967 U.S. Open at age 17 and made the cut at the Open in 1968. He had won the Pennsylvania Open twice. And within the past month, he played for the U.S. Walker Cup team in Scotland, stayed over and was runner-up in the British Amateur to fellow American Steve Melnyk.

Still, he was surprised as anyone to be atop the U.S. Open leaderboard with one round to play. "I've never had a lot of natural confidence in myself. I'm gradually building, though."

Simons, who had opened with a pair of 71s, burned up the front nine with a 31, and a birdie at the 10th moved him to five-under for the round. A bogey at the 12th could have foretold a Hinson-like fall down the stretch. Instead, the youngster birdied 13 and 16 and had a record-tying 64 in his sights. He didn't quite accomplish that, as he bogeyed 17 after a two-iron into a bunker. Still, his impressive round included seven birdies, all on putts of between six and 15 feet. Simons posted a 54-hole total of 207. Notably, his closest pursuer was Nicklaus with a 68 for a 209 total and a Sunday date with Simons in the final twosome.

Simons admitted that he idolized Nicklaus. "I don't know that I've had the experience enough to win the Open. Not with Jack Nicklaus breathing down my neck tomorrow."

Nicklaus had 16 pars and two birdies (Nos. 1 and 6) in a third round that wasn't quite as flawless as it sounds. He was fortunate that a poor wedge shot bounced over the creek on the fourth, and he missed four straight greens starting at the 12th before saving par every time.

Looking ahead to the final round, Nicklaus dismissed any suggestion that his beating an amateur was a foregone conclusion. "Don't come around here with this, 'All you've got to do is beat an amateur' stuff. Anything can happen. Don't think an amateur can't win—especially an amateur who can shoot 65 on this golf course."

The game's other current superstar, Trevino, had a close-up look at Simons' 65, as they played together in the third round. "He showed me something. He didn't play any lucky round," said Trevino. "He made me play golf to shoot a 69. I didn't want any amateur making me look bad."

The man they called the Merry Mex again got off to a hot start at two-under through four, and again squandered it, though not as badly as the day before. Two bogeys dropped him to an even-par 35 on the front nine. He birdied 10 and got back to two-under on the day by holing a 60-foot birdie putt on 16. Trevino joined Simons in making a bogey on 17. At 211, Trevino headed a group of four players tied for fourth, behind Nichols at 210.

The last time an amateur led the U.S. Open through three rounds was Marty Fleckman in 1967, and he shot an 80 on Sunday. Simons didn't collapse like that, but he couldn't summon anything like the magic of Saturday, going without a birdie in the final round. Still, he remained very much in the picture until the 72nd hole.

Through nine holes, Simons was one ahead of Nicklaus and two ahead of Trevino and Nichols. The amateur was two-over on the front nine, his first of two bogeys coming when he tried to hit a three-wood from the rough on the par-five second and barely moved the ball.

Nicklaus made a costly mistake of his own. He followed a birdie at the fourth with a drive into the creek to the left of the fifth fairway. After a penalty drop, he hit his next over the green and made a double bogey. Trevino balanced a birdie at the second with a bogey at the eighth in an even-par front nine.

Simons bogeyed the short par-four tenth after a tee shot into a fairway bunker to fall into a tie with Nicklaus. Trevino made it a three-way tie with a birdie on the 12th, where his eight-iron approach landed pin high, skipped 15 feet past, then grabbed and took the slope back down toward the hole, stopping 15 inches away. At that point, Rosburg—who was making a final-round move—and Colbert were one shot back.

Trevino left a 25-foot birdie putt on the 13th less than an inch short. On 14, he had another chance to move into the lead with a 10-foot birdie try. Always one to talk to the gallery, himself, or the golf ball, Lee was heard to say, "Oh, how I'd like to make you, baby." He did just that, moving to one-under for the tournament and a one-shot edge on Nicklaus and Simons.

Simons dropped to two behind with a bogey on 14, where he drove into the rough and couldn't reach the green with his second shot. Trevino and Nicklaus maintained their positions over the next few holes, but it wasn't easy. Lee knocked his first putt eight feet past on 15, then made the par putt coming back. He went over the green on 17, pitched to three feet and saved his par. Nicklaus lived up to his reputation as the best clutch putter who ever lived, holing par putts in the six-to-seven-foot range on 15, 16, and 17, the latter representing a bunker save.

Colbert had shot himself out of it with a three-putt bogey on 16. Rosburg had an 18-foot birdie putt on the 18th for a 67 that would have given him an even-par 280 total and a chance at a playoff if Trevino were to bogey. Instead, Rosburg three-putted for a 69, a two-over total and bad memories of the controversy on 18 in the second round that he felt cost him two shots.

When Trevino reached the 18th tee, he stuck his right hand out without looking behind him, expecting his caddie to hand him his driver. But the caddie—a college student who was a local Merion caddie—wasn't there yet, having stopped for a drink of water. "Here's a guy who ain't even playing, and he's choking," Trevino joked to the gallery.

Trevino hit his drive into the intermediate rough on the right. From his lie, he preferred a three-wood shot to a one-iron, but it was too much club and went over the green. He pitched to eight feet, and, as he was standing over the crucial putt, a loud crack broke the tense silence—part of the scoreboard had broken off under the weight of a spectator who had ascended it for a better view. After stepping away to collect himself, Trevino missed the putt, finishing with a 69 and 280 total.

Now Nicklaus and Simons strode to the 18th tee. Nicklaus was in a tie for the lead and Simons was one back, having narrowly missed a 15-foot putt on 17 that would have gained him a tie. Still with a chance to become the first amateur to win the U.S. Open since 1933, the Wake Forest golfer drove into the deep rough on the left. Just like on the second hole, he tried to hit a three-wood out of it, this time from necessity, as he needed a birdie. It came up well short of the green, still in the rough and Simons finished with a double bogey, a 76, and a T5 finish that didn't reflect how close he had come.

Nicklaus, by contrast, drove perfectly. There had been only one birdie all day on the tough 458-yard 18th, but Nicklaus had a chance after hitting a four-iron to 14 feet. No player had ever holed a putt on

18 to win the Open, and Nicklaus failed to become the first, his putt sliding by to the left.

"I felt after making those other two putts (on 16 and 17) that I would make this one, too," Jack said. Instead, he headed into a clash of titans in a playoff.

Nicklaus knew what he was up against. In February, he had played an exhibition with Trevino and told him that if he ever realized how good a player he was, it would "really make it tough for the rest of us to win."

Trevino had been on a hot streak ever since. But he knew what he was up against, too.

"I respect him more than I do any other player in the game," Lee said of Nicklaus. "I'm going to have to play as hard as I can if I win tomorrow. He's the greatest player to ever pick up a club."

Still, he added, in an optimistic note, "My chances are as good as Jack's. The pressure is on him."

The man with a hardscrabble past, which included a stint as a driving range assistant, no doubt looked forward to the man-to-man aspect of an 18-hole playoff. "I've been a hustler all my life," Trevino said. "The only difference is that this will be for $30,000 and in the old days if it was for more than five bucks it was really something."

Trevino's wild-and-crazy-guy personality was on display on the first tee Monday as the playoff was about to start. Trevino had bought a rubber snake for his daughter on a trip to the zoo back home in Texas, and he had put it in his golf bag. A photo in the *Philadelphia Inquirer* during the practice rounds showed him playfully dangling the snake from his golf club, joking about the deep rough at Merion. Now Lee decided to break the pre-playoff tension by tossing the snake toward Nicklaus as he sat near the first tee. Someone screamed, others laughed, as did Jack after being momentarily caught off guard.

The appropriateness of the gesture would be debated, but, in any case, it didn't throw Nicklaus off his game. Jack made a routine par on the first hole, a short par four, while Trevino hit his approach in a bunker, came out nicely to three feet, but missed the putt and fell one behind with a bogey.

The second and third holes were where Nicklaus made his costly mistakes, leaving shots in bunkers on both. He reached a greenside bunker in two on the par-five second. Facing a long bunker shot from a sloping lie with a lot of sand to carry, he didn't catch the shot cleanly and failed to escape the sand, resulting in a bogey. On the par-three third, he and Trevino hit into the same bunker. This time the shot was easier, but Jack flubbed it and ended up with a double bogey. Trevino, meanwhile, hit his bunker shot to three feet and saved par.

Trevino was one-over through three holes—and two strokes ahead. "I realized he was nervous, too," Lee would say about Nicklaus's bunker troubles.

The quality of golf improved from there, and while Nicklaus never caught up, Trevino was never able to pull away. Instead, it bounced back and forth from Nicklaus pulling within one to Trevino going back ahead by two.

Nicklaus birdied the tough fifth from six feet; Trevino answered with an approach to six inches for a birdie on the eighth. Nicklaus birdied the par-three ninth with a tee shot to two feet, but gave the stroke right back with a bogey on the 312-yard, par-four 10th. Jack inexplicably hit a 40-yard wedge shot fat, coming up short of the green, and ultimately missed a 12-foot par putt.

Nicklaus recovered with a birdie from 12 feet on the 11th to get back within one. It didn't last long, as Trevino holed a downhill 25-footer for a birdie on No. 12. The margin was two again.

Both missed birdie putts from inside 10 feet on the 13th, Nicklaus lipping out a six-footer. Trevino saved par from 10 feet on 14. Nicklaus hit his approach to 10 feet on the 15th, while Trevino was 25 feet away. In a crucial blow, Lee sank his second long putt on the back nine. Jack matched the birdie, but still trailed by two.

After pars on 16, Nicklaus hit his tee shot into a bunker on the 17th, while Trevino was on the fringe 60 feet from the hole. Facing a tough shot from a buried lie, Nicklaus hit a better bunker shot this time. He couldn't convert the nine-foot par putt, and Trevino secured a three-stroke lead by making a three-footer for par.

Trevino's second shot to 18 finished in the sand. A bunker faux pas of his own could open the door to Nicklaus, who had a nine-foot putt for a birdie. Not today. Lee blasted out to five feet and blew kisses to the gallery, finishing with a par for a 68, while Nicklaus parred for 71.

About his bunker shots on Nos. 2 and 3 and his poor wedge on 10, Nicklaus wrote in his autobiography, "All I could say was that I hit them fat. I did not know why then and I do not know why now. All three of those shots totally surprised me."

Golfers being what they are, however, it was another hole that haunted him the most in retrospect. If he hadn't made a careless double bogey on the 11th in the second round, he wouldn't have had to go to a playoff.

Trevino's post-round perspective was that "every dog has his day." He didn't miss a fairway after the fourth hole, and his 68 was bettered by only five rounds all week. His head-to-head triumph vaulted Trevino ahead of Nicklaus on the money list. In the next month, he would go on to add the Canadian Open and British Open titles in a hot streak for the ages. Nicklaus's February pep talk to Trevino had worked—to Jack's own detriment.

TOP-10 FINISHERS		
1	Lee Trevino	70-72-69-69—280*
2	Jack Nicklaus	69-72-68-71—280
T3	Jim Colbert	69-69-73-71—282
T3	Bob Rosburg	71-72-70-69—282
T5	George Archer	71-70-70-72—283
T5	Johnny Miller	70-73-70-70—283
T5	Jim Simons	71-71-65-76—283
8	Ray Floyd	71-75-67-71—284
T9	Gay Brewer	70-70-73-72—285
T9	Larry Hinson	71-71-70-73—285
T9	Bobby Nichols	69-72-69-75—285
T9	Bert Yancey	75-69-69-72—285

*Trevino won playoff, 68-71

1972

NICKLAUS TAMES PEBBLE BEACH

While Pebble Beach had been hailed as one of the most iconic of American courses since the 1920s, the USGA didn't bring the U.S. Open to its links until 1972. The concern over the decades mostly hinged on whether or not a sufficient number of fans would journey to the remote location of the Monterey Peninsula 120 miles south of San Francisco. Course owner Del Monte Properties had to make a financial guarantee to the USGA, which ultimately proved unnecessary, with season ticket sales exceeding 14,000.

It turned out that people were willing to make the trek to enjoy spectacular ocean views while watching players take on a great course in the national championship. For that matter, the event made for great television, too. With Pebble Beach featuring an inspiring stretch of seaside holes starting at No. 6, ABC decided to expand its coverage to the front nine for the first time.

Another concern was that this was the first time the U.S. Open would be played at a course open to the public. This would mean that the USGA would have less control over the preparation for the championship, and, therefore, likely compromise course conditioning. Fairways were narrowed as usual, and the rough was overseeded to produce U.S. Open style difficulties for those who found it. But the greens were a problem.

In order to achieve U.S. Open speeds, they were cut shorter than usual. As the championship neared, the grass became dangerously distressed. "This is the worst set of U.S. Open greens I've ever putted on," said two-time Open champion Billy Casper.

Perhaps a greater challenge than putting on the greens would be hitting them with approach shots. Pebble Beach has some of the smallest greens of any championship course. Combined with ocean breezes and U.S. Open firmness, that would make them exceptionally troublesome targets.

While much was unknown about an Open at Pebble Beach, one thing was certain: Jack Nicklaus was the favorite. Challenged by Trevino at the pedestal of the game in 1971, Nicklaus had reasserted himself by capturing the Masters among three victories in the opening months of 1972. What's more, Pebble Beach was avowedly his favorite course. He won the 1961 U.S. Amateur there and had added three titles at the Bing Crosby National Pro-Am, the PGA Tour event that Pebble Beach hosted, including the one held just four months before the Open.

For the second consecutive year, Nicklaus and Trevino were 1-2 on the money list heading into the championship. But Trevino, who vanquished Jack in their playoff duel at Merion in 1971, was a question mark as this year's event approached. He was hospitalized with pneumonia in his hometown of El Paso, Texas, starting on the Saturday before the Open, and not released until Tuesday morning.

The timing was terrible. As he lay in the hospital bed, the Open on his mind, Trevino sketched every green at Pebble Beach from memory. He also practiced his putting on a carpet he unrolled on his hospital room floor.

The defending champion finally arrived at Pebble Beach on Wednesday afternoon and got in a practice round. He was on so much medication that he remarked, in true Trevino style: "If I were a horse, they'd throw me out of the Kentucky Derby."

While his own preparation was in question, Trevino perhaps wishfully took a swipe at his rival. "I think Nicklaus is going to be stale. I think he's overtrained. He's been playing every day since Wednesday. I think the only way to train myself is under competition."

It was Nicklaus's usual practice to arrive midweek the week before a major for extra preparation. Usually, he went home for the weekend and then returned on Monday, but, with this U.S. Open on the West Coast, he didn't make the trip back to Florida. Not that he minded spending a couple of extra days at Pebble Beach.

"I feel better and more relaxed right now than I did at Augusta," he said on the eve of the championship.

Nicklaus had a relatively relaxing first round on Thursday, with two birdies, one bogey, and 15 pars. He two-putted from 10 feet for a birdie on the par-five second, hit his tee shot to four feet on the par-three fifth, bogeyed the eighth with a three-putt, and parred in on the more difficult back nine. Such steadiness was a valuable trait on a day when 48 players shot in the 80s and the average score was 78.0.

The best chance for scoring at Pebble Beach is on the first seven holes. After that, it's usually a matter of trying to hold on, something that not many were able to do. Ras Allen was one-under through seven holes and shot an 86; Bunky Henry one-under through four and careened to an 88. More relevant was the case of Homero Blancas, a Mexican-American born in Texas, like Trevino. The 34-year-old, who won in Phoenix earlier in the year, birdied six of seven holes starting with No. 2. He double bogeyed the other (No. 6), but was still four-under through eight. He missed a two-foot putt and bogeyed the ninth for a 33 on the front nine, then stumbled to a 41 on the back, including a triple bogey on 16.

The resulting 74 left Blancas three strokes behind six players tied for the lead on a day when no one could conquer Pebble. Joining Nicklaus at 71 were Kermit Zarley, Chi Chi Rodriguez, 1969 champion Orville Moody, Tom Shaw, and Mason Rudolph.

Trevino was also at 74 with three bogeys and only one birdie. "I should have had around 85. I probably should be in a morgue somewhere," said the not-so-merry Mex in a hoarse voice. He said he planned to go back to his hotel and sleep until an hour before his 1 p.m. tee time on Friday.

The wind was only moderate on Thursday, and the high scores were surprising to many. The scoreboard was showing that with a

U.S. Open setup, Pebble Beach was even more of a test than anticipated. The beauty was also a beast.

Three players managed to shoot in the 60s on Friday, but otherwise everything was pretty similar. Again, 48 players shot 80 or
worse, this time three of them in the 90s. The average score was 77.9.
And for the second straight day, there was a six-way tie for the lead
at the end of the round.

That logjam came at even-par 144, with no players able to break
par for 36 holes. Nicklaus remained a member of the leading sixsome,
though he wasn't happy with his 73. The others at 144 were Zarley,
Blancas, Bruce Crampton, Cesar Sanudo, and Lanny Wadkins.

Wadkins was in his rookie season on tour a year after he sat one
stroke out of the lead through 18 holes at Merion in 1971 on the way
to a top-15 finish as an amateur. Now he gained a share of the lead
through 36 holes thanks to a 68 in the second round. Blancas kept
his hot start going longer than in Round 1, sitting at three-under
with five birdies through 13 holes. He bogeyed 14 before steadying
the ship to par in for a 70.

Just as big news as the players at 144 was the lone player at
145—42-year-old Arnold Palmer. He got there with a 68, matching
Wadkins for the best score of the day, and, as it turned out, the week.

Trying to orchestrate a late-career hurrah with a second Open
title, Palmer had prepared like Nicklaus. Arnie arrived the previous
Wednesday and outdid even Jack by playing 27 holes for six straight
days, explaining that he wanted to prepare for every possible situation by seeing it in a practice round.

It didn't seem to work on the first day, when Palmer bogeyed the first
three holes and shot a 77. No amount of preparation could overcome
poor putting. His putting didn't seem much better at the outset on
Friday. Two-under through three holes, he missed makeable birdie
putts on Nos. 5, 6, and 7, then bogeyed the eighth on a missed
two-footer. "I was as mad as I've ever been on a golf course," he said
after the round.

Palmer took out his anger on Pebble. He finally made a long putt
on 12, sinking a 30-footer for a birdie, and struck the ball beautifully

for successful birdie putts inside six feet on 10, 17, and 18, with the lone blemish of a bogey on 15. Still the darling of the galleries, Arnie's Army was ready to roar on the weekend.

Another big name in the hunt was Trevino, who crept within two of the lead with a 72 after spending 18 hours in bed following the first round. Still feeling relatively weak, though a little bit better on Friday, he was driving it short but straight, missing only one fairway in two rounds. "I'm just slicing the ball into the fairways," he said.

Nicklaus was going along nicely at two-under for the round— three-under for the championship—through 13 holes before making three straight bogeys. On the par-five 14th, he hit a four-iron second shot from the left rough out of bounds on the right, eventually saving a bogey by holing a 20-foot putt. He three-putted for a bogey on 15, a gust of wind knocking him off balance and causing him to leave a 25-foot birdie putt six feet short, and missed the green on 16. A failed birdie effort from five feet on 17 didn't improve his mood, though he was satisfied to still have a share of the lead. "I like to think that I got my bad round out of my system."

Saturday was another day when even par was a good score, especially among the leaders, since the wind picked up late in the day. Even par is what Nicklaus shot, and it moved him into the lead by himself instead of sharing it with five others like he did in the first two rounds. The game's No. 1 player had led after every round of the Masters, and now led or shared the lead through three rounds of the U.S. Open.

"If you had told me earlier [that 216 would lead through 54 holes], I would have said you were cracked. I didn't expect this much wind in June. It's more than we get at the time of the Crosby [February]," he said.

Much like the first round, Nicklaus was steady, avoiding the bunches of bogeys that plagued nearly everyone else. His only bogeys came on the two par threes on the front nine, a three-putt from 22 feet on the fifth and a tee shot into a bunker on the seventh. His birdies were fairly routine on par fives, a two-putt on No. 2 and an up-and-down from a greenside bunker at 14. He narrowly avoided bogeys on the last two holes, negotiating a two-putt from 60 feet over a hump at 17 and watching his tee shot settle perilously close to the small cliff over the beach to the left of 18.

Trevino finished with a flourish with birdies on 17 and 18, just as Palmer did the day before. With the 218-yard 17th playing into the wind, Lee used a driver and intentionally hit a big fade, carving it to within 25 feet of the hole. A birdie from five feet on 18 gave him a 71, a 217 total, and a spot in Sunday's final twosome with Nicklaus, his playoff opponent of a year earlier.

Zarley could have claimed that date with Nicklaus. The 30-year-old two-time winner on the PGA Tour headed to the 17th at one-under but made a double bogey when his tee shot found a bunker and he failed to escape on his first attempt. He shot a 73 and a tie for second with Trevino and Australia's Crampton, who played the last eight holes in two-under for a 73.

Palmer also shot a respectable 73 to remain in the hunt, two strokes behind. He was tied with Johnny Miller, who, at that point in his career, owned two PGA Tour victories at age 25. Miller had the most birdies on the day—six—in shooting a 71. He would shoot a 79 on Sunday.

Blancas and Wadkins each had a share of the lead at some point of the front nine. The back nine continued to give Blancas fits, as he double bogeyed the 10th, sending him on a downward spiral to a 40, coming home for a 76—still not completely out of it at 220. Wadkins had a worse blowup, finishing with double bogeys on 15 and 16 and bogeys on 17 and 18 for a 79. Just like that, he was out of it.

Nicklaus wasn't sure that slow and steady would win the race in the final round. "Tomorrow I'll have to break par to win. So many guys are close to me, one of them is almost certain to have a hot round. I'll have to take more chances."

Little did he know that the weather would turn even worse on Sunday. Aggressive play wouldn't be called for, and even steady play would be impossible. Instead, it was more like survival of the fittest.

A couple of early starters did shoot decent numbers in the final round. The first man off the tee, Rudolph, carded a 70 to finish a strange sequence that started 71-80-86. And Jim Simons, still an amateur after his impressive showing at Merion in 1971, shot a 72 that moved him all the way up from T48 to a T15 finish. They played much of their rounds in reasonable conditions.

By the afternoon, the wind had picked up to such an extent that small-craft warnings were issued along the coast and a nearby regatta was canceled. The whipping wind meant double trouble. The USGA had cut the greens close and not watered them, based on a forecast of cloudy weather. Instead, it was sunny and the greens were becoming baked out, making approach shots nearly impossible to hold—that is, if you could control the approach shots in the wind to begin with.

"I can't recall a day like this when we were almost not playing golf," Nicklaus said after the round.

"I don't think tough is the word. Impossible is a better adjective," said Crampton. "Instead of aiming at the green, you were aiming at the golf course."

As he did at the start of their playoff at Merion, Trevino added some levity while he and Nicklaus prepared to play together in the final round. When Nicklaus took the spot next to him on the practice range, Trevino started intentionally topping three-woods. "Look at that, Jack. I can't get 'em up!" Trevino deadpanned.

Trevino wasn't able to put much pressure on Nicklaus in the final pairing, seeming to run out of gas after a trying week physically. The defending champion quickly fell from one stroke behind to four when he bogeyed the second hole and third holes, while Nicklaus hit a two-iron onto the green and two-putted for a birdie on the second. Lee hung in there long enough to be within three strokes of Jack through 12 holes before two late bogeys put an end to his chances as he shot a 78. It wasn't a total blowup round on a day when the average score was 78.8, but it wasn't good enough.

On the 325-yard par-four fourth, Nicklaus ran into the type of problem that would plague everyone at Pebble Beach on this day. His wedge approach bounded 25 feet past the pin on the firm green instead of checking up close, and he three-putted for a bogey.

The telecast began with Nicklaus on the tee on the par-three fifth at even par, one shot ahead of Palmer—who had birdied the third—and Zarley. Jack's downhill chip from the back fringe on the fifth skittered seven feet past, and he missed that one for a second straight bogey. Palmer had just bogeyed the par-five sixth after driving into the Carmel Bay water hazard on the right, so now Nicklaus and Zarley were tied for first, with Palmer, Blancas, and Crampton one behind.

Zarley plummeted down the leaderboard with bogeys on four straight holes starting at the seventh, where he stunningly missed a one-foot putt, followed by a miss from three feet on the next hole—there were no gimmes in this round. Zarley would finish with a 79.

The 120-yard seventh hole is set on a peninsula, completely exposed to the strong wind coming off the bay directly into the line of play. Nicklaus, his blond hair flying, selected a seven-iron and hit a punch shot with such an abbreviated follow through that the club barely went higher than his knees. Under the conditions, it was a fine shot, finishing 25 feet from the hole on the left fringe. Even better, he holed the putt for a birdie.

Adding two-putt pars on Nos. 8 and 9, Nicklaus was now pulling away as the seaside holes were taking a heavy toll. Besides Zarley's bogey string, Crampton bogeyed 6 and 10, Palmer followed his bogey at 6 with two more at 8 and 10, and Trevino bogeyed 6. Blancas, following his front nine/back nine pattern of the week, went out in two-under 34, then bogeyed 10 and double bogeyed 12 to fall to five-over.

Nicklaus suddenly had a four-stroke lead at even par. Soon, however, he would have big troubles of his own. ABC's otherwise extensive coverage didn't include the ninth hole or the tee shots on 10. It fell to announcer Jim McKay to verbally give the news to the viewing public: "We've just gotten word things may turn. Jack Nicklaus has put his tee shot in the water of Carmel Bay [on the 10th hole]. Stand by, it isn't over."

He didn't literally hit his ball into the water. Blown off balance by a gust of wind during his swing, Nicklaus pushed his drive over the cliff to the right of the fairway and onto the beach below, where it was unplayable. After a penalty drop from the lateral hazard, he faced a long third shot to the green on the 436-yard par four. Things went from bad to worse when his two-iron went to the right and didn't fly far enough to reach the green, finishing in the hazard for the second time on the hole. This time it landed at the base of a shorter cliff near the green, sitting on a ledge above the beach, fortunately with a lie good enough to be able to play it from the sandy rough. Now in view of the ABC cameras, he was able to hit it onto the green. Two putts later, he walked off with a double bogey and a lead that had been halved to two.

Nicklaus's mental game was as strong as anyone who has ever played, and he did his best to remain positive. "I simply thought, well, I had made my one mistake of the round. Everybody else was making at least one like that, maybe more, and so I refused to worry," he said later.

He would soon be tested again. After a par on 11, Nicklaus was a victim of the conditions on the 205-yard 12th, which has a shallow green with a bunker in front and a steep drop-off behind. He hit what he thought was a perfect three-iron into a left-to-right wind, but after landing pin high it took a big bounce and went over the green, rolling down to a terrible lie at the bottom of the slope. Frustrated, Nicklaus turned to USGA official P.J. Boatwright, who was accompanying the final pairing, and said, "What did you do with all the grass?"

There might not have been much grass on the green, but there was plenty where Nicklaus's ball settled. All he could do from there was hack it partway up the slope. Two holes ahead of him, Palmer had a 10-foot birdie putt on the 14th. Palmer was two strokes behind, so if Nicklaus made a double bogey—a distinct possibility since he faced a tough third shot to a green that sloped away from him— and Palmer made his putt, Arnie would suddenly have a one-stroke lead. ABC showed Palmer's putt and Nicklaus's pitch shot on a split screen. Both wearing yellow sweaters, they hit the shots at almost the same time. Palmer missed. Nicklaus couldn't stop his pitch from rolling 10 feet past the hole.

"Looking at the putt, it occurred to me for the first time all day that I might lose the championship," Nicklaus wrote in his autobiography. "Look, I told myself, you've just made one double bogey and you are not going to make another." Known to stand for a long time over putts, Jack stood even longer over this one "until the feeling of readiness finally arrived." Ready and able, Nicklaus made the putt. He was still alone in the lead, albeit by only one shot now.

At this point, Nicklaus was three-over, with Palmer four-over, and Blancas and Crampton five-over. Trevino was six-over, having made bogeys on 10 and 11 just when he could have gotten back into the thick of it.

Down the stretch, Nicklaus combined some good fortune with a couple of excellent shots. The friendly breaks came on his tee shots on 13 and 14. He went way left on 13, but his ball glanced off a spectator and came to rest on a dirt road instead of deep rough or a bunker. He hit the green and made a par. Trying to cut the dogleg on 14, his tee shot drifted to the right and finished just two yards from being out-of-bounds. He survived with another par, and, while he was making those two pars, his lead expanded.

Palmer hit poor tee shots on 15 and 16, leading to a pair of bogeys. Crampton bogeyed 14 and Blancas bogeyed 16, so Nicklaus now had a three-stroke lead.

In the next-to-last twosome, Crampton birdied 15 to pull within two. Nicklaus had an answer. He birdied the 15th as well, hitting his approach to 12 feet, holing the putt, and allowing himself to smile.

Nicklaus walked to the 17th tee with a three-stroke lead. Interestingly, he had tossed and turned in the early morning hours with a recurring bad dream about playing Pebble Beach's last two holes with a three-stroke lead. "I must have played 17 and 18 a hundred times or more," he wrote. Every one of those times in his nightmare, he played for a bogey on 17 by going for the right portion of the green instead of the pin cut on the back left behind a hump. Then on 18 he either hit his drive into the ocean on the left or out-of-bounds on the right, blowing the championship. "It was the worst dream I've ever had about golf."

Reality proved much different. Instead of aiming to the right on the 17th, he went for the flag with a one-iron—and hit one of the greatest shots in golf history. The degree of difficulty was off the charts. A one-iron is the hardest club to hit anyway (hardly anyone even carries one these days, replaced by hybrids even in the pros' bags), and this one was into the teeth of a strong wind and aimed at a narrow portion of the green where the hole was located behind a bunker. The ball flew arrow-straight, bounced once, hit the flagstick, and plopped down four inches from the hole for a tap-in birdie.

When Nicklaus kept his tee shot on 18 on dry land and in bounds, he was able to take a pleasant stroll up the seaside 18th. A three-putt bogey left him with a 74, a two-over 290 total, and a three-stroke victory. Crampton was alone in second after a 76 for 293, followed by Palmer (76) at 294, and Blancas (75) and Trevino (78) at 295.

Nicklaus's 74 was the best score among the last 32 players off the tee on Sunday. Those players averaged 79.6, with 13 of them shooting in the 80s, including an 87 by George Archer, third on the money list entering the championship.

"Watching everybody sort of demolish themselves, and I just kept playing golf, playing golf," Nicklaus said after the round.

Normally, too much carnage doesn't make for a great U.S. Open. While there's a degree of schadenfreude in watching the pros struggle like everyday golfers, there's a lack of excitement with an absence of birdies. And there are questions about the fairness of the course setup.

While the condition of the greens at Pebble Beach in 1972 could be criticized, there was an element of nature to the challenges faced by the players, with the wind howling off the water in a truly magnificent setting showcased for the first time in a U.S. Open. It made the struggles seem epic.

It also helped that the champion was the greatest player in the game, adding validation to the event. While he won with an over-par final round, Nicklaus birdied two of the last four holes and hit one of the most memorable golf shots of all time. Pebble Beach may have been the star of the show, but Jack Nicklaus was a more-than-worthy co-star.

TOP-10 FINISHERS

1	Jack Nicklaus	71-73-72-74—290
2	Bruce Crampton	74-70-73-76—293
3	Arnold Palmer	77-68-73-76—294
T4	Homero Blancas	74-70-76-75—295
T4	Lee Trevino	74-72-71-78—295
6	Kermit Zarley	71-73-73-79—296
7	Johnny Miller	74-73-71-79—297
8	Tom Weiskopf	73-74-73-78—298
T9	Chi Chi Rodriguez	71-75-78-75—299
T9	Cesar Sanudo	72-72-78-77—299

1973

MILLER TIME

T
he previous U.S. Open at Oakmont Country Club northeast of Pittsburgh, in 1962, was nearly won by local hero Arnold Palmer, who lost to Jack Nicklaus in a playoff. Now Palmer was 43 years old, and long dethroned as the king. He hadn't won a major championship since 1964. In 1972, for the first time in 17 years, he failed to win a PGA Tour event.

He did recapture some of the old magic to win the Bob Hope Desert Classic in February of 1973. However, heading into the U.S. Open, he hadn't finished better than T18 in any other event. Palmer didn't figure to be anything more than a sentimental favorite this time at Oakmont—but he proved to be so much more.

The favorites were the usual suspects of the early 1970s—Jack Nicklaus with four wins so far on the year and Lee Trevino with two wins and two seconds. They were joined by red-hot Tom Weiskopf, finally fulfilling his vast potential with a scorching streak of 1-2-1-1 in his last four tournaments, having won the Kemper Open and IVB-Philadelphia Classic in the two weeks prior to the Open.

Oakmont was hit by a heavy rainstorm on Tuesday, moderating the fearsome firmness and speed of the greens that the course is famous for (it had also been a rainy May). The putting surfaces recovered some of their danger by Thursday, when only one player broke 70. That was South Africa's 1965 U.S. Open champion Gary Player with a four-under-par 67.

Player's position atop the leaderboard was a surprise, considering he hadn't done much since undergoing surgery in January for a blockage between his kidney and bladder. After a long convalescence, he had played in only four events, just two in the U.S., and had missed the Masters. The gritty South African had fully prepared for the Open, however. He had spent the last eight days practicing at Oakmont, including some 36-hole days and sometimes playing two balls.

Player bolted out of the gate by going a stunning six-under through 11 holes with birdies on Nos. 1, 2, 4, 9, 10, and 11, five of them on putts between 10 and 20 feet. "It would be impossible for me to putt any better," he remarked. Player stalled after a poor drive on the par-five 12th led to a bogey, adding another bogey at 16. Still, he led by three strokes at the end of the day over Trevino, Ray Floyd, and Jim Colbert. Trevino noted he had played it safe by avoiding shooting at sucker pin placements and "two-putted from here to El Paso."

The 1962 playoff participants, Nicklaus and Palmer, were in the hunt with 71s. Nicklaus had a disappointing round until the 17th hole. Since 1962, that short par four had been lengthened by 30 yards to 322. The trees in the vicinity of the green had been removed, but the new tee was framed by a chute of trees. Combined with the additional yardage, those trees were expected to prevent anyone from attempting to cut the dogleg and drive the green.

Maybe for mere mortals. But in the practice rounds, Nicklaus concluded that, given the right conditions and circumstances, he could go for it. In the first round, with a following breeze and a standing of two-over par, Nicklaus figured the time was right. "That's a stupid shot," fellow competitor Bob Goalby told a marshal when he saw Nicklaus pull out the driver. Wrong. Nicklaus's tee shot flew long and straight, reached the green on one bounce, and settled 12 feet from the hole. He then summarily holed the eagle putt.

Palmer had recently refamiliarized himself with Oakmont, 39 miles from his home in Latrobe. He had played the course frequently in high school, but not after 1962, until, in mid-May of 1973, he was invited to join as a non-resident member (he still had to pay a $5,000 fee). In the weeks leading up to the Open, he had played in the club's "SWAT" competition several times. He also worked on his game with his club-professional father, Deacon. The practice and the work paid off with four birdies, two on approaches to two feet, another on a two-putt, and the fourth on an eight-footer. His ball-striking was a bit inconsistent, however, with three of his four bogeys coming after approach shots into bunkers, the other on a three-putt.

The big news Friday was more about the course than the players. The USGA had decided that the greens would be watered for five minutes Thursday evening to maintain the conditions they were in during the day. For reasons never determined—or at least never announced—they were soaked for much longer than that. Either a new automated sprinkler system malfunctioned, or human error was the culprit. In any case, members of the grounds crew were seen toweling off or squeegeeing the greens in the early hours of Friday morning.

"Let's just say the greens are softer than I would like to see them. They won't be watered tonight," said the USGA's P.J. Boatwright.

The condition of the greens was reflected in the scoring, as approach shots held much more easily than usual. There were 19 subpar scores, a record for any U.S. Open round to date on any course, certainly not what one would expect at Oakmont. Twelve of those rounds were in the 60s.

The lowest round was turned in by an unlikely source, Gene Borek, a club pro from Long Island, who shot a 65 after an opening 77. He made the field at the last minute as an alternate, after Dave Hill withdrew on Tuesday. Hill, who had made headlines for his harsh criticism of Hazeltine National at the 1970 U.S. Open, didn't bash Oakmont, but claimed he was tired from playing too much golf and wasn't mentally prepared to play such a tough course.

"First, I'd like to thank Dave Hill," Borek said to start his press conference after setting the competitive course record. Borek returned to earth the next day with an 80 on the way to a 38th-place finish.

Buddy Allin, playing with Borek, shot a 67, while Colbert had a 68 to move within one of the lead, still held by Player. "The greens are soft, and if you drive extremely well it's not that difficult a golf course," said Colbert, uttering words that had probably never been spoken of Oakmont.

The other rounds in the 60s were all 69s, so it's not as if many players went exceptionally low. Player joined the subpar crowd with a one-under 70 to lead at 137. He had two birdies, one bogey, and 15 pars on a day marked by fine scrambling, having missed seven greens.

Nicklaus was among the 69 shooters despite not being especially happy with the way he played. One-over through 11 holes and missing the green on the par-five 12th, he holed out from a bunker for a birdie and added two more birdies for a 33 on the back nine. "I haven't liked either of the first two days, but something has happened both days to turn it around."

Jack was tied for third with New Zealand left-hander Bob Charles and 26-year-old Johnny Miller, a promising talent who, at that point in his career, owned just two victories. Miller had made a spirited final-round run at the 1971 Masters and had shown the ability to go very low, as evidenced by a 61 at the 1970 Phoenix Open. But he had let some potential victories get away, most notably with a shank on the 15th hole of the final round at the 1972 Bing Crosby Pro-Am.

Known more as a ball-striker, it was his putting that carried him in opening rounds of 71 and 69 at Oakmont. Miller sank five putts of between 12 and 25 feet on Friday, three of them for birdies and two for pars. "If I start playing the way I've been putting, I'll be in business. This is the best I have ever putted," he said.

Miller played the first two rounds with Palmer, and his work on the greens made an impression. Arnie told his young playing partner that it was the best two putting rounds he had ever seen.

Palmer had a disappointing 71 in the second round. He was three-under through eight holes, then let it get away with bogeys on 12, 13, and 15, the first of them on a three-putt from 20 feet. "The three-putt green threw me off a little and seemed to cause my other problems." At 43, Palmer's confidence was much more fragile than it was in his prime. Still, at 142 through two rounds, he wasn't in bad position.

Trevino was also at 142 after a 72. He was hitting nearly every fairway and green, but had 19 putts on the back nine and wasn't feeling as good about his two-putts as he had felt after the first round. The man known as the Merry Mex seemed to be in a sour mood all week, but particularly more so on this day, as he strode briskly to the putting green after the round and declined all interview requests.

Saturday started with wet greens for the second straight day—this time because of rain, which fell for about four hours starting at 7 a.m. The first group went off as scheduled at 10:20 a.m., but once again the greens were softer than usual for Oakmont.

Not everyone took advantage, particularly not those who topped the 36-hole leaderboard. Rust, fatigue, or both caught up with Player. The man who was six-under for the first 11 holes in the first round played the first 11 holes in six-over in the third round on the way to a 77. Colbert also fell back with a 74. Nicklaus managed only one birdie in a 74 and bemoaned that "everything I tried today turned out badly."

Miller's day turned decidedly sour when, on the first tee, he reached into his golf bag for his yardage book and panicked when he realized he had left it at the house he was renting. He told his wife, Linda, to go back and get it. Miller's frustration grew as he made three bogeys and a double bogey to go five-over on the first six holes, left to guess what clubs to hit. He settled down with a birdie on the par-three eighth and appeared to turn things around with an eagle at the ninth.

Linda returned in time to hand him the yardage book as he made the turn. As it turned out, the lack of the book wasn't Miller's only problem on this day. He bogeyed Nos. 10 and 11 and went on to shoot a three-over 38 on the back nine for a 76.

The door was open, and four players walked through it with rounds in the 60s to create a quadruple tie for the lead at three-under 210.

One of those was Jerry Heard, a 26-year-old who, along with Miller and a few others of similar age and promise, were being called the Young Lions. Heard, in fact, had broken out as the leader of the group in 1972 when he scored his second and third PGA Tour victories and finished fifth on the money list. He opened with a 74 at Oakmont and promptly changed his clubs in mid-tournament, buying a new driver in the pro shop and changing the swing weight of his irons. "Lee [Trevino] told me my irons were too light and my driver was no good," Heard said.

Apparently, Trevino knew what he was talking about. Heard had a 70 on Friday and the best round of the day on Saturday with a 66, highlighted by an eagle at the ninth.

Less heralded was 34-year-old John Schlee, who earlier in the year scored his first PGA Tour win at the Hawaiian Open but whose best major championship finish was T36. Six strokes back after rounds of 73 and 70, Schlee's name was left off the list of scores in Saturday morning's *Pittsburgh Post-Gazette*. He surged into his share of the lead with a 67 that included nearly holing an iron shot at 11 and adding birdies at 14 and 17. Schlee was full of confidence, buoyed by his horoscope. "It says that June will be a good month and I will do well in outdoor athletic competition."

Palmer was paired with Julius Boros in the third round, and they shot matching 68s to form the veteran half of the four-way tie for the lead. If either were to go on to win, he would be the oldest U.S. Open champion to date, Palmer at 43 and Boros at 53.

Boros already was the oldest winner of the PGA Championship, achieving that at 48 in 1968, besting Palmer in the process. The syrupy-swinging Boros also owned a pair of U.S. Open titles: 1952 and 1963.

"I sure don't feel 53," said Boros, who preserved his three-under round with 15-foot par-saving putts on 15 and 17. "I'm not tired and the only thing that bothered me out there today was I heard some guy calling me an old man."

Palmer, of course, heard nothing but cheers and encouragement from the crowd. He had entered the tournament as the sentimental favorite, and now, based on his play through 54 holes, he was the real favorite.

The first eight holes were up and down, with two birdies and two bogeys, then Arnie reeled off three straight birdies starting at the ninth. The one on the 11th was a crowd pleaser, as he punched an eight-iron from the trees to 45 feet, then holed the lengthy putt. "When I got my round going, it felt like ten years ago," said an emboldened Palmer, who would be searching for a second U.S. Open title to go with his 1960 triumph.

The list of contenders also included the game's hottest player, Weiskopf, who stood one stroke off the lead after rounds of 73-69-69, and two-time U.S. Open champ Trevino, who was two back with a 70 for a 212 total after another round of relentlessly hitting fairways and greens without many birdies to show for it.

Next came Colbert, Charles, and Nicklaus at 214. Miller was six strokes back at 216 in a tie for 13th. It was an even more formidable deficit than a half-dozen strokes would normally be, considering that he needed to make up that much ground on four players, not just one or two.

"I was really down Sunday morning. I had almost no desire," Miller later said. "Here I had a chance to win the Open, and I'd gagged it." His wife didn't come to the course, instead staying with their infant child and packing up to be ready to go.

On the practice range before the round, Miller decided to try an open stance. Later that day, he said it was something he had employed early in the year and gotten away from. Years later, he said he heard a voice telling him to open his stance.

Whatever the motivation or its provenance, the change worked wonders. Miller hit a three-iron to five feet on the difficult first hole and made a birdie, then a nine-iron to within a foot on the short par-four second for another. "I thought it was a good way to start, but it didn't do that much for me," he said at the end of the day.

Another birdie followed at the third with a five-iron to 25 feet and a holed long putt. And yet another at the par-five fourth with a four-wood second shot into a greenside bunker and a blast out to one foot. Now he really was in business.

"All of a sudden, I knew I had a shot at the Open. That made me nervous, if you want to know the truth. I almost gagged on a couple of putts," he admitted.

Those troublesome moments came on the seventh and eighth holes after a pair of routine two-putt pars from 25 feet on Nos. 5 and 6. He failed on a six-foot birdie chance at the seventh and three-putted from 30 feet for a bogey on the eighth, missing a four-foot second putt.

"Maybe it was the best thing that happened to me. I got really irritated," he said. "I told myself I wasn't going to win the Open playing like a coward or a chicken."

Miller then promptly righted his round with a birdie on the par-five ninth, hitting a two-iron second shot to 40 feet and getting down in two putts. It gave him a four-under 32 on the front nine.

While Miller was creating a buzz by playing his way into contention, the leaders were jockeying for position early in their rounds. Heard briefly took the solo lead at four-under with a birdie on the second. Palmer joined him with a birdie at the par-five fourth on a five-foot putt, and it was Arnie's turn to take the solo lead when Heard bogeyed that relatively easy hole with a poor greenside bunker shot and a three-putt.

Palmer gave it right back with a bogey on the par-three sixth, hitting a bunker and missing from 12 feet. Now it was a five-way tie for first at three-under involving the four who started the round sharing the lead plus Weiskopf, who birdied the second hole.

The most adventurous (and circuitous) route over the opening holes was taken by Schlee. His opening tee shot sailed so far right that he thought it was probably out of bounds, so he hit a provisional ball, which found a fairway bunker. It turned out that his first shot had lodged in a hedge in bounds. That took the provisional out of play, but his best option under the unplayable ball rule was to return to the previous spot under a stroke-and-distance penalty. Emotions churning, he made the long walk back to the tee, and finally found the fairway and the green to make a double bogey.

After losing two strokes on a single hole, Schlee jumped right back into the fray by gaining two strokes on a single hole with a 20-foot eagle putt after a four-wood to the fourth. He bogeyed the fifth and continued his yoyo act with a birdie on the sixth to create the five-way tie.

By contrast, Boros was rolling along at three-under with pars on the first five holes. The 53-year-old then birdied the sixth to become the third player to take the solo lead at four-under. At this point, Miller had just birdied the 11th from 14 feet to get to two-under for the tournament and five-under for the round.

Miller drove into the rough on the 12th, a formidable par five of 603 yards. Only able to hit a seven-iron out of the deep stuff, he needed a four-iron for his third shot. No problem on this day; Miller drilled it to 15 feet and made the putt for yet another birdie, this one drawing him within one of the lead. "That was the turning point of the round," he would say.

Miller's precision with his irons continued on the par-three 13th, where he hit a four-iron to five feet. When the putt dropped, he had his eighth birdie of the round. He had come from nowhere into a tie for the lead.

Not to be forgotten, Trevino joined the pack of contenders at three-under with a birdie on the ninth to complete a two-under front nine with birdies on both par fives.

Weiskopf's bid for a third straight victory ran into apparent trouble when his second shot to the par-five ninth sailed so far to the right that the ball ended up inside a concession stand, perched on a table. A discussion with a rules official ensued, which took so long that the twosome of Palmer and Schlee were waived through.

Both hit the green with their second shots, Arnie 40 feet from the hole and Schlee 25 feet, and two-putted for birdies. Schlee had bogeyed the eighth in his rollercoaster front nine, so the birdie got him back to three-under, while Palmer's birdie pulled him into a tie for first at four-under.

Weiskopf ultimately was given free relief outside the concession stand. He still faced a tough pitch shot up a steep slope, but handled it adroitly, the ball landing just short of the green and rolling to six feet from the hole. He made the putt for a birdie that tied him for the lead with Miller, Palmer, and Boros.

The tie didn't last long. Up ahead, Miller, who called himself "Joe Feast or Famine," wasn't done feasting, as he made his ninth birdie of the day with a four-iron and a 20-foot putt on the 15th to become the first man to get to five-under.

His swing grooved, Miller strode confidently down the fairways, his blond hair flowing. He stayed laser-focused on the task at hand, a lesson he learned from his 1971 charge at the Masters, which fizzled down the stretch when he dwelled too much about winning and too little about the shots before him. He also wasn't as confident over the ball as he appeared to have been. "I kept saying to myself, 'Now, don't shank it,'" he said, remembering his lateral shot that kept him from winning the Crosby.

Boros had a chance to tie Miller for the lead if he could do what the other contenders had done, make a birdie at the ninth. After a long wait due to the Weiskopf ruling, the green finally cleared. Julius hooked his shot badly. It finished on the putting surface, but only because the ninth green at Oakmont is shared with the practice putting green. He was some 80 feet from the hole with a couple of slopes to negotiate. A two-putt from there would have been impressive; instead, Boros took three to get down and stayed at four-under.

Heard had bogeyed the sixth and was looking shaky when his drive at the ninth was hooked into the first fairway. He recovered, however, to hit a wedge third shot to 13 feet and birdied to get back to three-under.

Now the contenders started falling away. Weiskopf drove in the rough and ended up missing a six-foot par putt at the 10th to drop to three-under. Boros also bogeyed 10 and added another bogey at 12 to fall to two-under. Heard bogeyed 11 and 12, and now was just about out of it at one-under.

Miller remained resolute. He negotiated a two-putt from 45 feet to par the long par-three 16th. He hit a one-iron off the tee on 17 and a wedge to 10 feet but missed the birdie putt. On a day when he teed it up in obscurity on the first hole, Miller was the center of attention as he played the demanding 456-yard 18th. Could he make a par to finish off an amazing 63 and set a clubhouse target of five-under? He almost did even better.

After nailing a perfect drive, Miller's five-iron second shot finished 20 feet from the hole. His putt looked good all the way until it lipped out. That close to a 62, Miller settled for a 63—the lowest round shot to date at a U.S. Open in any round, let alone the final round with the championship on the line.

Minutes earlier, Palmer had a chance to tie Miller at five-under with a four-foot birdie putt on the 11th. He missed the left-to-right breaker on the low side, however, and soon received a shock.

After hitting what he thought was a perfect drive at 12, Palmer looked at a leaderboard. Not wearing his glasses or contact lenses, Palmer could dimly make out that there was a red "5" on the board. "Who the hell is five-under?" he asked Schlee. "Miller. Didn't you know?" his fellow competitor responded.

"I couldn't believe it," Palmer later said. "Nothing has hit me as hard or as quickly in all the tournaments I have been in. I thought I had the tournament under control. I thought the only guys I had to worry about were behind me, Weiskopf and Boros."

Soon, Palmer got another shock. He strode to a ball in the fairway that he assumed was his, but it turned out to be Schlee's. Palmer's drive had kicked into the left rough and into a nasty lie. He hacked it out, missed the green well to the left with a four-wood third shot, pitched 50 feet past, and bogeyed. Three-putt bogeys followed in short order on 13 and 14, and Palmer was done. There would be no storybook local hero angle. Would Miller's storybook final round hold up for the victory? It was looking better all the time.

Weiskopf slipped to two-under with a bogey on 14 where he misjudged his approach and three-putted from 50 feet. He returned to three-under with a birdie from 12 feet on 16. He needed two more birdies, though, and a 12-foot birdie miss on 17 ended his bid for a first major (he would get it a month later at the British Open). Trevino treaded water with pars on the back nine until the 17th, which he bogeyed to fall to two-under.

A couple other players had final rounds worthy of mention, though they never were in serious contention. Nicklaus birdied 16 and 17 for a 68 and a two-under final total. Lanny Wadkins had a round that nearly equaled Miller's. Starting the day at five-over, two strokes worse than Miller, Wadkins eagled both par fives on the front nine, both on putts in the 40-foot range, and shot a four-under 32. On the first five holes of the back nine, he birdied two of them (12 and 13) and failed to convert makeable birdie putts on the other three. A tap-in birdie at 17 got him to seven-under for the final round before a bogey on 18 left him with a 65.

It was down to Schlee as the last man with a chance to catch Miller. He bogeyed 13 with a three-putt from long range, then fought back with a three-iron to 10 feet and a birdie at 16 to get to four-under. Needing one more birdie to tie, he couldn't get a wedge approach close at the 17th. His second shot to the 18th bounded over the green, leaving a 40-foot chip shot that he needed to hole. Schlee came close enough to give Miller, who was standing and watching near the green, a momentary scare before the ball passed the hole inches to the left.

Palmer, incidentally, birdied the 18th to tie Nicklaus and Trevino in a star-studded trio in fourth, three strokes behind Miller, also trailing runner-up Schlee and third-place Weiskopf.

"If I ever thought there was one tournament I could win it's the U.S. Open. I have confidence because I've played well in the Open," said Miller, who finished T8 in the 1967 Open as a 19-year-old at San Francisco's Olympic Club, the course that Miller grew up playing. "The fairways are narrow, the rough high and the greens firm and fast; everything I like."

To shoot a 63 in those kinds of conditions was almost unfathomable. Granted, Oakmont wasn't quite as harsh as usual. But the greens had dried out somewhat after the sprinkler incident and rain of the previous two days, and approach shots weren't landing like darts. Wadkins's round showed that the course was somewhat vulnerable, but there were only four rounds in the 60s. The average score was 73.8, so Miller beat the field by a whopping 10.8 strokes (strokes gained, under the current metric). For the sake of comparison, Palmer's 65 to win at Cherry Hills in 1960 was 9.3 better than the average score of the round.

"It was definitely no fluke," said veteran Miller Barber, who played with Miller in the final round. "It was just an excellent round of golf. Everything he hit was right at the flag. He lipped out a few putts, too. It could easily have been a 60."

The victory served as a springboard for Miller, who went on to win eight times in 1974, four in 1975, and three in 1976 when he added the British Open as a second major. He shot a few more super-low rounds along the way, but the most memorable was his breakthrough at Oakmont.

TOP-10 FINISHERS		
1	Johnny Miller	71-69-76-63—279
2	John Schlee	73-70-67-70—280
3	Tom Weiskopf	73-69-69-70—281
T4	Jack Nicklaus	71-69-74-68—282
T4	Arnold Palmer	71-71-68-72—282
T4	Lee Trevino	70-72-70-70—282
T7	Julius Boros	73-69-68-73—283
T7	Jerry Heard	74-70-66-73—283
T7	Lanny Wadkins	74-69-75-65—283
10	Jim Colbert	70-68-74-72—284

1980

JACK IS BACK

J
ack Nicklaus entered the 1980 U.S. Open in the wake of nearly two years of disappointing play. Since winning the British Open and Philadelphia Classic back-to-back in July 1978, he had no victories. Perhaps even more alarming, he had only four top 10s in 21 PGA Tour starts since the beginning of 1979.

Nicklaus was 71st on the money list in 1979, a stunning fall for a player who had ranked in the top three every year but two since joining the Tour in 1962—and was fourth and ninth in those "down" years. He did come close in a couple of 1979 majors, one stroke out of a three-way playoff at the Masters and T2 at the British Open (the British Open earnings then didn't count in the PGA Tour money list). Overall, though, the results were such that when Jack took stock of himself at the end of the year, he decided that he wasn't working hard enough on his game.

Facing a choice between quitting the Tour or rededicating himself, Nicklaus chose the latter. Turning 40 in January 1980, he went to work with lifelong teacher Jack Grout, who fortuitously was wintering in Florida near Nicklaus for the first time in many years. Grout felt that Nicklaus's swing had gotten too upright, and. over the first three months of the year, the two Jacks spent innumerable hours striving to recover the swing that had made Nicklaus the greatest player in the game.

Nicklaus also zeroed in on his short game. He brought in Phil Rodgers, a contemporary player in their younger days who had become a short-game guru, to spend two weeks at his home for intensive sessions. Unlike his full-swing work, here Nicklaus was mostly trying to learn a new technique.

In March, Nicklaus lost a playoff to Ray Floyd at the Doral Open, seemingly a sign that the work was paying off. But that was his only top 10 in nine 1980 starts before the U.S. Open. In April, he was T33 at the Masters. In his next start, in May, he was T43 at the Byron Nelson Classic.

"The frustration at that point became overwhelming, sinking me into as depressed a mood as I can recall suffering," he wrote in his autobiography. After talking things over with his wife, Barbara, "the depression lifted and I decided to hang in."

Next came a T20 finish at the Nicklaus-hosted Memorial Tournament in Ohio, where the lone bright spot was a promising putting tip from Grout. The week before the U.S. Open, Nicklaus played in the Atlanta Classic, and shot a horrific 78 in the first round. He rebounded with a 67 on Friday, but still missed the cut.

Despite the struggles and overall mediocrity, Nicklaus was upbeat when he came to Baltusrol in New Jersey for the U.S. Open. For one thing, the venue had good vibes for him because he won the 1967 U.S. Open there. For another, he felt that something had clicked during the 67 in Atlanta, and he attributed the poor opening round to being too occupied with his putting and temporarily neglecting his long game. And, in any case, he always was excited for the Open.

Adding a fourth U.S. Open title to those he captured in 1962, 1967, and 1972 would enable Nicklaus to join Willie Anderson, Bobby Jones, and Ben Hogan as the only players to win that many. Not that he was very high on the list of favorites, considering his recent play. Far and away the favorite—though he had yet to win the U.S. Open— was Tom Watson, who had five victories in 1977, five in 1978, five in 1979, and already five in the first five months of 1980.

The conditions were favorable for scoring, thanks to a rainy spring that softened the bases of the greens, and further aided by additional rain on Monday and Tuesday nights of tournament week. Approach shots would be holding more than in a typical U.S. Open, allowing for more aggressive play.

It was conceivable that somebody could even threaten the Open 18-hole record of 63 established by Johnny Miller at Oakmont in 1973. As it happened, *two* players matched that score, which had been shot only once before in the history of the Open. And both threatened to break the record.

On Wednesday, Nicklaus had played a practice round with fellow Ohio State alum Tom Weiskopf. "I wanted to see what was wrong with 'the Ohio strongboy,'" Weiskopf would say the next day. He saw nothing wrong. "His precision of play was as sharp as I've ever seen."

Three years younger than Nicklaus at age 37, Weiskopf was experiencing a career downturn of his own. After winning 12 tournaments from 1971-78, Tom had gone winless in 1979 and, so far, in 1980. Unlike Nicklaus, recent results had been encouraging—Weiskopf had finished T4 at the Memorial.

Weiskopf's first round didn't get off to a promising start. He bogeyed the first hole, one of the toughest on Baltusrol's Lower Course, after an approach into a bunker on the 465-yard par four. He got that stroke back with a birdie from eight feet on the second hole and remained even par through five holes. Then Weiskopf went on a tear, with seven birdies on the next 12 holes. It started with a 35-foot putt at the sixth, and he added birdies at Nos. 8, 9, 10, 13, 15, and 17.

Nicklaus, who teed off 30 minutes after Weiskopf, kept hearing the roars ahead of him—and watching the red numbers grow higher next to his fellow Ohioan's name on the scoreboard. Walking down the 13th fairway and hearing yet another round of cheering—this time for Weiskopf's birdie on 15—Nicklaus's longtime caddie, Angelo Argea, offered tersely: "Answer him." Nicklaus did just that with a seven-iron to a foot from the hole for a birdie to get to five-under.

Weiskopf then joined in what became a game of call-and-response. While playing No. 17, Weiskopf took in a resounding celebration from Jack's Pack for a Nicklaus birdie from eight feet on 15. Tom proceeded to hit a wedge within two feet for a birdie on 17 to get to seven-under.

Now a birdie on the sometimes-reachable-in-two, 542-yard par-five 18th hole would give Weiskopf an Open record 62. That would earn him a $50,000 check from *Golf* magazine for anyone breaking the 18- or 72-hole record in this U.S. Open, a substantial amount considering that the first-place prize for the tournament was $55,000. Weiskopf drove into the trees on the right and hit a three-iron 70 yards short of the green. Trying to get his wedge shot close, he instead hit it into the bunker that the pin was tucked behind. Weiskopf did manage to get up and down from there, holing a three-foot putt to match Miller's record 63.

Nicklaus had also gotten off to a slow start to his round. He saved par on the first hole after missing the green, then bogeyed the short par-four second after a one-iron tee shot under a tree left him with no shot at the green. Jack quickly got under par with a birdie from three feet on the third and another from 35 feet on the fourth. A birdie from 11 feet at the seventh enabled him to shoot a two-under 32 on the front nine (Baltusrol played to a par of 34-36 for the nines, with the only two par fives on the course coming on the last two holes.)

Jack really got rolling with a 20-footer for a birdie on 11, a 14-footer for a birdie on 12, and the tap-in birdie on 13. He managed to remain five-under thanks to a bunker save on 14 after a blast to four feet, and reached six-under with the birdie at 15. Like Weiskopf ahead of him, Nicklaus birdied 17 (from 14 feet) to reach seven-under and give himself a chance for a 62.

Nicklaus didn't quite get to the green in two on the 18th, but he was just on the upslope in front of the green and pitched to three feet. Surely, the man known as the greatest clutch putter would sink that. Nope. Perhaps the golf gods conspired to keep a 62 in the U.S. Open as an unattainable number for the time being, as Nicklaus pushed the putt to the right and settled for a 63. "I chickened out," he admitted of the downhill left-to-right breaker, afraid of rolling too far past the hole if he missed. The 63 barrier wasn't broken until 2023, when Xander Schauffele and Rickie Fowler shot 62s.

The favorable scoring conditions take a little bit of a shine off the 63s, at least as far as overall consideration of the best rounds ever played in a U.S. Open. Still, it was an extraordinary showing by a couple of great players and a special first round.

Next on the leaderboard were three players at 66—Lon Hinkle, Keith Fergus, and Mark Hayes. Three more shot 67, including Floyd, who had a 30 on the front nine but couldn't keep it going. A group of four at 68 was headed by one of the other players in Nicklaus's three-some, Isao Aoki of Japan.

Watson made some noise with a hole-in-one on the fourth hole with an eight-iron, but that was the lone bright spot in a round of 71 that left him eight strokes off the lead.

Nicklaus began the second round as if he were going to pull away from the field, making a birdie on the first with a three-iron to five feet and a birdie on the second with a seven-iron to seven feet. That put him nine-under through 20 holes, an unprecedented pace for a U.S. Open. He slowed down with a three-putt bogey on the sixth and missed birdie chances on Nos. 8 and 9. Then he suddenly started going in the wrong direction.

After a bogey at 11, Jack hit his tee shot into the front bunker on the par-three 12th. From a buried lie, he got out of the bunker but not on the green, pitched on, and two-putted for a double bogey. On 13, he had a 20-foot putt for a birdie and somehow left it six feet short. For-tunately, he made the second putt. "I don't know what I would have shot if that putt hadn't dropped," he said after the round.

With that potentially bad bogey avoided, Nicklaus got back on track on the last five holes with four pars and a birdie from five feet on 17. It gave him a second-round 71 and a U.S. Open record 36-hole total of 134.

He no longer had Weiskopf to worry about. Tom double bogeyed the sixth—needing to one-putt just to do that after a bad drive and a succession of poor shots—and bogeyed 16 and 17 to stumble in with a 75.

With the greens quickening a bit and players noting that pin posi-tions were tougher, the best score of the day was 67, shot by Craig Stadler and Mike Reid. Aoki shot a noteworthy 68 to share second place at 136 with Reid, Hinkle, and Fergus.

At age 37, Aoki was a big star in Japan, where he had 25 wins on that nation's tour. He was starting to make somewhat of an impres-sion on the international scene with T7 finishes at the British Open in 1978 and 1979 and a victory in the 1978 World Match Play Cham-pionship in England. He wasn't very well known in the U.S., however, and had played in only one U.S. Open, finishing T36 in 1979.

If Aoki was known for anything, it was for his putting. Using an idiosyncratic style with the toe of the putter pointed upward, he demonstrated his prowess with the flatstick on the back nine of the second round. He one-putted the last six holes, with the middle four in that stretch from 18, 25, 30, and 18 feet. Those followed a three-foot birdie putt on 13, and he also birdied 14 and 16 to go along with three par saves down the stretch. Nicklaus noted that there wasn't much conversation between them except to say, "Nice putt."

Hinkle and Fergus both matched par 70, Hinkle making it hard for himself with a four-over front nine before rallying to go four-under on the back with birdies on three of the last five holes.

Watson highlighted his round with an eagle for the second consecutive day, this time holing a 100-foot pitch from in front of the 18th green. It came on the heels of a birdie on 17, turning a previously lackluster round into a 68 for a 139 total and a T9 placement, giving himself a chance heading into the weekend.

On Saturday, Nicklaus again had it going on the front nine. There was a blip near the beginning, with a bogey on the third hole, but that was followed by birdies on Nos. 4, 5, and 7, all on putts of between 20 and 25 feet, to take a three-stroke lead.

He said later that, as he strode down the 10th fairway, he felt "relaxed, confident, composed. I had a chance to run and hide from the field. Instead, I gave back the lead I had."

Nicklaus didn't make any birdies on the back nine, while bogeying the 14th (bunker) and 15th (three-putt). He set himself up to birdie the 18th after hitting the green in two, but uncharacteristically three-putted from 30 feet, going six feet past on the first putt and missing the birdie attempt.

Jack finished the round in a share of the lead. Considering his winless stretch and his back-nine troubles on Friday and Saturday, he wasn't as intimidating a figure heading into the final round as he had been in earlier years.

Tied with Nicklaus at 204 for 54 holes was Aoki, who shot his third straight 68 while playing with Jack. Their tie for the lead meant they would be paired for a fourth straight day in the final round. Aoki's ball-striking was better than on Friday, while his putting wasn't as impressive—until the last two holes. Coming off bogeys on 15 and 16 that dropped him to even par for the round, Aoki birdied 17 with a 30-foot putt that hit the hole, popped up in the air, and fell in. He then holed an 18-footer for a birdie on 18 to earn his share of the lead while Nicklaus was three-putting.

Hinkle, a long-hitting 30-year-old who had posted three victories in 1978-79, was one stroke behind after a 69 that included a two-putt birdie on the final hole. Two strokes back at 206 were Hayes, who eagled 18 for a 69; Fergus, who was briefly tied for the lead before a double bogey on the sixth on the way to a 70; and Watson, who continued moving closer to the front each day. This time he got off to a slow start with three-putt bogeys on the third and sixth before turning red-hot with five birdies on the next six holes, including four in a row on Nos. 10-13. A bogey on 16 was offset by a birdie on 18 for a 67. Nobody else was better than 209, as Baltusrol was stiffening a bit on the weekend. Weiskopf was now out of it after a third-round 76.

In his post-round interview, Watson speculated that Nicklaus might retire if he won—and that would "put more pressure on him than there is on me."

Nicklaus, in fact, had no such intention. A victory would only show him that he should keep going, because it would signal there were undoubtedly more wins to come. Actually, there might have been more pressure on Watson, gunning for his first U.S. Open title. Nicklaus knew how to win the Open, having done so three times, though his play over the last 23 months did leave him with a few nagging doubts.

As the contenders played the front nine, it was clear that Baltusrol was a sterner test than it had been in the early rounds, with the greens firming up just enough. By the end of the day, there were only five subpar rounds, compared to 19 in the first round, 16 in the second, and 11 in the third.

Of the six players entering the day within two strokes of the lead, five were over par on the front nine. Hayes faded quickly and was never a factor on the way to a 74. Hinkle bogeyed the fourth and sixth—his only two bogeys of the day, but he didn't make a single birdie until the 18th. Watson bogeyed No. 1, got the stroke back with a birdie on the second, then ended a string of pars with a bogey on the ninth.

Fergus was the only player to mount much of a challenge to the final twosome of Nicklaus and Aoki. The 26-year-old had been a standout at the University of Houston but was still looking for his first victory in his fourth year on the PGA Tour (he would finish his career with three wins). Fergus bogeyed the third hole but rallied with a birdie from six feet on the fourth, a par save after a bad drive on the sixth, and a birdie from eight feet on the seventh.

Most of the attention focused on the odd-couple pairing of Nicklaus and Aoki. The Japanese star drove into deep rough on the first hole into such a bad lie that he could only hack it out and leave himself a full wedge third shot to the par four. He hit a good one to seven feet and made the putt for a par save that seemed to bode well.

That putt wasn't a sign of things to come, however, as the touch on the greens that had served so well to this point abandoned Aoki for the rest of the front nine, where he missed four putts in the six- to eight-foot range. The first of those was an eight-foot par attempt at the second after he rolled a downhill 50-foot putt that far past. It was Aoki's only three-putt of the week. He went on to miss a seven-foot par putt on the fourth hole and failed to convert a seven-foot birdie try on the fifth.

Another Aoki bogey followed on the seventh, where a poor drive left him no chance to reach the green. He recovered to birdie No. 8 with an approach to one foot. The nine ended on a sour note when he tried to punch a fairway wood with an abbreviated swing on the 205-yard ninth, making poor contact and landing well short of the green in a bunker. He hit a nice sand shot, but missed the six-foot putt and made a bogey that left him with a three-over front nine.

Nicklaus started well enough with pars on the first two holes and a seven-iron to five feet on the third, which he converted for a birdie and a two-stroke lead. This wasn't going to be easy, though. A good-looking tee shot carried too far and went into the back bunker on the par-three fourth, leading to a bogey. He managed a par on the sixth with a five-foot putt after a drive in the rough and a second shot short. He couldn't do the same from the rough on the seventh, and a bogey dropped him into a tie for the lead with Fergus.

On the eighth hole, Nicklaus missed the fairway for the third straight time. In his autobiography, Jack wrote that periodically through his winless stretch a voice inside his head would say, "Are the wheels going to come off again?" The voice spoke up after the drive on No. 8.

"I was able to quiet it again with a precise diagnosis," wrote Nicklaus, who noticed that he was lifting his head a little too soon on his swing. "From that moment, using 'Head Steady' as my swing key, I never missed a shot."

Jack was able to hit the green with an eight-iron from the rough on the 374-yard eighth and two-putted for a par, followed by another routine par on the ninth for a one-over 35 on the front nine. Up ahead, Fergus had bogeyed the 10th, missing a three-foot putt, so Nicklaus held the solo lead at five-under for the championship.

Nicklaus and Aoki took a big step forward on the 10th. Nicklaus hit a seven-iron approach to three feet. Aoki's second shot to the par four bounced to the back fringe 20 feet from the hole—and he chipped in for a birdie. Nicklaus holed his birdie putt to reach six-under, while Aoki was four-under.

Fergus stayed at four-under on Nos. 11-16, missing a couple of good birdie chances along the way. Needing a birdie, he made a costly bogey on 17, hitting his wedge approach into a front bunker. A birdie on 18 gave him a four-under 276 total with a 70. Hinkle stayed at three-under on the back nine until giving himself a 15-foot eagle putt on 18. He didn't make it, setting for a 71 and 276 total.

Watson should have been the most dangerous contender, but he followed his bogey on the ninth by taking three from the fringe on the 10th for a bogey to fall to two-under. Birdies at 16 and 18 gave him a 70 and a total of 276 that probably wasn't going to be good enough as Nicklaus and Aoki were both looking solid on the back nine. That pair each made pars on the 11th through the 16th, Nicklaus hitting each green in regulation and Aoki needing a one-putt save only on the 15th, staying at six-under and four-under.

Nicklaus was receiving plenty of encouragement from the swelling gallery. His short birdie putt at the 10th was greeted with enthusiastic cheering and shouts of "Let's go, Jack!" It was a contrast with his 1967 victory at Baltusrol, when he outdueled fan favorite Arnold Palmer. On that occasion, Nicklaus was heckled by the gallery and one fan stood in the rough holding a sign that said, "Hit it Here, Jack." Now that he had established himself as perhaps the greatest player in the history of the game while engaging fans and media with a pleasant personality—and was no longer supplanting a beloved icon—Nicklaus had become a fan favorite. And the fans wanted to be a part of history, as the man who was now an icon was shooting for a fourth U.S. Open title.

Coming to the finish of a pair of par fives with a two-stroke lead, Nicklaus's main thought was that he wanted to be playing 18 ahead by two. He had a feeling Aoki would birdie 17—which would mean he would need a birdie himself to maintain the margin.

The 630-yard 17th could be trouble in the case of a poor drive, which might bring cross bunkers into play and leave a very long third shot after a lay-up second. Both players took care of that with fine drives and were in good shape in two. Aoki put the pressure on by hitting his third shot to eight feet. Nicklaus hit a sand wedge to 23 feet right of the hole.

Figuring that Aoki would make his putt, Nicklaus stalked his birdie try, took his stance, and stood over the ball for 20 seconds with his usual intense concentration, looking up at the hole three times. He finally made the stroke and watched the ball roll into the center of the hole. Nicklaus raised his putter in the air and strode forward with a big smile on his face. His wife said she had never seen that expression on his face after making a putt before—a combination of ecstasy and relief. Nicklaus was right—Aoki did make his birdie putt. So, the duo headed to the 18th tee two strokes apart.

Nicklaus played 18 conservatively with a three-wood off the tee and a three-iron 60 yards short of the green. He hit his third shot to 10 feet and awaited Aoki's shot from about 55 yards in the right rough. Isao's only chance at victory was to hole it for an eagle—and he nearly did! The ball landed short of the hole on a nearly perfect line, missing by only six inches to the left as it rolled past the cup and settled three feet behind it.

Nicklaus didn't need to make the putt, but he did. The gallery went crazy. They had already broken through the ropes to surround the very edge of the green. When Nicklaus's putt fell, fans started to rush the green. With Aoki still needing to hit his putt, Jack raised his hands to stop the crowd, and they heeded his signal.

There was still a commotion that needed to settle down, with Nicklaus encouraging Aoki in the meanwhile. Aoki made his three-footer, which didn't seem to mean a lot, as he would have finished second either way. But, actually, it did mean something. That $50,000 from *Golf* magazine would be awarded to anybody who broke the old 72-hole record of 275. Aoki's putt gave him a three-under back nine, a round of 70, and, important monetarily, a 274 total. Both he and Nicklaus, who finished at 272, received $50,000. For Aoki, that was more than second-place money of $29,500.

The crowd broke out in shouts of "Jack! Jack! Jack!" as Nicklaus was guided through them to the scorer's tent to sign his scorecard and be interviewed for television. On the message portion of the 18th hole leaderboard, they put up "JACK IS BACK."

"This year I thought an awful lot about not playing anymore. But today . . . and the way I played . . . and these people . . . I've got to keep playing," Nicklaus told ABC-TV's Bill Fleming.

He did keep playing, and kept winning, adding a fifth PGA Championship title two months later.

TOP-10 FINISHERS		
1	Jack Nicklaus	63-71-70-68—272
2	Isao Aoki	68-68-68-70—274
T3	Keith Fergus	66-70-70-70—276
T3	Lon Hinkle	66-70-69-71—276
T3	Tom Watson	71-68-67-70—276
T6	Mark Hayes	66-71-69-74—280
T6	Mike Reid	69-67-75-69—280
T8	Hale Irwin	70-70-73-69—282
T8	Mike Morley	73-68-69-72—282
T8	Andy North	68-75-72-67—282
T8	Ed Sneed	72-70-70-70—282

1982

DUEL BY THE SEA

A s an undergrad at Stanford, Tom Watson would get up before dawn and make the nearly two-hour drive to Pebble Beach Golf Links to grab the first tee time. When he reached the 17th hole, he would fantasize about playing the last two holes, vying to win the U.S. Open.

"I would say to myself, 'You've got to play these holes one-under to win the Open.' Of course, I'd always play them two-over," Watson said.

Watson was on the Stanford golf team from 1969-71, when it was known that the Open would be played at Pebble for the first time in 1972. As a PGA Tour rookie, Watson played in that 1972 Open, finishing T29. He would have a better chance to live out his fantasy when the championship returned to Pebble Beach in 1982.

By then, he had taken over from 1972 Open champion Jack Nicklaus as the best player in the game. Watson was the Player of the Year for four straight seasons from 1977 through 1980 and nearly as good in 1981, when he won the Masters and two other tournaments. At 32, he was in his prime.

Nicklaus, at 42, was past his career peak. He was still a formidable threat, as he showed in 1980 when he won the U.S. Open and PGA Championship. Watson appeared to have his number, though, having outdueled Nicklaus in the memorable two-man dogfight for the 1977 British Open title, known as the "Duel in the Sun," and relegated Jack to runner-up status in the 1977 and 1981 Masters.

The biggest title that had eluded Watson to date was the U.S. Open. He couldn't convert a 54-hole lead in 1974 or a 36-hole lead in 1975 into victory; in several other years, slow starts doomed his title chances though he finished in the top ten.

Both Watson and Nicklaus had strong track records at Pebble Beach. Watson won the PGA Tour's annual event at Pebble, the Bing Crosby National Pro-Am, in 1977 and 1978. Nicklaus won that tournament in 1967, 1972, and 1973 as well as the 1961 U.S. Amateur and 1972 U.S. Open. A Watson-Nicklaus showdown at the 1982 U.S. Open would be the ideal storyline.

That scenario didn't seem likely after the first round. Nicklaus had a 74 with a 39 on the back nine. Watson was three-over through 14 with two birdies and five bogeys before making birdies on 15, 16, and 17 for a 72.

Watson's score was a pretty good one on a breezy day when nobody shot in the 60s. The co-leaders were Bill Rogers and Bruce Devlin at 70. Rogers was coming off a big year in 1981 when he broke Watson's hold on Player of the Year honors, winning the British Open and three other tournaments. He had taken a step backward so far in 1982, however, with only two top-ten finishes. The 44-year-old Devlin wasn't even playing the tour full-time, having become a commentator for NBC golf broadcasts. When he played, it wasn't going well. His best finish in eight tournaments in 1982 was T45; he had missed the cut in his last two events with a scoring average of 76.5.

This was a different Devlin at the U.S. Open, one who more resembled his former self, winner of eight PGA Tour events from 1964 to 1972. In the second round, the lanky Aussie put together a 69 to take the 36-hole lead at 139. It was a round with a couple of dramatic changes in direction. Devlin played the first eight holes in four-under, then bogeyed four of the next five before turning it around to birdie 15, 17, and 18. His pitching wedge approach landed in the hole but popped out on 18; in the first round, he lipped out a three-wood on the par-five second hole on the way to an eagle.

A common theme at Pebble Beach is that the first seven holes are ripe for scoring before the challenge really kicks in. Danny Edwards had nines of 31-40 in the first round, and George Burns had an even more dramatic rise and fall in the second round with 30-42 (he birdied six straight holes starting at No. 2). Watson failed to exploit the vulnerable portion of the course, but he was making up for it by playing the hard part well. On Thursday, he was one-over on the front nine; on Friday, he was two-over, and holed a 20-foot bogey putt on No. 9 to do that. He birdied the 14th and 17th and parred the rest of the back nine for a 34 and a 72 to stand at even par for the championship despite a shaky ball-striking round in which he only hit five fairways.

Nicklaus was more solid, with a three-birdie, one-bogey 70 to join Watson in a tie for eighth at 144. After only seven players broke par in the first round, there were 16 subpar scores in a calmer second round. The best was Larry Rinker with a 67 to claim second at 141. Scott Simpson was next at 142 after a 69, while Rogers slipped to a 73 and was in a four-way tie at 143.

With overnight rain and practically no wind on Saturday, 21 players broke par, with 14 of them shooting in the 60s. Devlin, however, went backward with a 75 that didn't include a single birdie. The best rounds of the day were 67s by Lanny Wadkins and Peter Oosterhuis; the most consequential was a 68 by Watson that vaulted him into a tie for the lead at four-under 212 with Rogers, who posted a 69.

A number of players fired and fell back. Andy North got to three-under on the round and tied for first at four-under for the tournament through seven holes, then went eight-over for the rest of the round to shoot a 77. Rinker reached four-under with a birdie at the second, but bogeyed the fifth and double bogeyed the ninth on the way to a 75. Simpson was tied for the lead at three-under before bogeys at 10 and 11. And hometown boy Bobby Clampett was looking to make good, going three-under on the front nine and earning a share of the lead at that point. The 22-year-old—who grew up nearby in Monterey and was in his second PGA Tour season after an amateur career that labeled him as a phenom—retreated with a 39 on the back nine.

Rogers also shot a 33 on the front with birdies on Nos. 2, 4, and 6. He managed to hold it together for an even-par back nine to gain his share of the lead, though a missed birdie putt from five feet on the 18th was a lost opportunity. He birdied the 14th from three feet and the 15th from 30 feet to offset bogeys on 10 and 17.

Watson finally made some hay on the easier holes with birdies on Nos. 3, 4, and 7 with putts of between 12 and 16 feet, then he added a birdie from 18 feet on the difficult eighth. He bogeyed the first and ninth, however, missing a four-foot putt on the latter, to shoot a 34 on the front. He hit a three-iron to three feet and birdied the par-three 12th, then bogeyed the par-five 14th after driving into the rough and missing the green with a seven-iron third shot. He finished in style with birdies on 16 and 18, sinking a 10-foot putt on the finishing hole for a 34 on the back nine.

"The 3-iron I hit on No. 12 could be the key to my tournament. Sometimes it only takes one good swing to win a tournament, to turn things around... One shot, in the right place, can give you the confidence you need to win an Open," Watson said.

The previous year's Open had come down to a battle between Burns and eventual winner David Graham, who had a brilliant final round at Merion. There was a larger group of contenders this time around, but the two were again solidly in the mix through 54 holes, tied for third at 214, Burns with a 70 and Graham a 69 that featured birdies on 14, 16, and 18. Joining them in a quartet of players two strokes back were Devlin and Simpson.

Nicklaus stayed in the hunt for what would be a fifth U.S. Open title, and a second at Pebble Beach, with a relatively uneventful 71 for a 215 total. He birdied the second with a tap-in and the 10th from 20 feet and bogeyed the 12th when he missed from three feet. The rest of the holes were pars, including missed birdie chances from inside 20 feet on the last four holes.

"I'm not disturbed the way I'm rolling the ball," said Nicklaus after the round. "These greens are very difficult to read. I've only been playing them for 21 years, and one of these years I'll learn how to putt them."

Calvin Peete was also at 215, while a group of five players harbored hopes at four strokes back at 216—Wadkins, Clampett, Rinker, Dan Pohl, and Craig Stadler.

Watson started the final round well with a birdie on the par-five second, reaching a greenside bunker in two and making a 10-foot putt, then gave it right back with a bogey on the third where he hit his short-iron approach fat and into a bunker.

Devlin made a surprising early move with birdies on the second and fourth to get to four-under. When Watson bogeyed the third, the Aussie veteran was tied with Watson and Rogers for the lead.

All were about to be eclipsed, however, by a stirring front-nine charge by Nicklaus. The round started poorly with a bogey on the first, where he missed the green with a pitching wedge, and a par on the vulnerable second, where he drove into the rough and couldn't get to the green in two.

Suddenly, his putter heated up just in time. A 15-foot birdie putt fell on the third, and he followed with a birdie from 24 feet on the fourth. A six-iron to two feet on the sixth produced a third straight birdie. Jack made it four in a row with a one-iron second shot to the par-five sixth and two putts from 35 feet. The ascending red numbers by Nicklaus's name on the leaderboard and the thunderous gallery roars captured the attention of everybody on the grounds, especially his fellow competitors. The four-time Open champion was now tied for the lead with Watson, Rogers, and Devlin at four-under.

Jack moved to the 120-yard seventh, hit a pitching wedge to 11 feet, and made the putt for a fifth straight birdie. Shades of his old rival Arnold Palmer at Cherry Hills in 1960, it looked like Nicklaus was going to ride a front-nine birdie run to an Open title.

The solo lead didn't last long, as Rogers birdied the fourth from eight feet to tie Jack at five-under. Nicklaus then ended his birdie streak with an unexpected lapse. He missed the eighth green to the right, chipped to nine feet, and missed the putt to drop to four-under.

Meanwhile, Watson treaded water at four-under with a string of pars, a couple of the frustrating variety. He couldn't get up and down from a greenside bunker in two on the par-five fifth and missed a two-foot birdie putt on the seventh. "It was a missed opportunity, but there was nothing to do but put it out of mind," said Watson said of the short-putt gaffe. The putting problems persisted when he missed a 10-foot birdie putt on the ninth.

Conversely, he was happy to get a par on the 10th. His seven-iron approach was short and right, finishing on a shelf below the green, and his pitch from long grass just made it to the fringe 25 feet from the hole. He drained it. "The putt looked like it breaks right, but I knew from experience it was straight," Watson said. "Finally—my first really good putt of the day!"

Wadkins, Graham, and Pohl all reached three-under during the front nine but didn't manage to stay there. Clampett got to two-under with a birdie on 11, then double bogeyed the 12th. A couple of birdies down the stretch got him back to two-under too late to threaten for the title. Devlin spoiled his hot start with a bogey at the seventh and double bogey at the ninth to fall to one-under and wasn't a factor on the back nine.

Rogers dropped to a tie for the lead at four-under with a bogey at the ninth, missing an eight-foot putt. He also failed to sink a five-footer to bogey the 10th and a three-footer to bogey the 12th. The championship battle was left to Watson and Nicklaus, a dream scenario for golf fans.

The 11th hole looked to be a turning point. Nicklaus three-putted from 20 feet, missing a three-footer and slipping to three-under with a bogey. Watson followed his long par putt on the 10th by holing a 22-foot birdie putt on 11 to reach five-under.

However, Watson bogeyed the 12th from a bunker and, a few minutes later, Nicklaus birdied the 15th from 15 feet. Now they were both four-under again.

Watson moved back ahead with a birdie at the 14th on yet another long putt. A relatively poor sand wedge approach left him on the back fringe 35 feet from the hole with a double-breaking putt. It broke left at the beginning, then took a bigger break to the right and fell into the hole for a birdie, and Watson was pumped.

"I knew it was down to a shoot-out with the greatest player of all time, and I drew on old positive memories. I thought back to the 1977 British Open at Turnberry," he said later.

Nicklaus, playing ahead of him, would set the target number. Jack hit the last eight greens in regulation, but the 15th was his only birdie on the back nine. He missed an eight-foot putt on 14 and couldn't convert putts of about 18 feet on each of the last three holes. Still, he wore a satisfied smile as he walked off the 18th green and tossed his ball into the gallery, having posted a 69 for a four-under 284 total. The smile widened as a Watson bogey on 16 was posted on the scoreboard next to the 18th green, which now showed a red "4" for both Tom and Jack.

Watson's bogey was the result of a drive into a fairway bunker, with the ball resting so close to the front lip that he had to hit out almost sideways. That shot finished on a downslope in the fairway, leaving a very tough sand-wedge third shot to a front hole location that made it very difficult to stop it close. The ball ended up on the back of the green, leaving a 50-foot putt with a big left-to-right break that Watson called the most difficult putt he had had all week. He made it look easy, stopping the putt less than a foot from the hole. "Human beings would have three-putted," said fellow competitor Rogers, who had a close-up view. It was a bogey, but at least a double bogey had been averted.

With the par-three 17th playing into the wind and the hole located on a narrow back left corner, Watson decided on a two-iron. He pulled the shot and ended up in the rough, only 20 feet from the hole. The short distance from the hole wasn't really good news. It meant that there was little green to work with on a shot from the heavy grass.

"When I saw where the ball landed, I thought all I could do was hack it out and make a long putt to save par," Watson said after the round. "Then, when I got to the ball, I saw that it was sitting up in the grass so I could get the leading edge under the ball. That's all I wanted."

He felt so good that when caddie Bruce Edwards said, "Get it close," Watson responded, "I'm going to make it."

The shot landed softly on the green and rolled on a perfect line toward the hole. Before the ball even dropped, Watson said to Edwards, "I told you so!" When the ball fell into the cup, Watson raised his putter and dashed across the green in celebration.

Nicklaus was stunned. He had just been interviewed by Jack Whitaker on ABC-TV, at the conclusion of which Whitaker said, "Well, Jack, we're going to wait here with you, and you're on the edge of your fifth Open win. And it's a pleasure to be in your time, I'll tell you."

"I saw where Tom's ball landed on 17, and I knew I had no worse than a tie," Nicklaus said after the round. "There was no way in the world he could save par there, so I figured he'd have to birdie 18 just to get in a playoff."

Nicklaus's attention wandered before Watson played his pitch shot. He looked up at the TV monitor in time to see Watson running across the green and figured the shot had lipped out. "I can't believe anyone could have holed it... He could drop a thousand balls from that spot and never roll one in."

In his autobiography, Nicklaus admitted that he had underestimated Watson's chances. "It stunned me, but really it shouldn't have because I'd always known that what separates the great from the good players is their ability to visualize and will themselves into making superb shots when they most need them."

Now instead of coming to the 18th hole needing a birdie to tie, Watson just needed a par to win, and could afford to play the 540-yard par five conservatively. He hit a three-wood off the tee, then a seven-iron, and a nine-iron 20 feet from the hole. For good measure, he holed the putt for a round of 70, a six-under 282 total, and a two-stroke victory.

As Watson walked off the green, Nicklaus put his arm around his rival's shoulder and good-naturedly said to the man who seemed to have his number, "You little son-of-a-bitch, you're something else. I'm proud of you."

Nicklaus had won the 1972 U.S. Open at Pebble Beach with a shot for the ages on the 17th hole; now he had lost the Open on another shot for the ages on the same piece of ground next to Carmel Bay.

"I've been dreaming of this moment since I was 10 years old," said Watson after finally winning a U.S. Open. "It made it even sweeter to beat Jack Nicklaus."

TOP-10 FINISHERS		
1	Tom Watson	72-72-68-70—282
2	Jack Nicklaus	74-70-71-69—284
T3	Bobby Clampett	71-73-72-70—286
T3	Dan Pohl	72-74-70-70—286
T3	Bill Rogers	70-73-69-74—286
T6	David Graham	73-72-69-73—287
T6	Jay Haas	75-74-70-68—287
T6	Gary Koch	78-73-69-67—287
T6	Lanny Wadkins	73-76-67-71—287
T10	Bruce Devlin	70-69-75-74—288
T10	Calvin Peete	71-72-72-73—288

1986

SHOOTOUT
AT SHINNECOCK

S hinnecock Hills hosted the second U.S. Open in 1896. It was played on the original course measuring just 4,423 yards with a field of 35 players in those early days of golf in America.

In 1916, the eastern Long Island club enlisted Charles Blair Macdonald—along with his associate Seth Raynor—to remodel the course, expanding its length to roughly 6,000 yards. In 1931, the club acquired adjacent land and had an essentially new course laid out by William Flynn. That course was a gem, but it would remain a hidden one for decades until the USGA brought the Walker Cup there in 1977.

Frank Hannigan of the USGA was so impressed by Shinnecock Hills at the Walker Cup that he felt the U.S. Open should be played there. A major roadblock was that the club membership was small and seasonal, most not living locally and only arriving for the summer. In those days, the USGA was responsible only for setting up the course and running the competition, with the host club handling the rest. There was no way Shinnecock Hills could set up and man the committees needed for that. The only way for a U.S. Open to come there would be for the USGA to run all aspects of the event itself.

The USGA resolved to do just that, deciding in 1981 to award the 1986 championship to Shinnecock Hills. Overall supervision of the event would fall to Hannigan, who was elevated to USGA executive director in 1983.

The club's location is served by a single two-lane road, so the logistics included finding a place for parking, assuring that the Long Island Railroad would run expanded service during the event, managing traffic, and building a pedestrian footbridge over that lone road. Impressively, the USGA pulled it off with very few hitches.

The trouble was worth it, as the course received nearly universal praise. While not an exact facsimile of a Scottish links, it was as close as America had, and it gave this U.S. Open a different feel than usual.

"It's the best course I've ever seen in my life," Ray Floyd told his wife Maria after his first practice round. "It's so good, they can't mess it up."

The Floyds had an interesting drive across Long Island on Sunday evening after the Westchester Classic north of New York City, where Ray held a share of the 54-hole lead but shot a 77 on Sunday. It was a horrid performance by a man who had developed a reputation as one of the game's great front-runners. Maria asked him why it happened. Ray didn't want to talk about it; he just wanted to put it behind him. Maria insisted, and Ray ended up pulling the car onto the shoulder, at first to argue, and then to address why he'd blown the tournament. After evaluating it, he decided he had entered the round overconfident and then couldn't handle it when things started going the wrong way.

The first round of the Open was a different sort of challenge. It was the worst weather anyone could remember for a U.S. Open. The wind was 20 to 30 mph, with higher gusts and rain off and on, with the temperature dipping into the bone-chilling 40s. The 447-yard ninth hole played into the wind, and few could even reach its elevated green in two shots as the average score was 4.88. The parallel 450-yard 18th was even harder, playing to 4.92.

Floyd hit only five greens in regulation and had to chip and putt well to shoot a five-over 75 with 25 putts. Scrambling skills were a must on this day when it was so hard to hit greens that only two players hit more than nine in regulation. The players with the best scores,

Bob Tway at 70 and Greg Norman at 71, hit eight and seven greens, respectively.

Jack Nicklaus, who two months earlier won a thrilling Masters at age 46, hit only four greens in regulation. What's more, he lost a ball on the 10th hole after his drive drifted to the right into an area of long grass and bushes. Even with the help of a good-sized gallery, the ball couldn't be found in the allowed five-minute span and Nicklaus had to go back to the tee to hit another ball because he hadn't played a provisional. He had survived the front nine with a 36, but with a double bogey on 10 and another double on 13, he had a 41 on the back nine for a 77.

Tway, a tall second-year tour player, had won the Westchester event for his second victory of the year and career. He got to two-under by holing putts in the 20-to-25-foot range on 11 and 12 before bogeys on 13 and 15 and an appropriate finish with a 10-foot par-saving putt on 18. Norman said that his 71 felt like a three-under round. The average score was 77.8, with 45 players shooting in the 80s.

The weather calmed for the second round, with much less wind coming from a more benign direction. Nine players broke par, including Joey Sindelar, who followed an opening 81 with a day's best 66. The players who came into the interview area were keen to talk about the contrast between Thursday and Friday.

"Yesterday trying to fight the wind, rain and cold, it was a matter of survival. I lost all feel. You're just trying to get in without hurting yourself," said Floyd after a 68 that included 16 pars and two birdies. "When I took off my outer sweater in the morning, my mind clicked and I said, hey, it's golf." Trevino also shot a 68 and said he was just as pleased with the 74 he shot in the first round when there were five holes he couldn't even reach in regulation

Norman moved to a three-stroke lead with a 68 that could have been even better. He was ahead by five after a 31 on the front nine when he needed only nine putts. He had four birdies, two on 15-foot putts and two on short ones. He chipped or blasted out of a bunker close to the hole to save three pars and saved another with a chip-in after his first try rolled back off the green. Ironically, his back nine was more solid, with seven two-putt pars. The other two holes were bogeys, though, for a 37. He finished the day at one-under 139; next came Trevino and 1985 runner-up Denis Watson at 142. Floyd was at 143 along with Tway, who had a disappointing 73, and 1982 champion Tom Watson trying to recover from a bit of a slump after dominating the game in the early '80s (he would fade out of it on Sunday).

Norman was on a roll in 1986 with victories in Las Vegas and the Kemper Open in May and June, the latter two weeks before the U.S. Open in his last start before Shinnecock Hills. He had joined the PGA Tour in 1984 after success in his native Australia and on the European Tour. While impressing with his long and straight driving and his attacking style, the blond Shark was still looking for his first major, having lost the 1984 U.S. Open in a playoff to Fuzzy Zoeller and finished T2 at the 1986 Masters after leading through 54 holes.

On Saturday, Norman's round followed a similar pattern as it had the day before. He birdied the fifth (eight feet) and eighth (30 feet) along with three par saves on the front for a 33 that put him five strokes ahead of playing companion Trevino. Greg bogeyed 10, and his lead was cut to three when Trevino birdied 11. Soon, they were tied.

Norman drove way to the right on the 377-yard 13th. From a marginal lie, he made better contact than he figured on, and went well over the green. He couldn't control his pitch from there, which rolled off the green on the other side. His fourth shot was a nice chip, but he missed a four-foot putt and made a double bogey. Trevino was watching all of this after hitting a seven-iron approach to two feet, and, when he tapped that in, it was a whole new ballgame.

Already stewing from losing the lead, Norman lost his composure when a spectator heckled him, yelling, "Norman, you're choking!" as he waited to hit his second shot on the 14th. The Shark strode over to the gallery rope and said, "If you want to say something to me, say it after the round when I can do something about it."

Nothing more came of it, and Norman settled down to par the last five holes for a 71 and an even-par 210 total. Trevino made pars through 17, then bogeyed 18 for a 69 and 211 total that yielded the 54-hole lead to Norman.

Trevino was tied by Hal Sutton, who charged in with a 31 on the back nine for a 66. Sutton was another two-time winner so far in 1986, giving him a total of seven PGA Tour wins at age 28, including the 1983 Players and PGA Championships. After an even-par front nine, he chipped in for a birdie at No. 10 and added three birdies on putts of nine to 12 feet. Tway was two shots back at 212 after a 69 marred by missing a par putt from three feet on the 17th.

Floyd felt he played very well in shooting a 70, despite grumbling about a couple of tough lies after drives that barely missed the fairway. A holed bunker shot for a birdie at 15 kept him in the loop, as he finished three strokes back. Mark McCumber was also at 213 after a 68 that could have been better if not for bogeys on 16 and 18. Payne Stewart joined the pack at three back after recovering from an opening 76 with rounds of 68 and 69.

Ben Crenshaw, a golf-design aficionado who called Shinnecock Hills "blessed golf terrain" made a similar move with 76-69-69 to stand four behind. He holed a six-iron for an eagle on the 14th but gave it right back with a double bogey on the next hole.

Crenshaw created a stir in the final round when he birdied four straight holes culminating on the sixth to get to even par for the championship and a share of the lead. He was one of seven players who made it to even par at some point during their first six holes. All seven were bouncing back and forth between even par and one-over during that span, the lead shared by whichever of them happened to be even par at the moment. It was the beginning of a wild day when 10 players would hold at least a share of the lead during the round. And, at two brief points, eight had shared it simultaneously.

"I haven't seen anything like it. It was wild. You weren't sure where you stood," Trevino would later say, looking back at the experience.

At 46, Trevino was looking to duplicate Nicklaus's age-defying feat at the Masters. He was off to a good start with a birdie on the first hole to get to even. He would bogey the third and birdie the sixth.

Sutton also quickly reached even par with a birdie on the first, a 394-yard par four that was vulnerable this day with an accessible hole location. His back-and-forth act included a bogey at the fourth, a birdie at the fifth, and a bogey at the sixth.

Tway needed two birdies to get to even par, and he got them at the first and at the par-five fifth before a bogey at No. 7.

McCumber and Stewart needed three early birdies to get an "E" by their name on the leaderboard, and they got them in the same places—Nos. 1, 3, and 5. Stewart took a step back with a bogey on the sixth, McCumber with a bogey on the seventh. Crenshaw came the farthest to reach even par from starting at four-over, but, once he got there at No. 6, he promptly bogeyed the next hole.

Norman, meanwhile, started at even par, but couldn't take advantage of his 54-hole lead. He bogeyed the third with a three-putt from 20 feet, couldn't birdie the par-five fifth after his second shot went way left, and bogeyed the sixth to go two-over. The Aussie recovered briefly with a birdie at the seventh to get to one-over, creating a seven-way tie for the lead at that moment as no others managed to hold on to their even-par position,

Tway broke out of that logjam with a seven-foot birdie putt at the eighth. He became the first player to lead by himself since Norman's brief lead at the very outset.

Tway's solo lead quickly evaporated—and in frustrating fashion. He hit a very good approach to the tough ninth, leaving a 12-foot putt for a birdie. The downhill attempt rolled three feet past, and he missed the comebacker.

Within minutes before and after Tway slipped to one-over, two other players joined the one-over group—and they were nearly finished with their rounds. Lanny Wadkins started at six-over and shot a quiet one-under 34 on the front nine. Then he birdied 11, 14, 15, and 16, the latter on a 15-foot putt, to enter the fray. Chip Beck also began at six-over and remained there with a 35 on the front, but caught fire with birdies on 10, 11, 12, 13, and 15, three of them on putts between 25 and 30 feet.

Wadkins, the 1977 PGA champion, had won three times in 1985 when he was Player of the Year. Beck, like Floyd, hailed from Fayetteville, North Carolina, and his swing teacher was Ray's father, L.B., who owned a driving range.

Trevino, playing with Tway, bogeyed the ninth and fell to two-over. It was now an eight-way tie for the lead among Norman, Sutton, Tway,

McCumber, Stewart, Crenshaw, Beck, and Wadkins at one-over, with Trevino, Floyd, and Denis Watson at two-over. It was truly anyone's U.S. Open.

The first to drop out of the tie was Crenshaw with a bogey at 12. The way things were going, it was perhaps not a surprise that an eight-way tie was restored when Floyd joined the party by sinking an 18-foot birdie putt on the par-three 11th. This time it was only momentary. Playing with Floyd, Stewart had hit his tee shot to three feet on 11. When he knocked in the putt, Stewart had the lead at even par. At about the same time, Norman's 10-foot putt for a par lipped out on the ninth hole and he fell to two-over. A minute later, Sutton birdied the ninth from nine feet to tie Stewart for the lead at even par.

ABC television was doing a mostly admirable job jumping all over the course in its coverage to show the many leaders and keep viewers with somewhat of a grip on the confusing goings on. Floyd hadn't gotten a lot of airtime, however, as he never held a share of the lead on the front nine. They did show his birdie from eight feet on the fourth hole that got him to two-over. Other than that, Floyd was rolling along steadily with pars on the other eight front-nine holes. He missed a birdie chance from five feet after getting close to the green in two at the par-five fifth. Conversely, he made a key par on the ninth hole—not shown on television—by holing a 10-foot putt after a drive into the deep rough, a lay-up, and a full sand wedge to the green.

Floyd and Stewart, playing together in the fourth-from-last twosome, were about to emerge from the large cast of characters into leading roles down the stretch. At age 43, Floyd was looking to add to his legacy. He had won the PGA Championship in 1969 and 1982 and the Masters in 1976 among 19 PGA Tour victories to date. His U.S. Open record wasn't stellar with just two top-10s in 21 appearances, though he did have 10 other top-25s. It was a bit of a mystery why he hadn't contended more often, especially considering his record in the PGA Championship where the course setups were similar.

Stewart was 29 and had won only two events on the PGA Tour. Those were relatively minor events in 1982 and 1983, his first two years on tour. He was known for his style, easily distinguishable in his plus fours and Hogan cap, and was becoming known for coming close in tournaments but lacking the knack for winning them. He was in the top 20 on the money list in 1984 and 1985 and entered the U.S. Open with top-10 finishes in eight of his last nine starts, including a playoff loss at Colonial in May.

Payne birdied the long par-four 12th hole with a 12-foot putt to reach one-under, becoming the first player to break the even-par barrier in the final round. Floyd was in danger of losing two strokes to Stewart there, which would have left him three behind. His tee shot found a fairway bunker, forcing a lay-up with his second shot. A sand wedge approach left him with a 20-foot putt for a par, which he made, though again none of his shots on the hole were shown on television.

The championship took a drastic turn on the 13th, a 377-yard par four, after which Floyd could no longer be ignored. Ray laid well back with a one-iron off the tee, then fired a six-iron at a fairly dangerous pin position on the right side of the green, finishing four feet from the hole. Stewart was also aggressive with his nine-iron approach, but the ball didn't land softly and bounced onto the fringe, finishing close to the long rough, which would affect his backswing on the chip shot. Payne nearly holed the chip, which caught the lip and finished three feet past. After Floyd made his birdie putt, Stewart missed the short one, and the two were at even par with Sutton, who was in trouble on the 12th. Sutton had to pitch out after a drive under a small bush, eventually making a bogey and leaving Floyd and Stewart in front.

Beck, finishing at about the same time, had a great chance to post an even-par 280 total with a five-foot birdie putt after a marvelous approach to the 18th. The downhill breaker slid off to the right and he settled for a 65 and 281 total. A half hour earlier, Wadkins had saved par with a chip and four-foot putt to also post a 65 and 281. Now all they could do was wait.

"I hope the wind blows like hell," Wadkins told the press. "Unfortunately, there are a lot of arrows out there. One might be a bullseye."

Stewart soon made a second straight bogey, one that gave hope to Wadkins and Beck as he retreated to one-over, leaving Floyd the only man at even par. Stewart's bogey on 14 was similar to the one on 13, with an approach shot that bounded over the green, a decent chip, and a missed putt, this one from five feet. Floyd also was over the green in two on the par four, chipping to four feet and making the putt for the solo lead.

In the following two twosomes, McCumber and Tway both recovered from bogeys at 13 with birdies at 14, creating a six-way tie one stroke behind Floyd, joining Wadkins, Beck, Stewart, and Sutton.

Others had fallen by the wayside. Norman bogeyed the 10th—holing a 20-foot putt to do that—and when he added bogeys on 11 and 13 he was out of it, ultimately shooting a 75 to tie for 12th. After the round, he said he came out "flat" and couldn't generate much emotion, an odd statement for the final round of the U.S. Open. He would finally claim a major title a month later at the British Open. But it was a year that could have been better. He led through 54 holes of all four majors, yet captured just one.

Trevino, after his slip to two-over at the ninth, bogeyed 14 to fall to three-over. He birdied 15 before parring in for a 282 total and a T4.

Floyd had a chance to get under par when he hit a pitching wedge approach to six feet on the 15th, but he missed the birdie putt while Stewart stayed alive with a bunker save on a 12-foot putt. After that pause, the Floyd rally and Stewart retreat would resume on the 16th.

Floyd had an eight-iron approach to the 544-yard hole after conservative shots with a three-wood and one-iron. Distracted while standing over the ball, he turned and shouted at a group of photographers, "Don't take snapshots until I hit, please!" Bothered but apparently unaffected, he hit a beautiful shot that cut through the wind and stopped 12 feet from the hole. Floyd calmly drained the putt to get to one-under. Stewart was on the wrong end of another two-stroke swing when he missed a three-foot par putt to fall to two-over.

Over the course of four holes, Stewart had lost five strokes to his playing companion. After the round, Payne admitted he was overwhelmed by Floyd's intensity. "When he's playing like he did today, you can see it in his eyes. They get real big."

Stewart wasn't the only one who noticed. Ray's wife Maria called the look The Stare, and after the final round she told a reporter from

Newsday that she saw it when Ray was walking from the 10th green to the 11th tee and didn't notice her. "His eyes glaze. He looks at me and he looks right through me. It means he's in the game mentally."

In the succeeding twosomes, McCumber and Tway would double bogey the par-five 16th in the same manner. They drove in the rough, hacked it out to leave a longer than usual third shot, which they pulled to the left of a greenside bunker, leaving a nearly impossible pitch over the bunker from a downhill lie, which they dumped into the bunker. They finished T8 at 284. Tway would go on to win the PGA Championship by holing a bunker shot on the 72nd hole to beat Norman and earn Player of the Year honors with four victories.

Also posting a 284 total was Nicklaus, who began the day at six-over, the same as Wadkins and Beck. Jack made some noise with two early birdies but couldn't make more of a run and ended up with a two-under round. Still, it was a 67-68 weekend. If not for the lost ball and the back-nine 41 in the first round, he could have threatened to pull off a second straight major at age 46.

Crenshaw lurked at two-over until a bogey at 18 left him at 283. Stewart would later join him in a T6 after a bogey at 18 made him four-over on the last six holes in a round of 70. In the final twosome, Sutton bogeyed 15 to fall to two-over, which is where he would finish in a tie for fourth with Trevino.

Of the players who were in the first eight-way tie for the lead at one-over, only Wadkins and Beck finished one-over. The other six all went backward as the wind picked up, the pressure mounted, and Floyd surged ahead of them. What had appeared to be the most wide-open Open ever turned into a no-sweat wait for Floyd after he finished with routine pars on 17 and 18. By that time, there was nobody in the remaining three twosomes with a chance to catch him.

At age 43 and nine months, Floyd became the oldest U.S. Open champion to date (surpassed in 1990 by 45-year-old Hale Irwin). "I truly felt if it didn't happen here, it wouldn't happen," he said after the round. "It was probably my last chance. Maybe not, but probably."

Looking back on it nine years later, he said, accurately, that it wasn't just the number of players but their identity that made the victory something to be especially proud of. "The quality of the players will always stay in my mind. Even now I look at those names and think of how many were in contention and how good each of them was, and I still say, 'Wow! That was something special.'"

TOP-10 FINISHERS		
1	Ray Floyd	75-68-70-66—279
T2	Chip Beck	75-73-68-65—281
T2	Lanny Wadkins	74-70-72-65—281
T4	Hal Sutton	75-70-66-71—282
T4	Lee Trevino	74-68-69-71—282
T6	Ben Crenshaw	76-69-69-69—283
T6	Payne Stewart	76-68-69-70—283
T8	Bernhard Langer	74-70-70-70—284
T8	Mark McCumber	74-71-68-71—284
T8	Jack Nicklaus	77-72-67-68—284
T8	Bob Tway	70-73-69-72—284

1990

HALE THE THREE-TIME CHAMP

I n 1989, Curtis Strange became the first player since Ben Hogan in 1951 to successfully defend a U.S. Open title. Now he headed to Medinah Country Club outside Chicago to try to become the first since Willie Anderson (1903-05) to win three in a row.

"The odds are very much against me, but whether I play good or bad, you'll know I gave it my best," Strange said before the tournament. "I've been thinking about this week for a year. Not a day has gone by when it hasn't been on my mind. It has consumed me for the last couple of months."

Hale Irwin was also seeking a third U.S. Open victory. His two had come in 1974 and 1979, and he wasn't considered a hot prospect at Medinah. His last tour victory was at the 1985 Memorial, and he hadn't finished in the top 70 money winners in any of the four ensuing years. His 1990 campaign was shaping up a little better—he was 49th in earnings leading up to the Open, with a T5 at the Players Championship and a T3 in the Kemper Open in his last start.

The USGA had given Irwin, who turned 45 earlier in the month, a special exemption from qualifying, since his 10-year exemption from winning in 1979 had just expired. It was the type of honor occasionally meted out to past champions in the twilight of their careers—no recipient of a special exemption had ever finished better than 12th.

Medinah's No. 3 Course hosted the U.S. Open in 1949 and 1975. The club had to make some changes to the course to be considered for a third Open. The USGA didn't like the original 18th hole, a sharp dogleg par four that put an iron in the players' hands off the tee and lacked space around the green for a large grandstand.

Both the 18th tee and green were moved, with the change to the tee location leading to other changes. The old 17th green wasn't close enough to the new 18th tee, so a new par-three 17th was built. Some renumbering of holes ensued, with the former 17th now becoming the 13th, while the old 14th hole, a par three, was tossed, and the old 15th, a short par four, was greatly extended to become a par-five 14th.

In the end, the changes turned Medinah from a par-71 layout to a par-72. The USGA didn't elect to play any of the par fives as par fours in the championship, as it sometimes did. In fact, course setup head P.J. Boatwright, fearing that tree-lined Medinah was too hard, set up the U.S. Open course at 7,195 yards instead of the full 7,336 yards the redesigned course stretched from the tips. Perhaps the prime example was the new 14th, which was 590 yards on the club scorecard from the back tee but was played at 545 yards for the Open.

The course played tough in practice rounds, with greens that were very firm. An inch-and-a-half of rain on Wednesday turned Medinah from a lion into a lamb, as the greens became receptive targets for approach shots.

"I was hoping [the greens] would soften up from Tuesday, but I knew the USGA wouldn't do it. I guess God took care of it," said Tim Simpson, one of three players to shoot 66 and share the first-round lead as a U.S. Open record was set with 39 subpar rounds.

"If there was ever a day you could get at this golf course, today was the day," said Jeff Sluman, who also shot 66 as did 1987 champion Scott Simpson.

Far back at 73 was Strange, whose bid for a three-peat was being hampered by shaky putting. He missed four putts of about four feet, three of them second putts and one birdie attempt.

Tim Simpson's round could have been even better. He hit every fairway, missed only one green, and was putting from the fringe on that one. The 35-year-old had been on tour since 1977 but had only come into his own in 1989, when he scored his second and third victories and ranked sixth on the money list, having never previously notched better than 31st. He was keeping up the pace in 1990 with six top-10s before the U.S. Open, including a playoff loss at Doral.

Scott Simpson made four of his seven birdies after iron shots within four feet. Sluman's 66 was more of a scramble, at least at the beginning, as he made two par putts of 15 feet on the first three holes before settling down.

After the round, a group of Medinah members met with Boatwright and asked him to make the course harder. While realizing that the soft greens were one reason for the low scoring, they were displeased that the course wasn't played at its full length, that the rough had been trimmed on Wednesday, and they felt the pin positions could have been tougher. Boatwright didn't relent on the course length, nor do anything diabolical with the pin positions in subsequent rounds.

The record for subpar rounds only lasted one day, as 47 were recorded on in Friday's second round and the cut came at a U.S. Open record low of one-over par. With little sun on either Thursday or Friday, the greens remained soft. That the course was a par 72 with four par fives offering birdie opportunities also made it easier to get to red figures than a typical U.S. Open, where par is more often 70 or 71 with two or three par fives.

No player had ever reached 10-under par at any point of a U.S. Open. Ben Hogan in 1948 and Jack Nicklaus in 1980 came close with nine-under before winning at eight-under. Two reached nine-under on Friday at Medinah, and Tim Simpson finished there with a 69 for a 135 total to take the solo lead.

While his ball-striking wasn't as impeccable as it was in the first round, Simpson's putter heated up, as he made four putts of at least 15 feet. He made several scrambling pars, but had his first bogey of the tournament on a three-putt.

The other player to reach nine-under was Mark Brooks, who got there by playing the first eight holes in five-under Friday after an opening 68. The 27-year-old had missed the cut in all seven of his major championship appearances up to this point (he would go on to win the 1996 PGA Championship and finish second in the 2001 U.S. Open). He played the last 10 holes in three-over to end the day in fourth place at 138.

Sluman, who had been in a slump since winning the 1988 PGA Championship, played a bogey-free 70 to claim second at 136. Mike Donald was at 137, also after a 70.

The under-par second round was welcome for Donald, who in April at the Masters had followed a first-round 64 with an ugly 82. After an opening 67 at Medinah, Donald received a telegram from a former pro-am partner in Boston, which read, "Forget about the Masters, you can do it."

"How am I supposed to forget about it, if that's the first thing he mentions," asked Donald.

The Masters debacle wasn't the first for Donald in a major. He tied for the first-round lead at the 1984 U.S. Open with a 68, then shot a 78 in the second round. He finished T34—and that was his best showing in 11 major championship starts.

Overall, Donald's career had traced a similar trajectory to Tim Simpson's. Joining the tour in 1980, over his first nine years he finished in the top 70 on the money list just once (46th in 1984). Finally, in 1989, Donald scored his first victory, at the Anheuser-Busch Golf Classic, and ranked 22nd in earnings. He entered 18 events in 1990 before the U.S. Open with only one top-10, a fifth in Atlanta two weeks before Medinah.

Donald was one-over on the front nine of the second round before birdies on 11, 17, and 18, sinking 10-foot putts on the latter two for a 33 on the back nine and a measure of redemption.

Irwin also shot 37-33, with birdies on 14, 16, and 17, earning an invitation to the press tent after posting a 139 total, good for a tie for fifth with Scott Simpson. "I don't know about the rest of you, but I don't think I'm over the hill," Irwin told the assembled writers after getting questions about his age. "I still think I can play."

Strange was yet another player shooting a 70. He began the day with no certainty of making the cut, and his prospects didn't look bright after a bogey on the first hole with a familiar missed putt of four feet. His putter came around with a pair of 20-foot birdie putts on the front nine and an encouraging finish by holing a 40-foot birdie putt on 18.

"I'm not finished yet. I'm not one to throw in the towel and say I'll catch you next week," he said after the round. "That grinding I did to make the cut can carry over to the next two days."

Strange's momentum did carry over to Saturday when he shot a 68. With the field bunching up, that brought him within two strokes of the lead. A three-peat was suddenly well within reach.

Curtis hit every fairway and missed only one green. Through 12 holes, he had 11 pars and one birdie, then he heated up down the stretch with birdies on 13 (15 feet), 16 (four-iron to four feet), and 17 (20 feet). The latter putt was a big breaker on a hole and green that gave several players fits.

The scoring was again low, with an average of 72.3, but there were a couple of signs that things were changing. While there were 15 rounds in the 60s, nobody did better than 68. There were seven of those, with most coming from earlier starters, as winds picked up in the afternoon. Of the last six twosomes off the tee, only one player, Billy Ray Brown with a 69, broke par.

Scott Simpson and Sluman both reached nine-under during the round. Simpson's rise and fall was the most dramatic. The 1987 champion started the day at five-under, having shot a 73 in the second round, and played the first seven holes in four-under with five birdies and a bogey. He parred through the 15th, and then disaster struck with a bogey-triple bogey-bogey finish for a round of 32-41—73.

The triple bogey on the 168-yard par three 17th started with a tee shot that flew the green and plugged into a bunker, leaving Simpson in a devilish situation with a green that sloped sharply away from him and water taunting him on the other side. He didn't get out of the bunker with his first attempt, and the next one sent the ball across the green to the rough, followed by a chip on and then two putts to end the misery.

The previous day, Ian Woosnam came to the 17th seven-under for the tournament and also made a triple bogey without a ball in the water (two chips and three putts). He double bogeyed it on Saturday, with those five strokes over par accounting for his entire 54-hole deficit relative to the lead, which was shared by Donald and Brown at 209.

Sluman's moment at nine-under was short-lived after making a birdie on the first hole to get there. He stumbled to a 39 on the front nine in an erratic round with seven bogeys and five birdies for a 74 that left him at 210. Tim Simpson was also at 210 after bogeys at 16 and 17 saddled him with a 75.

The troubles of the two Simpsons and Sluman, and the inability of anybody to finish at better than seven-under created a bottleneck at the top of the leaderboard heading into the final round. Brooks (72) and three-time major champion Larry Nelson (69) made it a quartet at 210, one behind the leading duo. Six players, including Strange, were two back at 211. Seven more were at 212, eight at 213, and four at 214, making a total of 31 players within five shots.

Donald had two birdies and two bogeys in a round of 72 that gave him a share of the lead. "The rest of the field reacted like it was a U.S. Open," he said. "It turned out my pars were pretty good."

He and Brown were an unlikely duo at the top, with one PGA Tour victory between them. Brown won the NCAA Championship as a freshman at the University of Houston in 1982. His first two years on tour were underwhelming, with only one top-10 finish each in 1988 and 1989. Things were finally looking up in 1990 with three thirds and a fifth in the first five months of the year, but this was just the second major championship and first U.S. Open that the 27-year-old had ever played.

Major champions Strange, Fuzzy Zoeller, Larry Mize, Nick Faldo, Scott Simpson, Seve Ballesteros, Irwin, and Jack Nicklaus were all lurking within four strokes. So were future major champions Jose Maria Olazabal and Paul Azinger, each ranked in the top 10 in the world. At age 50, Nicklaus was 10 years removed from his last major title, but he shot a 68 in the third round to pull within four and felt he had a chance. He had shot 27-under par the previous week in winning on the senior tour but would finish with a 76 here.

The most dangerous of those champions, besides Strange, was Faldo, who had won his second consecutive Masters in April and lost a playoff to Strange at the 1988 U.S. Open. After his opening rounds of 72-72, Faldo on Friday described his weekend prospects: "I've got to shoot two really good rounds—67, 68." He delivered with a 68 on

Saturday and was three strokes back, albeit with 12 players ahead of him.

Irwin was little more than an afterthought, having shot a 74 in the third round to stand four strokes off the lead in a tie for 20th. He was paired on Sunday with a man who was five strokes back but seemed more of a threat—Greg Norman, the No. 1-ranked player in the world with two victories so far in 1990. Norman had barely made the cut with rounds of 72-73, holing a three-foot putt on the 18th hole to survive on Friday, then moved up with a 69 on Saturday. Their Sunday tee time was two hours ahead of the final pairing.

Norman thrust himself into contention midway through the front nine. He birdied the par-five fifth from close to the green in two, birdied the par-four sixth with a great second shot out of the trees, and birdied the par-three eighth with a 40-foot putt. It added up to a 33 on the front nine. When Norman birdied the par-five 10th, he moved to six-under for the tournament and one shot behind co-leaders Donald and Brown, who had just teed off on the first hole.

Norman was now one of five players at six-under, joining the quartet of Brooks, Nelson, Sluman and Tim Simpson, who had all only completed one hole. Faldo made it six players at six-under when he birdied the fifth to go two-under for the day. There were also three players at five-under, and a group of seven at four-under, comprising a hefty group of contenders to be sorted out.

Donald pulled away from the scrum with birdies on the first two holes, sinking a 12-foot putt on the first and hitting a three-iron to three feet on the second, becoming the fifth player to reach nine-under for the tournament. He would hold there for a long stretch, meaning a significant charge forward would be required for anybody in the following pack to challenge.

Irwin, seemingly out of it at three-under par and six strokes behind with eight holes to play, was up to the task. His front-nine 36 included a bogey at the second hole, a birdie from eight feet at the seventh, and a par save at the ninth that didn't seem especially significant at the time. Irwin's three-wood tee shot hit the branch of a tree there; he couldn't reach the 429-yard hole with a four-wood second, and he ended up making a 10-foot par putt.

Hale's back-nine charge began with some dazzling iron play—a seven-iron to six feet on the 11th hole, a five-iron to four feet on the 12th, and a four-iron to three feet on the 13th for a third straight birdie. He made it four in a row with a pitching wedge to 12 feet on the par-five 14th and a clutch putt.

Norman got a birdie himself on the 13th, but badly screwed up on 14. He deliberated whether to hit a driver from the fairway on his second shot to get close to the green, then decided to lay up with a three-iron. He hit an awful shot, far to the right. It was the kind of miss that plagued him at key moments in his career. The ball finished in the trees, with no chance to reach the green in three, and he ended up with a bogey. While Norman dropped to six-under, Irwin climbed to seven-under with a two-stroke swing between them on the 14th.

Strange was hanging in there at five-under at this point with a bogey at the second and a birdie at the fifth, but he was about to unravel. The two-time defender three-putted for a bogey on the seventh and also bogeyed the ninth. A 37 on the back nine netted him a 75 for a T21. "I expected myself to come through today, and I didn't," he said. For the week, he ranked first in fairways hit and tied for first in greens in regulation. His biggest problem was on the greens though his ball-striking wasn't quite as pure in the final round.

While Strange's bid for a third consecutive Open was faltering, Faldo's pursuit of a back-to-back major title was mounting. The Englishman followed a 34 on the front nine with a 20-foot birdie putt from the fringe on the 11th to pull within two strokes at seven-under.

Meanwhile, Brown, and especially Donald, were holding up surprisingly well in the final pairing. After his two opening birdies, Donald parred the rest of the front nine, hitting every green and burning the edge on three of his birdie putts.

Brown admitted to ABC television reporter Jerry Pate that he was so nervous before the round that he felt like throwing up. He made some mistakes in a front-nine 37, but almost matched them with two birdies. The first birdie was on No. 5, then Brown made a bad double bogey on the other par five on the front nine, No. 7. He drove into a bad lie in the rough, didn't escape the rough with his second shot, and eventually three-putted. Showing resilience, he birdied the eighth from 15 feet; showing nerves, he bogeyed the ninth after a poor approach and taking three from the fringe to stand at six-under.

Around the time Donald and Brown were making the turn, Irwin was heading up the 18th fairway. He was still seven-under, having holed a par putt of seven feet on the 15th and missed birdie putts of 10 and 18 feet on the next two holes (Norman bogeyed 17 to end his chances).

Irwin's seven-iron approach to the 440-yard 18th settled 45 feet short and right of the hole. His putt rolled up and over a ridge, then broke about five feet right to left—and dropped into the center of the hole for a birdie. Irwin's reaction was priceless. The former college football cornerback at the University of Colorado ran around the front part of the green, arms aloft, then dashed over to the gallery ropes to the right of the green and exchanged high fives with several fans, ran back onto the green, then blew a kiss to the sky.

"I don't know how you can be stoic after something like that," he told the press afterward. "In 22 years of [tour] golf, I've never made a putt like that to win or come close to winning."

The thriller of a putt climaxed a back-nine 31 and a round of 67. Over the next two hours, Irwin went to the TV tower to be interviewed, then the press tent for another interview, then back to the TV tower, where he was asked to give commentary not only on his round but also on the play of those trying to beat or match his eight-under finishing total.

Shortly after Irwin's game-changing birdie, Faldo birdied the 14th from seven feet to reach eight-under, then Brown birdied the 11th from four feet to get to seven-under. Faldo, playing about an hour ahead of the final twosome, faltered with a bogey on 16, pulling his approach shot 60 feet left of the hole, leaving his first putt six feet short, and missing that one.

Faldo hit his approach shot to 15 feet on 18, needing a birdie to match Irwin at eight-under in the clubhouse. His putt tracked toward the hole, and Nick thought he'd made it. The ball caught the right edge of the hole and spun out. There would be no U.S. Open title for Faldo to add to his British Open crown of 1987 (he would go on to win that event a month later and again in 1992).

Donald kept chugging along at nine-under one way or another, following his long string of two-putt pars with a couple of great saving putts. He drove into the trees on the par-four 12th, had to punch out and hit a full third shot to the green, then holed a 15-foot putt. Another poor drive at the par-five 14th led to a longer than usual third shot, which he knocked over the green. A chip left him 18 feet from the hole, and he made it from there. The journeyman was playing as if he belonged on the big stage.

Donald finally stumbled on the 16th hole. His three-iron approach was pushed into the right bunker, he came out to 12 feet, but had apparently exhausted his ration of par-saving putts on the back nine, this one halting short of the cup's front edge. The bogey dropped Donald to eight-under, tied with Irwin. Brown also made a bogey from the bunker to fall to six-under.

Brown revived his chances with a birdie on the 17th, where his nine-iron tee shot landed near the back of the green and ran down the slope back toward the hole, finishing two feet from the cup. Donald two-putted from 15 feet for a par.

Walking toward the 18th tee, Donald said to his caddie—his brother Pete—"This is what we've practiced 20 years for." His three-wood tee shot looked like it might be headed for the deep rough on the right, but it got a favorable bounce to the left and well forward, leaving an eight-iron to the green from the intermediate rough. He hung that a little to the right, not wanting to flirt with the left bunker, and ended up 40 feet from the hole, not far from where Irwin had been. Donald couldn't conjure up Irwin's magic, with his putt rolling three feet past.

Now Brown had a chance to finish at eight-under, having hit a fine approach shot to 12 feet in a similar spot from where Faldo had narrowly missed. Like Faldo, Brown thought he'd made it but his just missed on the left, and he finished one shot behind with a closing 72.

Donald faced a knee-knocker to force an 18-hole Monday playoff and was up to the task. With the wind picking up considerably in the afternoon and the pressure mounting, Donald's 71 was the only sub-par round in the last six pairings and Brown had the only even-par round. The other 10 players among the last dozen on the course averaged 74.8.

Irwin had finished one shot out of a playoff in the 1975 U.S. Open at Medinah, won by Lou Graham over John Mahaffey; now he was in a playoff. He was glad the U.S. Open had stuck with the 18-hole format rather than switching to sudden death, as at the Masters or PGA Championship, or a three- or four-hole playoff at the British Open. After a two-hour wait, it would have been difficult to get warm again.

Donald started the playoff the same way he started the final round, with a birdie on the 385-yard opening hole, this time with a pitching wedge to five feet. Instead of following it up with another birdie, as he did on Sunday, he gave the stroke right back with a three-putt bogey from 60 feet on the second hole, missing a second putt of eight feet.

Donald made another bogey on the fourth hole, missing a six-foot putt after chipping on. Irwin made routine pars on the first four holes before joining Donald at one-over, thanks to a bogey on the par-five fifth. He tried to hit a four-wood out of a questionable lie in the rough, and moved the ball only nine yards, later admitting he should have hit an eight-iron. Wasting a stroke there, he ended up on the green in four and missed a 20-foot putt.

The sloppy nature of the playoff continued on the sixth hole with a bogey from Donald, who drove into the left rough, hit his second into a bunker, and missed a 10-foot putt.

Both made two-putt pars on the seventh and saved pars on the eighth, Irwin in unusual fashion. Hale knocked his tee shot on the 190-yard hole underneath the grandstand behind the green, got a drop, pitched on to eight feet, and made the putt to match Donald, who chipped within a foot.

The ninth hole brought the only two-stroke swing of the playoff, Donald sinking a 20-foot birdie putt and Irwin getting into trouble with a drive in the rough and ultimately missing a six-foot par attempt. Now Donald was one-over, and Irwin dropped to two-over.

After pars on the 10th, both bogeyed No. 11. Irwin was in trouble all the way, in the rough and then a bunker on the par four, two-putting from 25 feet. Wasting a golden opportunity to gain a stroke, Donald three-putted from 25 feet, missing a four-footer.

Normally a straight driver, Irwin's long game abandoned him in the middle of the round. He missed the fairway for the fourth straight hole on the par-four 12th, eventually getting on the green in four and making a four-foot putt for a bogey.

Both parred the 13th, and Irwin finally made his first birdie of the day on the 14th, which was matched by Donald. They were each close to the green in two on the par five, with Donald making a 12-foot putt and Irwin converting from four feet.

Routine pars on the 15th left Irwin facing a two-stroke deficit with three to play. The 16th was the toughest hole during the championship, playing to a 4.31 average. At 426 yards, it wasn't the longest par four, but the sharp dogleg left made for a long, uphill second shot if the drive favored the right side of the fairway. That's where Irwin's tee shot ended up, and his second required a two-iron draw around overhanging branches.

He hit a beauty, cutting through the wind, landing on the green, and running to within six feet of the hole. Irwin holed the putt, gaining a stroke on Donald, who preserved a one-shot lead with a chip to two feet for a par. The two-iron is supposed to be a hard club to hit, but apparently not for Irwin. He clinched his 1974 Open victory with a two-iron to the 72nd hole at Winged Foot and spiced his 1979 win with a two-iron to three feet for a birdie in the third round on the 13th hole at Inverness.

Donald missed a chance to go back ahead by two on 17 when he failed to convert a 12-foot birdie putt, while Irwin chipped close from the fringe to make a par.

Irwin couldn't produce any heroics on the 18th hole this time, two-putting from 30 feet for a par. It was up to Donald to make a par to claim the title—and he couldn't do it. A drive to the left got him in trouble and his five-iron second shot found the left front bunker. His shot from there served up an 18-foot putt. Like Faldo and Brown on the finishing hole on Sunday, Donald thought the putt was going to fall. When it didn't, he and Irwin both finished the 18 holes with two-over 74s.

The USGA had decided way back in 1953 that if an 18-hole playoff ended in a tie, it would go to sudden death. This would be the first time the rule was exercised.

The extra-hole affair started on No. 1, one of the more vulnerable par fours on the course. Donald had an inkling one of them would birdie it. He had done so in three of the last four rounds. But not this time. His second shot came up 35 feet short, leaving a tough putt over a ridge. Donald hit a nice approach putt, but it didn't matter. Irwin had hit a sand wedge from 103 yards to 10 feet. When the putt found the hole, Hale had earned his third U.S. Open title. After playing the first 12 holes of the playoff in four-over, he was three-under on the last seven.

At 45, Irwin became the oldest player to ever capture the U.S. Open, and the first to ever do so by holing a 45-foot putt on the 72nd hole—though the splendid two-iron the next day also had something to do with it.

TOP-10 FINISHERS		
1	Hale Irwin	69-70-74-67—280*
2	Mike Donald	67-70-72-71—280
T3	Billy Ray Brown	69-71-69-72—281
T3	Nick Faldo	72-72-68-69—281
T5	Mark Brooks	68-70-72-73—283
T5	Greg Norman	72-73-69-69—283
T5	Tim Simpson	66-69-75-73—283
T8	Scott Hoch	70-73-69-72—284
T8	Steve Jones	67-76-74-67—284
T8	Jose Maria Olazabal	73-69-69-73—284
T8	Tom Sieckmann	70-74-68-72—284
T8	Craig Stadler	71-70-72-71—284
T8	Fuzzy Zoeller	73-70-68-73—284

*Irwin won playoff on first sudden death hole after he and Donald both shot 74

1999

PAYNE'S PERFECT PUTT

T he No. 2 Course at Pinehurst in North Carolina was the masterwork of Donald Ross, one of golf's seminal and influential architects. Yet, it took nearly a century for the U.S. Open to come to Pinehurst.

The reasons were two-fold: location and agronomy. The Southeast isn't an easy place to maintain grass in the summer, and, from its 1907 opening until 1935, the No. 2 Course had sand greens. The conversion to grass enabled Ross, who lived next to the third hole, to get creative and endow the new putting surfaces with slopes that made them smaller targets than their actual size. Most notably, the greens were built up with drop-offs to the sides, back, or front.

Still, with the resort's courses closed in the summer until the 1960s, the U.S. Open was out of the question. In any case, the Open didn't even come to the Southeast until 1976 at Atlanta Athletic Club. That experience strengthened the USGA's resolve to avoid holding the event on a course with Bermuda grass greens, which could not be made fast enough for the preferred Open setup.

This left Pinehurst in a situation where there was no right answer. The resort switched from Bermuda to bentgrass greens in 1972, but they required heavy watering in the summertime, resulting in greens too soft for an Open. PGA Tour events were held on No. 2 in the 1970s and early 1980s, with scores as low as 62 and Hale Irwin winning one year at 20-under par.

The greens were switched back to Bermuda in 1979, then to back to bentgrass in 1987. By that time, the USGA was considering an Open at No. 2. A second strike against Pinehurst had been its remote location, at least 70 miles from North Carolina's major cities. However, Opens on the Monterey Peninsula at Pebble Beach in 1972 and 1982 and eastern Long Island's Shinnecock Hills in 1986 had eased those concerns.

The USGA pulled the trigger in 1993, awarding the 1999 U.S. Open to No. 2. It did so with the agreement that the resort and the USGA would closely monitor developments in agronomy with an eye to making the greens both fast and firm during the summer.

Fortuitously, in the early 1990s, a new strain of bentgrass, Penn G-2, was cultivated, designed to survive the summer heat with less water than required by previous strains. It hadn't been used on a golf course until Pinehurst converted the greens on its No. 4 Course to Penn G-2 as a trial. Pleased with the results there, the greens on No. 2 were rebuilt in 1994-95 and grassed with G-2.

With the conditioning secured, the USGA made some key decisions in altering its usual U.S. Open setup. Normally, U.S. Open greens are surrounded by heavy rough. At No. 2, however, it was decided to leave the greenside areas as short grass so that the ball was free to run well off the putting surface. That would both retain the course's character and bring imagination into play, as competitors would encounter numerous types of short-game shots with multiple options.

In practice rounds, players tried virtually every club in their bags for chips and pitches (putting from well off the green was also an option). Tiger Woods settled on a three-wood as his usual club of choice for rolling shots from around the greens. Phil Mickelson, by contrast, favored his 62-degree wedge, while using a technique that enabled him to hit low shots with the lofted club.

Payne Stewart came to Pinehurst on the weekend before the Open because he missed the cut at the PGA Tour's Memphis event. Perhaps that was a blessing in disguise. On Saturday and Sunday at Pinehurst, Stewart didn't play normal practice rounds; instead, he walked the course with his coach Chuck Cook, carrying his wedges and seven-, eight-, and nine-irons to try various shots from around the greens. Not only did that increase his comfort level with the shots he would need to play, but he and Cook also used the time to note in Stewart's yardage book the spots around the greens that he definitely needed to avoid, coloring them in blue on the hole diagrams.

Stewart had won the U.S. Open in 1991, but fresher in everyone's minds—including Stewart's—was that he had blown a four-stroke lead in the final round in 1998 at Olympic Club in San Francisco, losing by one stroke to Lee Janzen. While not successful, that bid at Olympic was part of a quest to revive his career in his early 40s, yet also a reminder that he was as well-known for his many runner-up finishes as for his two major titles.

Stewart earned the nickname "Avis" in his early career, finishing second 10 times from 1982 to 1988 against three victories, with a fadeout down the stretch of the 1986 U.S. Open also part of his story. He seemingly got over the hump in 1989-91 with five victories, including the 1989 PGA Championship and 1991 U.S. Open. Yet, Stewart entered 1999 with only one win since that 1991 Open triumph.

Those 1992-98 years were a mixed bag, with a couple seasons of poor play and others just not quite good enough. The runner-up tag returned in 1996-98 with four seconds and no victories. In early 1999, Stewart finally got a win at the AT&T Pebble Beach Pro-Am, which was shortened to 54 holes when the scheduled final round was rained out. At the age of 42, he entered the U.S. Open having added second-place finishes in March and April, proof that his game was in good shape but still leaving him with something to prove.

Stewart was only on the periphery of attention heading into the Open. Mickelson, winner of 12 tournaments in his first six years on Tour (plus an earlier Tour win as an amateur) was in the news for just showing up. His wife, Amy, was due to give birth to their first child ten days after the final round of the Open. The couple met with their doctor on Tuesday morning, and, only when they were told that it was unlikely she'd deliver early, did Mickelson fly from his Arizona home to North Carolina.

Mickelson told reporters that he would immediately fly back home if Amy went into labor, no matter his position in the tournament. "I have a once in a lifetime opportunity to be there, whereas the U.S. Open takes place every year," said Mickelson. Phil was carrying a beeper everywhere he went, including in his golf bag during the tournament, and had a private plane ready at the local airport.

Tiger Woods also was a focus in tournament preview stories. At age 23, he was a certified phenom, with a runaway victory in the 1997 Masters in his rookie season on his record. Tiger hadn't yet been able to add another major title, however, and he hadn't finished better than T18 in four U.S. Opens, including two as a pro. It was believed that his long-hitting game, while spectacular, was less suited to the Open's precision-requiring setups.

Pinehurst, however, provided reason for optimism about Tiger's chances. The fairways were slightly wider than usual and the rough, which had originally been planned to be cut at four inches, was trimmed to three inches in a decision made only a week before the championship. The idea behind the shorter rough was to give players the option of going for the green rather than just pitching out of the rough. The challenge was that No. 2's crowned greens would be hard to hit from the rough, and going over the green led to a difficult recovery on nearly every hole.

At the time, Woods wasn't the No. 1 player in the world; he was second in the Official World Golf Ranking. The top dog was David Duval, who was on a roll with three wins in 1997, four in 1998, and four already in the first half of 1999. Impressive as that was, he was still looking for his first major title.

Duval and Mickelson, playing together, were on top after the first round, shooting three-under 67s to tie for the lead with two players who were destined to fade from view, Billy Mayfair and Paul Goydos. Rain on Wednesday night left the greens softer than the USGA would have preferred, leading to 23 subpar rounds. Still, No. 2 was providing a significant test, as nobody was able to go extremely low.

While they shot the same score, Duval and Mickelson arrived at 67 in different fashion. Duval didn't make a bogey, hit 15 greens in regulation, and the longest of his three birdie putts was 15 feet.

Mickelson, still looking for his first major championship title at age 29, chipped in for a birdie on the fifth hole, holed birdie putts of 30 and 18 feet, and sank a par putt of 15 feet on the 18th. The birdie on the fifth moved him to three-under before bogeys on the sixth and eighth, with birdies on 13 and 14 to right the ship.

Woods and Stewart headed a group of five players at 68. Woods did more than his share of scrambling, finishing with 24 putts, and moved close to the lead by hitting his approach shots close on the last two holes for a pair of birdies. Stewart was steadier, with fewer greens missed, but squandered a chance to hold the lead as he missed a four-foot birdie putt on 17 and bogeyed 18.

Notably, one of Stewart's birdies came when he hit a pitching wedge out of a sand-filled divot on the third hole. In 1998, he made a costly bogey from a sand-filled divot on the 12th hole in his disastrous final round at Olympic. At Pinehurst, he made a point of practicing from sand-filled divots on the range.

The greens started drying out on Friday, there was some wind, and the scores went up considerably. Only three players broke par, and the scoring average was 75.44 compared to 72.86 in the first round. Some players, including Woods, complained about pin positions; others, including Stewart, said they were fine. Tom Meeks, the USGA official in charge of course setup, said the hole locations were difficult because the greens at No. 2 are difficult.

There was no argument that the course was bringing the cream to the top. Duval (70), Mickelson (70), and Stewart (69) were tied at the top at 137. Next in line were Woods, 1998 PGA champion Vijay Singh, Hal Sutton, and Mayfair at 139.

Stewart had a very good day with the putter, enabling him to break par in the tough conditions. He one-putted for pars on the first three holes, hit a wedge to two feet for a birdie on the par-five fourth, and made par from a sand-filled divot on the fifth, one of the toughest holes on the course. A birdie from 12 feet on No. 7 put him two-under on the round, though he gave two strokes back with bogeys on 8 and 9.

He went one-under on the back with a birdie from 15 feet on the 18th and eight pars, four of them by holing putts between six and 12 feet. The most hard-earned was on the 489-yard 16th, the longest par four in U.S. Open history to date and playing into the wind this day. Stewart drove into the rough, could only hit an eight-iron out, then hit a 100-yard shot to six feet. He saved par from a bunker on the 12th, from right of the green on the 14th, and holed an eight-foot second putt on the 18th for a 69 that matched the best score of the day.

Duval's round wasn't nearly as steady as his first—he had only three pars on the front nine—but he ended up pleased with a 70. He was two-under through five (thanks to a pair of 30-foot birdie putts), double bogeyed the sixth when his bunker shot rolled over the green, birdied the seventh and eighth, and bogeyed the ninth. He bounced back from two bogeys on the back nine with a birdie on 17 to earn a share of the lead.

Mickelson said he felt starting the day that 70 would be "an exceptional score." He had four par saves, including one on the fifth hole that typified the challenges around the greens at Pinehurst. From over the green, he faced a chip shot where, if he were to come up short, the ball would catch a slope and roll off the green to the left, but, if he went just slightly past the hole, the ball would roll off the front of the green. He heaved a sigh of relief after getting it to stop five feet from the hole and making par. Other than that, it was two birdies and two bogeys leaving him with the even-par round he wanted.

In the movement just behind the leaders, Woods slipped slightly backward with a 71, though he felt he hit the ball better than he had the day before, while Singh remained two off the lead by adding a 70 to an opening 69.

If the course played tough in the second round, it played *really* tough in Saturday's third round. There was only one subpar score, a 69 by Steve Stricker, the scoring average was 75.97, and the 68 players in the post-cut field combined for only 80 birdies. The percentage of greens hit in regulation was a cumulative 41.6.

Wind was a factor, but it's not as if it were at gale force—the breezes topped out at around 15 mph. It was more that the increasing firmness of the greens amplified the inherent difficulty of the course itself, particularly the challenge of approach shots. "A birdie today is out of the question unless you chip in, hole a bunker shot, or make a 30-foot putt," said John Cook. "You're not going to hit it close from anywhere on the fairway."

Stewart took sole possession of the lead, and he only needed a two-over 72 to do it, leaving him the only player under par for 54 holes at one-under 209.

"I enjoy playing where pars get rewards, no matter how you make them," Payne said. "My adrenaline gets flowing more, my concentration is better, and all of those things put me in the position I'm in now."

Stewart had been diagnosed with attention deficit disorder earlier in his career. His sports psychologist, Richard Coop, said the reason Payne performed better in major championships than in regular events was that the greater demands in majors forced him to concentrate better. And his U.S. Open record was particularly strong because he enjoyed battling to shoot around par.

In the third round, Payne was even par through seven holes with one bogey and one birdie when he hit a bad patch with consecutive bogeys on Nos. 8, 9, and 10. A key moment came on the par-four 11th where he bunkered his approach shot, blasted out to 10 feet, and made the putt to avoid a fourth straight bogey. He steadied the ship with all pars through the 17th and finished in style with a birdie from 15 feet on the 18th.

Mickelson took a two-stroke lead with an even-par 35 on the front nine. He bogeyed 11 and ran into a three-bogey stretch of his own on 15, 16, and 17, missing all three greens and failing to convert par putts in the 8-to-10-foot range. While his ball-striking was shaky throughout the round, it just happened that he was making par saves early and not late. Phil salvaged something with an eight-iron to six feet and a birdie on the 18th for a 73 that put him alone in second place, one behind Stewart, and in the final twosome for the fourth round.

"I've been looking forward to the final group of the U.S. Open since I started playing junior golf," Mickelson said.

The other 36-hole co-leader, Duval, went backward early with a double bogey on the fifth along with three bogeys on the first eight holes to be five-over for the round at that point. He steadied himself with what almost counted as a charge on this day, with pars on the last 10 holes. He had no birdies in a 75, but was just three strokes off the lead at 212 heading into the final round.

"I never panicked," said Duval. "I knew everybody was going to struggle. I just happened to be early,"

Woods struggled even earlier, but for a shorter time. He double bogeyed the first hole and bogeyed the second, the double coming when one of his three-wood chips, with which he had been very successful so far, ran over the green. He recovered with a birdie at the par-five fourth, followed by nine straight pars. Another bounceback, a birdie on 15 that followed a bogey on 14, gave Tiger a 72 that left him two behind, just as he had started the day.

Singh was even par through 14 holes and at one-under for the tournament was one shot out of the lead held by Mickelson. Vijay bogeyed 15, 16, and 17, just like Mickelson, and, with a par on 18, finished with a 73 to stand three back.

The lone par-breaker of the day, Stricker, couldn't avoid trouble near the end, either. He bogeyed 16 and 17, admitting he got too greedy with aggressive approach shots on those two holes. He found the hole from long distance early, holing a 40-foot putt for a birdie at the second and an eight-iron from a fairway bunker for an eagle at the third. His 69 netted him a tie for fifth at 212 with Duval and Singh.

Only one player shot a par round of 70, Tim Herron following a 69-72 start for a 211 total that earned him a tie for third with Woods. Nobody managed a 71, which meant that the two-over 72s by Stewart and Woods matched the third-best score of a difficult Saturday (Miguel Angel Jimenez had the only other 72).

Sunday brought a change in the weather with temperatures in the 60s, unusually cool for North Carolina in June. A light rain early in the leaders' rounds turned to a mist in the late afternoon. With greens slightly more receptive, the scoring average of the field was a stroke lower at 74.97—still difficult, and yielding only two subpar scores, both one-under 69s.

The conditions reminded many of St. Andrews in Scotland, perhaps appropriate because in spirit Pinehurst—a true golf town—is the closest thing America has to Scotland's Auld Grey Toon.

While Stewart warmed up on the range, he felt his rain jacket was hampering his swing. No problem. He scrounged up a pair of scissors and cut off the sleeves at the elbows. After hitting a few more balls, he was still uncomfortable and promptly slashed the sleeves at the shoulders. The stylish Stewart would play the final round in his usual plus fours and a bespoke sleeveless rain vest.

On the practice green, Payne worked on keeping his head down while putting. After the third round, his wife, Tracey, had told him he was looking up too soon on his putts during that not-so-good putting round. She had watched Saturday's play on television, because it was tough to see the action on the course with the large crowds. Tracey was not a golfer, and rarely gave her husband advice, but she knew enough to feel comfortable relaying this observation.

After the third round, a writer wryly asked Stewart if he was happy Janzen wasn't on the leaderboard—Stewart had finished second to Janzen twice in the U.S. Open, in 1993 and 1998. Payne smiled. "Yeah, that's alright, you know."

Still, Stewart faced no easy task as he headed to the final round intent on faring better with the 54-hole lead than he had a year ago. The opposition was formidable. Duval, Woods, and Singh were all in striking distance, and they were Nos. 1, 2, and 4 respectively in the Official World Golf Ranking. Mickelson, who was closest and would be in the final pairing with Stewart, was 11th. Payne himself was 13th. An epic battle of golf heavyweights loomed on this Sunday.

Duval was the first to mount a challenge. He birdied the second hole and added another birdie at the third, drawing within a stroke before Stewart finished the first hole. The world No. 1 flamed out quickly, however, with bogeys on the sixth and eighth and a double bogey on the ninth on the way to a 75 and a T7 finish.

Stewart started very well with a three-wood off the first tee, a seven-iron to 15 feet, and a holed putt for a birdie. He gave it right back on the second hole, and it could have been worse. His three-iron approach was too far right and rolled all the way down one of the many drop-off slopes surrounding the greens. This was the only time all week that he hit into one of the "don't go there" areas he had colored in his yardage book. His pitch wasn't hit hard enough, rolling back down off the green but, fortunately, not all the way back to his feet. From partway down the slope, he was able to use a putter, getting his fourth stroke to six feet from the hole, and making the key bogey putt. Stewart quickly got back to two-under for the championship with a beautiful nine-iron to two feet for a birdie on the third.

Mickelson headed to the course in the last twosome of the final round still carrying the beeper and insisting he'd be out of there if he got word from Amy. He got off to a shaky ball-striking start, missing the first two greens but saving par with putts of 10 and eight feet.

Woods had the potential for a great start, with birdies from three feet on the first and four feet on the fourth. He offset those, however, with bogeys on Nos. 2 and 5, both coming when he mis-clubbed and knocked his approach shots over the greens. Alongside him, Herron stayed in touch through five holes before a double bogey at the sixth knocked him out of it for good as he finished with a 75.

Stewart parred the last six holes of the front nine, three of them routine and three saves—a bunker shot to inches on the fourth, a putter from the front fringe 80 feet away to four feet on the eighth, and a bunker shot to seven feet on the ninth. Mickelson was one-under on those six holes, with three par saves, two routine pars, and a birdie from 20 feet on the eighth.

As the last twosome made the turn, Stewart was two-under and Mickelson one-under. Up ahead Singh, after pars on the first seven holes, made the only birdie on the eighth that day and added another birdie on No. 10 to move into third place at even par, with Woods at one-over. Four of the game's top names were battling for the title.

The 610-yard 10th was no pushover par five, but it's also not one where a player would expect to make a bogey after hitting two good shots. Stewart and Mickelson both missed the green, however, by hitting their wedge shots fat. From an awkward stance near a bunker, Stewart pitched to 15 feet and missed the par putt. Mickelson hit a bunker shot to seven feet and made the putt to save a par and tie Stewart for the lead.

Payne came up short of the 11th green, used a putter from the fringe, and made a four-foot putt for a par. He couldn't salvage par on the 12th. A poor drive in the rough left him with no chance to reach the green, and he ultimately missed a 15-foot par putt. Now Mickelson was one ahead of Stewart and Singh, with Woods three behind thanks to an awful three-putt from 15 feet on the 11th, missing a two-footer.

Tiger got that stroke back with a 20-foot birdie on 14 and Stewart regained a tie for the lead with a 15-foot birdie on 13. After his scrambling first 10 holes, Mickelson found his fairway-and-greens game for two-putt pars on Nos. 11 to 15. Singh remained at even par, first with saves from a bunker at 11, a long pitch shot at 12, and the back fringe at 13, then a lipped-out birdie putt at 14.

Singh was the first contender to come to the tough 16th. He drove into the rough and tried to hit a three-wood from there. Failing to make good contact, Singh came up well short, wedged to 20 feet, and missed the putt to fall to one-over.

Meanwhile, Stewart's scrambling continued with another drive into the right rough on 14, where he ended up making a 10-foot par putt to retain a share of the lead. He couldn't save par with a nine-footer at the par-three 15th after missing the green to the left with a four-iron. Mickelson was back in front by himself—and might have gone ahead by two, but his beautifully struck putt from 35 feet on 15 cruelly hit the lip and spun out.

Woods's length paid off at the 16th. Where nearly everyone else was needing a two-iron or more to reach the green, he got there with a four-iron to 12 feet. When the putt fell, he was at even par, one behind Mickelson and tied with Stewart.

Tiger wasn't quite ready to claim his first U.S. Open title, however. On the 191-yard 17th, he pulled his six-iron tee shot into a bunker. Woods came out nicely to four feet, then missed the putt to fall to one-over. He parred 18 to finish at one-over 281, along with Singh.

Neither Stewart nor Mickelson could hit the green from the fairway on 16, with Stewart's two-iron well short and left and Mickelson's three-iron just short and right. Stewart knocked his wedge shot 25 feet past, later saying that he did a dumb thing by trying to hole it, leaving himself a tough downhill putt. Mickelson's pitch came up eight feet short.

Stewart's putt was a double breaker down a slope that would make it tough to stop the ball close to the hole. "You couldn't *read* that putt, much less make it," Stewart's caddie Mike Hicks would later say. Stewart somehow found the right line and stroked the putt perfectly, the ball diving into the hole with some speed. Mickelson couldn't answer, pulling his putt to the right and making a bogey. Instead of a potential two-stroke lead for Phil, the pair were tied heading to the 17th tee.

Payne went first and put the pressure on with a six-iron that stopped three-and-a-half feet from the hole. It was reminiscent of his final-round tee shot on the par-three 17th at Hazeltine National in 1991, where he was also tied for the lead and covered the flag with a shot that finished five feet behind the hole. He missed that birdie putt, eventually winning the title in a playoff against Scott Simpson. This time he converted. The birdie gave him a one-stroke lead over Mickelson, who answered Stewart's tee shot with a fine one of his own to seven feet, but he missed the putt.

When Stewart hit his tee shot on the 446-yard, par-four 18th, he thought it was in the fairway. But he failed to make solid enough contact to reach the fairway of the slight dogleg on the line he hit it. The ball found the primary rough just a few inches short of the intermediate cut—and settled down into the worst lie he had all week. Upon reaching the ball, Stewart didn't show any frustration at his bad luck. He was all business, a sign that he was in a good place mentally as he pursued a second Open championship.

"There was no chance to even think about going for the green, so I took my medicine," Stewart said later. That meant hitting a nine-iron out, leaving him 73 yards from the hole. He aimed his lob-wedge shot from there slightly left of the hole for safety and for a better spot to putt from. Payne pulled the shot slightly, but wasn't dissatisfied with leaving himself a 15-foot putt for a par.

Mickelson had hit his second shot to 30 feet. He made a good effort at the birdie putt, tapping in for a par that left Stewart with a putt to win the U.S. Open.

At Olympic 12 months earlier, Payne had a 25-foot birdie putt on the 72nd hole to force a playoff and didn't make it. That one was a big breaker. This putt he had tried in practice rounds and knew it broke very slightly to the right. Aiming just inside the left edge, he felt it was a makeable putt. Still, no player had ever made a putt of this length on the final green to win a U.S. Open. "The odds are quite good that there will be a playoff," Johnny Miller said on the NBC telecast.

Stewart closed his eyes and made two practice strokes, a routine he followed all day. He stood over the ball, made the stroke, and concentrated on keeping his head still. He looked up as the ball was a few feet from the hole—and saw that it was clearly tracking into the cup. When the putt dropped, he stepped forward and thrust his right arm into the air. Moments later, his caddie, Hicks, jumped into his arms. Stewart hoisted him in a celebration that mimicked pitcher Don Larsen and catcher Yogi Berra after Larsen's perfect game in the 1956 World Series.

Mickelson then congratulated Stewart, who grabbed Phil behind the head and said, "Good luck with the baby! There's nothing like being a father!"

Next was an emotional hug and kiss from his wife, Tracey. "I kept my head down! All day! I did it!" exclaimed Payne in recognition of Tracey's advice.

In the television interview that followed on the 18th green, Stewart pondered a question and replied, "I don't know what to say," and turned to the crowd and yelled, "Woo!"—an exclamation appropriate for the most exciting finish in U.S. Open history.

Stewart's putts on 16 and 18 were the decisive blows, but the ones on 13 and 14 shouldn't be forgotten—that's four putts made from at least 10 feet on the last six holes. He had 24 putts for the round, 12 on each side, and didn't miss a putt inside nine feet.

Mickelson uncharacteristically had a round of mostly pars, 16 of them to go with one birdie and one bogey. It wasn't exactly a steady round, as he kept himself in it with one-putt pars early. He solidified his ball-striking as the round went on, but the problem was that he only left himself one birdie putt inside 18 feet all day—the one he missed on the 17th. He would have to wait until 2004 to win his first major, that coming at the Masters.

At least Mickelson's beeper didn't go off on Sunday. What he didn't realize was that Amy had contractions on Saturday night and went to the hospital. Not wanting to call Phil away from a chance to win the U.S. Open, she consulted with a doctor who prescribed medication which caused the contractions to slow and then stop.

Phil flew home on Sunday night. It turned out Amy's water broke on Monday morning, and the baby was born that day. If Stewart hadn't made the putt on 18, resulting in a playoff the next day, Phil would have been called away.

The sad epilogue to this U.S. Open story is that Stewart tragically died in an airplane accident four months later, when the private plane in which he was riding lost cabin pressure and eventually crashed. It was a life ended much too soon, but he gave us many U.S. Open memories, most of all a putt for the ages.

TOP-10 FINISHERS		
1	Payne Stewart	68-69-72-70—279
2	Phil Mickelson	67-70-73-70—280
T3	Vijay Singh	69-70-73-69—281
T3	Tiger Woods	68-71-72-70—281
5	Steve Stricker	70-73-69-73—285
6	Tim Herron	69-72-70-75—286
T7	Hal Sutton	69-70-76-72—287
T7	David Duval	67-70-75-75—287
T7	Jeff Maggert	71-69-74-73—287
T10	Darren Clarke	73-70-74-71—288
T10	Billy Mayfair	67-72-74-75—288

2000

TIGER'S DOMINATION

A fter playing a practice round with Tiger Woods on Wednesday at Pebble Beach, Paul Goydos predicted to a couple of reporters that Woods would win by 10 shots. Tiger's game was firing on all cylinders and, crucially, he had more game than anyone else to begin with.

Tiger had won 11 of his last 20 PGA Tour starts. It was a phenomenal pace, especially given the greater depth of talent on the tour over the past couple of decades—an evolution that had led many to doubt that one golfer would ever again dominate the game. Yet, at age 24, he was dominating more than Jack Nicklaus or Arnold Palmer had in their prime.

Tiger's standards were high. So high that, despite putting well in the practice rounds, he spent two-and-a-half hours on the practice green late Wednesday afternoon, because he didn't like the way he was making putts. "It just didn't feel right," he said. "It didn't feel like I was rolling the ball. It was kind of skidding a little bit." During the long practice session, Woods decided his hands were too low, and, by raising his hands, he was able to keep his putter more level which got the ball rolling the way he wanted it.

When he made a couple of putts on the front nine of the first round on Thursday, Woods's confidence, already high, soared even higher.

By the end of the day, he had put together a round of 65 to take a lead he would never relinquish.

His first birdie came on a tap-in after a sand wedge approach to the fourth hole, and he stayed in red figures by holing an eight-footer for a par on the seventh. That was followed by a 20-foot birdie putt at No. 8, a birdie from 15 feet on the 10th, and a par save from 12 feet on the 11th. Ball-striking returned to center stage with three birdies coming home, a nine-iron to one foot at 13 and tap-in birdies on both back-nine par fives, Nos. 14 and 18. A driver from the fairway got him close to the 14th in two, and he narrowly missed the green with a four-iron second shot on 18. The four-under back nine was preserved with par saves from six feet on 15 and 12 feet on 17.

As good as his putting was, Woods was even more pleased with his driving, as he missed only three fairways. The rough, originally planned for three inches, had been grown instead to four-and-a-half inches, and was definitely to be avoided. Also toughening the course, relative to par, was the second hole playing as a par four instead of a par five as in past Opens and in regular play, so par was 71 instead of 72.

With relatively little wind, there were some other good scores, including a 66 by Miguel Angel Jimenez. Like most players, Jimenez got a lot of questions about Woods in his post-round press conference. The 37-year-old Spaniard grew tired of it.

"You would think there is only one player here," he complained. "There are 156 of the best players in the world here."

Jimenez, a mainstay on the European Tour with limited experience in the U.S., had lost to Woods in a playoff the previous November at the WGC-American Express in Spain.

Every U.S. Open at Pebble Beach seems to produce a player getting off to a sizzling start before the harder holes kick in. This time it was Hal Sutton, and in more spectacular fashion than most. He holed an eight-iron at the first hole for an eagle on his way to being six-under through 13 holes. A double bogey at 14 and bogeys at 16 and 18 left the 42-year-old former PGA champion with a 69.

The story of the day was Bobby Clampett's unlikely prominence on the leaderboard. That Clampett would even be in the field at Pebble Beach was against all odds, let alone shoot a 68 in the first round. A young phenom on the tour in the early 1980s, Clampett's career had flamed out after only one victory, and the now 40-year-old was an announcer for CBS and essentially retired from competition. He had played in only 10 events since 1996, and none in the last 20 months. He hadn't played in a U.S. Open since 1986. But Clampett grew up in Monterey and played his high school golf matches at Pebble Beach, and, as a young pro, finished third in the 1982 U.S. Open there. He had to get through local and sectional qualifying to make the 2000 field and made it into the sectional as first alternate only because his friend Bill Glasson withdrew as a favor.

Clampett played the first 10 holes in four-under in the first round. "I was fighting back tears all through the front nine," he said. The local kid, now wading into middle age, held it together pretty well down the stretch, with a bogey on 16 the only blemish.

On the other hand, there was the woeful tale of John Daly. The volatile 1991 PGA champion was three-over through 17 holes before hitting his drive out of bounds to the right on 18, then hooking his next two shots from the tee into the ocean on the left. Now playing his seventh stroke, he switched to an iron and found the fairway—only to hit his next shot into the water. He dropped into the sand next to the hazard, but too close to the seawall, forcing him to play his next shot left-handed. By the time he was finished, he had a 14 on the hole and an 83 for the round.

A year earlier at Pinehurst, Daly shot an 83 in the final round, including an 11 on the eighth hole with a two-stroke penalty for hitting a moving ball that was rolling back down off the green toward him. He vowed never to play another U.S. Open, but showed up at Pebble Beach. This time, he simply withdrew after the first round with almost no word, except to be heard saying, "Get me to the airport fast," as he stormed out of the scoring trailer.

The round was suspended due to fog just before 4 p.m. when Jeff Maggert called a USGA official to the 10th tee because he couldn't see the landing area. Play was never resumed, and more than half the field had to finish their first rounds on Friday. At its conclusion, Woods and Jimenez remained 1-2, with John Huston at 67, and Loren Roberts and 55-year-old Hale Irwin joining Clampett at 68.

With another fog delay pushing tee times back on Friday morning, Woods's tee time for the second round was 4:40 p.m., so he wouldn't be able to play all 18 holes that day. He got in 12 holes and played them three-under for a nine-under total to increase his lead over Jimenez (who had played seven holes) to three strokes. Notably, he was seven strokes clear of the next closest players, Thomas Bjorn and Angel Cabrera.

One moment stood out. Woods drove into the right rough on the par-five sixth. He was 208 yards from the hole, the ball lying in heavy rough, with a tree and cliff face between him and the green. The situation seemed to call for a lay-up. "I know for sure no other player would attempt that shot going for the green," Woods's caddie Steve Williams said later.

Woods went for it, taking a mighty swing with a seven-iron, and knocking it onto the green 15 feet from the hole. "Guys, this is not a fair fight," NBC on-course announcer Roger Maltbie said, no doubt shaking his head at what he had just seen.

Two putts from there produced one of five birdies on the first 12 holes, against a pair of bogeys. After a par save from 15 feet on the second, Tiger continued his hot putting with a 30-foot birdie at No. 3. He bogeyed the par-three fifth from a bunker, got back under par for the day with the birdie at the sixth, gained another stroke with a birdie from 10 feet at the seventh, and lost one with a bogey on the ninth from a poor chip and missed 12-footer. Woods finished the day in a flourish, hitting his approach to three feet for a birdie on 11 and holing a 30-foot putt on the par-three 12th, where he hit his tee shot 30 seconds before the horn suspended play and used his option to finish the hole before stopping.

The two late birdies moved him from one ahead of Jimenez to three ahead. The Spaniard was one-under for the seven holes he played on Friday to stay within striking distance. Saturday morning's conclusion of the second round was a different story. Jimenez played his 11 holes in four-over to shoot a 74.

Woods had a slipup of his own at the end of the second round. He hooked his tee shot into the ocean on the 18th hole and let loose with a few choice expletives that were caught on the tee microphone for the television audience. It was particularly cringeworthy since NBC had preempted children's programming to telecast the Open on Saturday morning. Woods recovered to take only four more strokes after teeing up a second ball, making a bogey that preserved a round in the 60s with a 69 (he also bogeyed the par-five 14th and birdied the 15th Saturday morning).

Williams later revealed an unusual situation that unfolded on the 18th hole. After Woods hit his drive into the drink, he was down to one last ball, but he didn't know it. The previous evening, Tiger had grabbed some balls from his bag to practice putting in his room, but forgot to put them back. His caddie was unaware of it until Woods, already out on the course, gave a ball to a young fan. Williams then noticed that there were only two balls left. After the tee shot into the water, without explaining that Tiger was down to his last ball, Williams tried to convince Woods to hit an iron off the tee for safety. Woods went with the driver, and fortunately hit a good one. If he had lost his last ball in the water or out of bounds, he would have been subject to a two-stroke penalty in either of two scenarios. Borrowing a ball from another player in his group would have been a penalty, because it would have been a different make and model, and pros aren't allowed to switch during a round. And, if Williams or anyone else had gone to fetch one of Tiger's balls, there would have been a penalty for undue delay.

As it was, Woods was able to finish 36 holes with a six-stroke lead, the first of several U.S. Open records he would set. He was at eight-under 134, while the next closest were Jimenez and Bjorn at 140, followed by Jose Maria Olazabal and Kirk Triplett at 141. Pebble Beach was taking a toll. Clampett followed his opening 68 with a 77; Irwin and Roberts slid from 68 to 78; Huston went from 67 to 75.

Scoring soared higher in the third round when the wind picked up. Pebble Beach's greens are small and when they dry out they are tough to hit and hold—and that's if you can cope with the wind well enough to land the ball on the green in the first place. The field hit less than

43 percent of the greens in the third round, and the scoring average was 77.12. The seaside par fours, Nos. 8, 9, and 10, lived up to their "Cliffs of Doom" nickname. The eighth and ninth each played to a 4.825 average, tying for the hardest on the course, and the tenth was right behind at 4.698. In the field of 63, only three players were even par or better on Nos. 8-10.

Sixteen players shot in the 80s, including an 82 by Bjorn playing with Woods in the final twosome. Only one player was under par, Ernie Els, shooting a three-under 68 to move into second place with a two-over 215 total. That left him 10 strokes behind Woods, who matched par 71 and set 54-hole U.S. Open records for margin of lead and relative-to-par scoring (eight-under).

Tiger somehow managed to hit 12 of 14 fairways, using irons off a number of tees to increase his chances of finding the short grass, and 12 greens in regulation. He fell victim to the conditions on the third hole, however, making triple bogey. While he felt he hit a good seven-iron approach, it drifted left of the green in the wind and ended in a terrible lie in tall grass next to a bunker. He tried to hit out sideways and barely moved the ball. His next swipe at it didn't quite reach the green, he chipped on, and two-putted.

The good news for Woods was that he had just birdied the tough second hole, and he still had a five-stroke lead after the third-hole debacle. That was as slim as his lead would ever get. He birdied the par-five sixth and short par-three seventh, both from 12 feet, to get back to even par for the round.

Woods went bogey-birdie-bogey on the course's toughest stretch, Nos. 8-10, holing a 15-foot putt for one of only two birdies by the field on the ninth. He survived a second shot into the hazard right of the green on the 10th, able to play out of the long grass above the beach and two-putt for a bogey. From there, he birdied the 14th and saved par with one-putts on 16 and 17 for his even-par round.

Els holed out from the fairway for an eagle on the par-four fourth and overcame three bogeys for what he called "the best 68 I ever shot." Still, he knew he had no chance to catch Woods in the final round.

"He's in another dimension," said the 1994 and '97 U.S. Open champion. "I considered squeezing Tiger in a bear hug, or arm wrestling him, or just tackling him, but that wouldn't work because on top of everything else, Tiger is getting stronger every day. I don't know what we're going to do with him."

Jimenez didn't have any birdies as he shot a 76 and was tied for third, 11 strokes off the lead, with Padraig Harrington.

With a 10-stroke cushion, there was no question that Tiger Woods would win this championship. But what would motivate him in the final round? Would it be exceeding his 12-stroke victory margin in the 1997 Masters, where he had a nine-stroke lead through 54 holes? Would it be beating or at least matching the U.S. Open 72-hole record of 272? Or would it be simply ensuring a performance worthy of a champion—shooting a subpar round rather than limping home with a mid-70s score but still winning? Instead, his goal, as he stated after the round, was to not make any bogeys.

That's a tall task at any U.S. Open—perhaps even more so at this one, where greens were hard to hit, and scores were higher than usual. But the way Woods was hitting the ball, combined with his short-game prowess and the way his putting was grooved this week, it wasn't an entirely unrealistic target.

Tiger parred the first nine holes and was a lot closer to making birdies than bogeys. He hit eight of the nine greens in regulation, missing 12-foot birdie putts on the first two holes and a 15-footer on the eighth. The other five putts for birdies were longer, but, in his post-round press conference, he described them all as either "hanging on the lip" or "dead center, short." The only green he missed was on the par-five sixth hole, where his second shot settled in long grass next to a fairway bunker 60 yards from the green and he went over the green from there. He pitched on and made a six-foot par putt.

Woods then heated up with four birdies on the next five holes. While this was a tournament without any suspense surrounding the outcome, Woods was nonetheless putting on a show for the spectators and television audience, mesmerized by witnessing a performance for the ages.

He birdied the 10th after a pitching wedge to 10 feet and narrowly missed a 12-foot birdie putt on the 11th. On the tough par-three 12th, he hit a five-iron to 18 feet and made that for a birdie. He caught a break on the 13th, getting a nice lie in the rough, and took advantage by hitting a sand wedge to one foot. Woods laid up with his second shot on the par-five 14th, hit a sand wedge to eight feet, and made the putt to get to four-under on the day. If he could land four pars coming in from there, he would tie the U.S. Open record of 272 and set a record of 12-under par (the two previous 272s, Jack Nicklaus in 1980 and Lee Janzen in 1993, were eight-under); and, fulfill his goal of a bogey-free round.

His tee shot found the rough on 15, but it became a routine par with a pitching wedge to 30 feet and two putts. He had to work harder for pars on 16 and 17. His three-iron tee shot on the par-four 16th finished in the first cut of rough. From there, he caught a flier, and his second shot sailed over the green, leaving a tough pitch that went 15 feet past. When he holed the putt, he flourished his signature fist pump and displayed a countenance of pure determination.

"One of the biggest moments of the day was when I buried that putt on 16," he said after the round. "I worked so hard not to make a bogey. If I missed that putt, I would have been ticked at myself."

He also had to save par on the par-three 17th, where he hit a four-iron into a bunker short and left of the hole location, a conservative shot because he didn't want to go long. That left a relatively easy bunker shot, which he made look even easier, blasting out to six inches from the hole. The 18th was a walk of coronation, making a conservative par with a four-iron off the tee, an eight-iron lay-up, a pitching wedge to 20 feet, and two putts for a 67 and that 272 total.

By the way, Els and Jimenez tied at the "top" of the other tournament, the one for mere mortals, Jimenez with a 71 and Els a 72 to finish at three-over 287.

The 15-stroke victory margin was a record for any major championship, surpassing the 13-stroke win by Old Tom Morris in the 1862 British Open in an entirely different era against a field of eight players.

When asked which was more impressive, the 15-stroke margin or 12-under total, Woods opted for the latter. He said the key to his scoring was sinking key par putts in every round. "Those big par putts, you have to make them in a U.S. Open," he said. "You're going to have 8- or 10-footers or longer for par. If you make those, they feel better than a birdie."

Some measures of Woods's dominance: He had the best score in the field in the first and fourth rounds, matched the best score in the second round, and matched the second-best score in the third round. He led the field in driving distance on the two measured holes at 299.3 yards; next best was 292.8. He hit 51 greens in regulation; nobody else hit more than 44. Even while hitting all those greens, and therefore having fewer opportunities for up-and-down one-putts, he was T6 in putts per round with 27.5 and didn't have any three-putts. He had seven bogeys or worse; the next best was 13.

"If I played out of my mind, I probably would have lost by five, six, seven shots," said Els. "It seems like we're not playing in the same ballpark now."

While this would remain his most impressive performance, Woods was, in some ways, just getting started. The U.S. Open was his first of four consecutive major championship wins—the "Tiger Slam" of 2000-01.

TOP-10 FINISHERS		
1	Tiger Woods	65-69-71-67—272
T2	Ernie Els	74-73-68-72—287
T2	Miguel Angel Jimenez	66-74-76-71—287
4	John Huston	67-75-76-70—288
T5	Padraig Harrington	73-71-72-73—289
T5	Lee Westwood	71-71-76-71—289
7	Nick Faldo	69-74-76-71—290
T8	Stewart Cink	77-72-72-70—291
T8	David Duval	75-71-74-71—291
T8	Loren Roberts	68-78-73-72—291
T8	Vijay Singh	70-73-80-68—291

2008

A WOUNDED TIGER
PREVAILS

T wo days after the 2008 Masters, Tiger Woods had arthroscopic surgery on his left knee to repair damaged cartilage. At the time, he didn't reveal that he had ruptured the ACL in the same leg in July 2007. Electing to play through it, Woods won seven of his next eight PGA Tour events in 2007-8. He was that dominant.

Following that win streak, Woods finished fifth at Doral and second at the Masters. After the April surgery, he had hoped to return for the Memorial Tournament in late May but wasn't ready. Instead, his first round of golf came on the Wednesday before U.S. Open week at the Open site, Torrey Pines in San Diego, where he played 17½ holes riding a cart.

The next test was walking, which he did for nine holes on Sunday. He also walked nine holes on Monday and nine more on Tuesday. "Is it fully recovered? Probably not," he said in a brief talk with reporters on Tuesday. The next day, he only hit practice balls.

Woods could afford such limited preparation since he already knew the course. Torrey Pines was the annual site of the PGA Tour event then known as the Buick Invitational, which Tiger, at just 32, had already won six times. In fact, he had won it for the fourth year in a row that January, by six strokes this time, less than five months before the Open. He had grown up not far away in Southern California and had won his age division at the Junior World Golf

Championship at Torrey Pines six times. If he could walk, he wasn't going to miss a U.S. Open at this course.

The USGA had selected Torrey Pines, which is owned by the City of San Diego, as a follow-up to the highly successful 2002 U.S. Open at the Bethpage Black. The New York state-owned course hosted the first Open that was neither at a private club nor a resort. As at Bethpage, Rees Jones had been hired for architectural work.

While the preparation of Bethpage mostly involved restoring what had become a rundown facility, Torrey Pines was more of a redesign. Jones moved some holes closer to the coastline cliffs and added yardage by building new tees.

The scorecard yardage was now a robust 7,643; however, it wouldn't play that long on any day of the championship. Mike Davis had taken over as the USGA's course setup man two years previously, and he was a believer in day-to-day variety in tee locations. At two of the three par fives at Torrey Pines, he would move the tees up on a couple of days to bring the greens more in two-shot range, thereby introducing a greater risk/reward element. Davis found other ways to mix things up. As a fan of the drivable par four, he envisioned and carried out a completely different version of the 435-yard 14th hole as a 267-yard par four, which would be used one of the four days (two of five, as it turned out). The 195-yard third would be played at 135 one day, and several other holes also were moved up on certain days.

Graduated rough was another Davis innovation. Instead of heavy rough lining the fairways just past a narrow strip of short rough, Davis introduced a wide band of intermediate rough before the really deep stuff. The idea was to more heavily penalize the very wild drive, while the player who didn't miss the fairway by so much would have a better shot at the green—albeit with more difficulty to control than a shot from the short grass.

Still, the course would play harder than it did in the regular PGA Tour event. The greens would be firmer and faster in June than in January, the fairways firmer and narrower, the deep rough deeper. Breaking par in any round would be an accomplishment.

Eleven players broke par of 71 in the first round, led by 68s from two unlikely sources: 33-year-old mini-tour pro Justin Hicks and

PGA Tour rookie Kevin Streelman, neither of them ranked in the top 600 in the world. They were both one-day wonders, shooting 80 and 77, respectively, in the second round. The 2006 champion, Geoff Ogilvy, headed four players at 69. Two-time champion Ernie Els was the most notable of five players at 70.

Most of the day's attention focused on the threesome of Woods, Phil Mickelson, and Adam Scott, as the USGA decided to group the world ranking's Nos. 1, 2, and 3 players. Mickelson was essentially a co-star with Woods, having grown up in the San Diego area, playing Torrey Pines in his youth, and owning three PGA Tour victories there, with three major titles so far in his career at 37, and two wins already in 2008.

Scott was sort of the "other guy", especially since his play was hampered by a hand injury incurred the week before. He shot a 73.

Mickelson drew notice with his quirky calculations of what clubs to carry. The man who won the 2006 Masters with two drivers in his bag went driverless among his allotted 14 clubs at Torrey Pines. His thinking was that finding the fairway was paramount to distance. Whether or not the strategy was good—and it was at least questionable—Mickelson's execution was very poor. He hit only two of the first 10 fairways and 12 of 28 in the first two rounds. He did manage a 71 in the first round, which was the best score in the feature group, but followed it with a 75 on Friday and ultimately finished T18.

Woods posted a first-round 72 on a day that got off to a bad start. He double bogeyed the first hole, a tough par four, with a badly hooked drive, a hack from the rough back to the fairway, a wedge over the green, a chip on, and two putts. Tiger righted himself with a birdie on the fourth with a fantastic five-iron shot from a fairway bunker to two feet, and he added birdies on Nos. 8 and 9 for a one-under 35 on the front nine.

Yet his troubles weren't over. Tiger made a second double bogey on 14, this one thanks to a flubbed pitch shot from just short of the green that didn't make the putting surface. He saved a stroke with a 20-foot par putt on 15, but failed to pick up a stroke when he three-putted for a par on 18 after hitting the par-five with a seven-iron second shot.

Woods said that the most important thing he learned that day was that he could walk 18 holes.

"To make two double bogeys and a three-putt and only be four back, that's a great position to be in because I know I can clean that up tomorrow," he said.

Away from the spotlight, 45-year-old Rocco Mediate cobbled together a fine 69. Two weeks earlier, he had earned a place in the field with a birdie on the first hole of an 11-for-7 playoff in sectional qualifying. He owned five PGA Tour victories, yet none since 2002, and had struggled with both his game and a bad back in recent years.

After a poor 2006, the garrulous Mediate did a tryout as a commentator for Golf Channel in early 2007, but ultimately abandoned that opportunity to focus on his game. His back improved during the year, and so did his game, as he reentered the top 100 on the money list for the first time in three years. But he again struggled at the start of 2008, making just two cuts in his first nine starts. By the U.S. Open, he had improved that to 8-of-16, and, more importantly, finished T6 at the Memorial in his last start. Still, he was down to 158th in the world ranking.

Mediate had never fared well at Torrey Pines, with a best finish of T37 in seven appearances. But he did have two top-10s in the U.S. Open, which was one of his favorite events, and he said the way the course was set up for this Open was "perfect." Starting on the back nine, he had two birdies and one bogey, then birdied Nos. 3 and 4 to get to three-under before a bogey at the seventh from a fairway bunker.

Mediate would reach four-under for the championship during the second round, which was as far in the red as anyone would get. He did it with birdie putts of 25 feet on the second hole and 30 feet on the fourth, though he was disappointed to miss some birdie chances from less than 20 feet elsewhere on the front nine. He went the other way with bogeys on 10, 12, and 17, all with drives in the left rough, before finishing with a birdie on 18. Once a medium-length hitter, Rocco was now one of the shorter hitters on Tour in his mid-40s. The par-five 18th was at the outer limits of his ability to reach in two, but he did it on this day with a good drive and a solid three-wood to set up the birdie.

Woods, teeing off 30 minutes later than Mediate, slipped to three-over for the championship on his first nine, while Mediate was getting to four-under. Starting on the back nine, Woods three-putted the 10th hole for a bogey then added another bogey on 12.

Tiger's day took a turn for the better with an eagle on the 13th. A new back tee on the edge of the canyon added 70 yards to the hole, making it 614 on the scorecard. On this day, it was set up at around 600 yards. Woods crushed a drive nearly 360 yards, then hit a majestic, high five-wood that landed softly and stopped seven feet from the hole.

The reprieve was temporary. Bogeys on 16 and 17 returned him to a three-over total, and he called a failure to birdie 18 a third straight mistake.

There would be no such mistakes after making the turn to play the front nine, at least not after the tee shot on No. 1, which settled in the right rough close to a tree. His stance put his left foot on a cement cart path, but he didn't take the option of a free drop because it would have put him behind the tree. Despite metal spikes slipping on the paved path and his bad left knee buckling during the swing, he hit an eight-iron to 18 feet from the hole and made the birdie putt.

Birdies followed on the second (25 feet), fourth (20 feet), and fifth (16 feet) holes. "I was just trying to get back to even par for the tournament. All of a sudden, putts started flying in from everywhere," he said after the round. He added a finishing birdie on the par-five ninth after going over the green in two and chipping to six feet to card a spectacular 30 on the nine. The 68 total put him at two-under 140, tied with Mediate.

Rocco expressed a desire to play with Woods in the third round. When all was said and done, it didn't work out that way. Australia's Stuart Appleby finished the round in first place with a long birdie putt on 18 giving him a 70 and a three-under 139 total. Since Mediate was the first player in with 140, that put him with Appleby in the final third-round pairing. Woods ended up with Sweden's Robert

Karlsson, who shot a second straight 70 to become the third of three players at two-under.

Appleby fared no better with the lead than Hicks and Streelman before him, skying to a 79 in the third round. For the second straight day, Mediate got as far as four-under on Saturday, once again the only player to do so before slipping back. Lee Westwood, who began the day at 141, was the steadiest player among the leaders. It would be left to Woods to finish with a flourish and create the biggest buzz heading into the final round.

Mediate was an everyman type of character, and the crowd quickly got behind him with frequent shouts of "Rocco!" as he made his way around the course. The object of their affection would respond with an appreciative grin, clearly enjoying himself even under the pressure of trying to win a U.S. Open. He got off to a good start with a birdie from 12 feet on the second hole and recovered from a three-putt bogey on the third to birdie the fifth from 12 feet to make the turn at one-under 34. When he birdied No. 10 from eight feet, he moved to a four-under total and a three-stroke lead as other contenders were succumbing to Torrey's difficulties.

Rocco would soon have his own scrapes with the course. He three-putted for a bogey on 13 and double bogeyed 15 with a drive into a bad spot on the left, a hack that advanced the ball but still remained in the rough, a third shot short of the green, a pitch, and two putts. When he bogeyed the par-three 16th after his tee shot found a tough lie in a bunker, he was two-over on the day and back to even par in the championship. A birdie on 17 from 15 feet gave him a 72, a one-under 212 total, and improved his mood.

"I just can't begin to tell you guys how much fun I'm having out there," he told the press afterward. "This has been an amazing experience."

Mediate's back-nine retreat enabled Westwood to pass him. At age 35, the Englishman had overcome a mid-career slump that saw him drop from the top 10 in the world ranking in 1998-2000 to outside the top 200 for a period in 2003. He was now ranked 20th in the world after claiming his 17th and 18th career European Tour wins in 2007, but his best finish in a major was fourth in the 2004 British Open (he would have seven top-three major finishes ahead of him, but no victories).

Westwood had two birdies and one bogey in an opening 70 and three birdies and three bogeys in a second-round 71. The steadiness continued Saturday with eight pars on the front nine, with the lone blemish a three-putt bogey from just 12 feet on the eighth. He birdied the 10th from eight feet and pitched to three feet for a birdie on the par-five 13th. That got him to two-under, and with a string of pars down the stretch, he found himself in front when Mediate, three two-somes behind him, double bogeyed 15. Westwood missed a chance to extend the lead when he couldn't convert a four-foot birdie putt on 18, settling for a two-birdie, one-under 70.

In contrast to Westwood, Woods's play again was volatile. The first hole of the round continued to haunt him, as he posted another double bogey. He drove into the rough again, and while this time got his second shot near the green, he still turned it into a double with a flubbed chip shot. Tiger visited the rough and a greenside bunker on the way to a bogey at the fourth. He birdied the seventh, but a three-putt par at the ninth left him with a two-over 37 on the front nine. A bogey at the 12th put him five strokes behind Mediate, playing just behind him.

Woods blocked his tee shot so far to the right on 13 that there was a concession stand in his line of play for the next shot, enabling a free drop. He dropped in trampled-down grass into a lie good enough, he figured, to reach the green or the back bunker with a five-iron. He hit a good one, managing to stop the ball on the back fringe, leaving a treacherous putt of 65 feet to a front hole location that had bedeviled the players all day. "How crazy is this putt?" said NBC analyst Johnny Miller, asking announcer Bob Murphy in the 13th hole tower for a read on the downhill big-breaker. Woods tapped the ball gently for such a long putt, sending it on its way on a line well to the right. Over the last 15 feet, it took a hard left turn and tracked perfectly into the center of the cup for an eagle, triggering a double-armed, uppercut fist-pump from Tiger.

Woods wasn't finished with the downs of an up-and-down day, with another rough-to-bunker bogey on the 14th. Coming to the 17th, he trailed Westwood by two. Another poor tee shot led to an approach that this time barely missed a greenside bunker, settling in the rough on the bank above it. His pitch shot flew high, took one bounce, and landed in the cup for an unexpected birdie. Woods immediately started laughing, as he knew he had hit the pitch shot too hard and would have faced at least a 10-foot par putt if the hole hadn't gotten in the way. "Pure luck," he would call it after the round.

Now one behind Westwood with the reachable par-five 18th to play, the heroics weren't finished. Woods's condition was adding to the drama. He had winced on several tee shots and was clearly limping as he played the 17th. The USGA's Davis, who was walking with Woods's twosome, asked Tiger if he needed to take a five-minute break before playing 18.

Woods declined, saying, "It's not going to make a difference." His drive found the fairway, and he hit a nice high five-wood to the green, but didn't watch the ball land and finish 35 feet above the hole as he grimaced and looked down toward the ground in pain.

In a mirror image of the eagle putt at 13, Woods sent it on a left-to-right downhill path, the ball again taking the break on a perfect line and falling into the cup. The gallery roar was again huge, but Tiger's reaction was more subdued, simply a fist clenched in front of him and a look of satisfaction on his face. The second eagle on the last six holes—with a chip-in birdie thrown in for good measure—gave Tiger a 70 and vaulted him past Westwood into the 54-hole lead.

Mediate had birdied 17 to temporarily gain a tie for second with Woods before Tiger's closing eagle. As it was, Rocco finished 54 holes in third place, two behind Woods and one back of Westwood. Woods was still giving interviews in the first of two press areas when Mediate approached to take his turn. "Mr. Woods! Mr. Woods!" Rocco called out, with his own question for the leader. "Are you out of your mind with what you're doing out there?"

In his own interview, Mediate was well aware that in the final round he would be up against a player who was 13-for-13 in major championships when holding the 54-hole lead.

"You never know," he said of his prospects in the final round. "But it'll take something crazy. It's going to take a ridiculous round by one of us to beat him."

The one wildcard was the shape of Woods's left knee. When asked if it was getting worse, he said, "Yes, it is." The good thing, sort of, was that the pain of the golf swing came after impact, so it didn't necessarily affect the flight of the ball.

Mediate again expressed that he wished he were playing with Woods the next day. That sentiment was surprising to some, considering that many players had struggled when paired with Woods down the stretch of a major. But, said Mediate, "I've played some of my best golf with him." Not in a major, of course. And on this Sunday, it would be Westwood in the final twosome with Woods, while Mediate played just ahead with Ogilvy, who at 214 was four out of the lead and two behind second place.

The final round was essentially a three-man battle. Ogilvy did pull within one of the lead through seven holes, but fell back with bogeys on Nos. 9 and 10, leaving it in the hands of Woods, Mediate, and Westwood.

Tiger opened the door to the others with another terrible start, his third double bogey on the first hole, this one the ugliest. His drive was way left again. He was uncertain about how the ball would react out of the lie but didn't expect what happened—the hosel of the club turned over at impact, causing the ball to come out to the left and hit a tree not far ahead of him, deflecting it further left. Trying to escape that predicament, Woods hit another tree on his next shot. Finally, he was able to hack his way out of the rough with his fourth shot but didn't quite reach the green. A pitch and three-foot putt secured a double bogey instead of a possible triple.

Woods had played his opening hole of the four rounds in seven-over: double bogeys in each of the three starts on No. 1 and a bogey on No. 10 the day he started there. On this day, it didn't get much better on the second hole. On that relatively benign par four of 389 yards, his tee shot flew into the right rough. He was able to hit the green with his second shot but was 60 feet from the hole. Woods three-putted for a bogey from there, missing a second putt from five feet.

Tiger's limp was conspicuous, particularly after the tee shot on No. 2. Some wondered if he was going to be able to finish the round, a notion that Woods later dismissed. "I was always going to finish," he said.

It was Mediate who took advantage of the early opening with an approach shot to five feet on the second hole and a resulting birdie to get to two-under for the championship. It gave him the lead because Westwood bogeyed the first with a drive and second shot that both went to the right. Through two holes, Lee was now one-under for the championship while Woods had dropped to even par.

Woods steadied himself with pars on the next six holes, four of them routine two-putts, one a relatively easy up and down from the fairway just short of the sixth green, and a nice bunker shot to three feet on the eighth. His playing companion, Westwood, also parred those six holes, hitting the green on five of them with a short par-saving putt on the other.

Mediate struggled through that stretch, missing four of the six greens. He had two par saves from five feet but bogeyed the fifth and sixth when he missed from nine and six feet. Rocco was now tied with Woods at even par, while Westwood held the lead at one-under.

The tees were up on several holes, with the course playing at 7,280 yards, about 360 less than its maximum length. The par-five ninth, 612 yards on the scorecard, was set up at significantly less than that, making it easily reachable for Woods, who hit his second shot to 30 feet and two-putted for a birdie. Westwood matched the birdie, reaching a greenside bunker in two, blasting to five feet and making the putt to retain the lead. Ahead of them, Mediate had missed the green in three, saving par with a six-foot putt.

Rocco made up for that missed opportunity with a birdie on the 10th from six feet. Westwood bogeyed that hole, finding a fairway bunker and blading his second shot over the green. Woods missed a 10-foot birdie chance on the 10th, then birdied the 221-yard 11th, where his tee shot landed past the hole on the fringe and took a slope back down toward the hole, finishing six feet away. Mediate and Westwood both missed the 11th green, but got their pars, Rocco with a 12-foot putt and Lee a sand blast to within a foot.

The birdie gave Woods the lead at two-under, having gone two-under on the nine holes since his terrible start, with Westwood and Mediate one behind. Westwood fell another stroke back with a bogey on the long par-four 12th, one of the toughest holes at Torrey Pines. Woods and Mediate hit the green and made pars.

Just when it looked like Woods had things under control, suddenly he didn't, as the tournament's vibe of unpredictability persisted. The 13th played at its full 614 yards, but after a big drive down the hill Woods hit a five-wood second shot in an effort to get close to the green. He pulled it drastically to the left into the ice plant ground-cover, an area marked as a lateral hazard. A minute earlier, Westwood had done the same thing. Both took penalty drops at a place from which getting the next shot close was impossible, and both made bogeys. For Westwood, it was his third bogey in four holes.

In the twosome ahead, Mediate had made a par on 13, so he ultimately picked up a stroke on the other two on the hole. It could have been better, though. Rocco, who laid up in two, hit a wedge approach to three-and-a-half feet, and missed the birdie putt.

While Woods and Westwood were on the 13th green, Mediate was finishing the 14th, which the USGA had turned into a 267-yard par four for the final round. Calling it a drivable par four was an understatement; a driver was too much club. There was more trouble close to the green than would be found on a lengthy par three, though—a canyon hazard on three sides and two bunkers in front leaving a narrow alley to a shallow, angled green. "We thought it would be interesting to force the players to make a decision on whether or not to try for the green under the gun on a Sunday at the Open," said Davis.

Mediate went for it with a three-wood and came pretty close to hitting the green, finishing in the left front bunker. He splashed out to two feet and made the birdie putt to get to two-under. A couple minutes later, Woods and Westwood holed out their bogeys on 13, falling to one-under and one-over, respectively.

Rocco was in the lead with four holes to play in the Open. At that adrenaline-pumping moment, Mediate had to stop and wait on the 15th tee. In the twosome ahead, Hunter Mahan had hit his tee shot way left, had trouble finding his ball, and, after finding it, needed a complicated relief ruling that required calling in a rules official. The wait on the tee stretched to ten minutes, with Mediate pacing restlessly back and forth, perhaps thinking of his third-round double bogey on this hole—as well as what it would mean to win the U.S. Open. When it was finally clear to play, Rocco, likely unsettled, hooked his tee shot into a bad spot on the left, with no chance for a second shot anywhere close to the green.

Meanwhile, Woods and Westwood settled on their strategies on the 14th tee. Tiger figured he was between a three-wood and a five-wood. He would need to either hit a cut shot with the former or a draw with the latter, either of which could bring more trouble into play, so he laid up with a seven-iron. Westwood pulled out his three-wood and hit a great shot to the green 20 feet short of the hole. Woods wedged to 18 feet and made a par, while Westwood two-putted for a birdie to move to even par.

On 15, Mediate hit a lovely wedge third shot from 80 yards to six feet from the hole. He pulled the par putt to the left, falling to one-under, tied for the lead with Woods and one ahead of Westwood. Tiger was having his own troubles, having hit his tee shot into the gallery on the right. From trampled rough, he hit his shot over a tree situated in front of him but came up well short of the green with little chance to get close. A pitch and two putts from 15 feet left him with a bogey. Mediate was back ahead by one over both players in the final twosome.

All three parred the par-three 16th, Mediate with a chip and three-foot putt, Woods with a chip and five-foot putt, and Westwood with a two-putt. All three parred the 17th, with Mediate coming oh-so-close to a birdie that would have put him ahead by two. First, his approach shot from 172 yards was right at the hole, coming within a foot of the cup as it rolled past, stopping 12 feet behind the hole. The putt looked good as it approached the hole, but just slid by on the left side. "When it was halfway there—I'll never forget this—the thought flashed through my head, 'I'm going to win the U.S. Open,'" Mediate told John Feinstein for their co-authored book about the Open, *Are You Kidding Me?* After the miss, he needed to gather himself and make a four-foot comebacker.

In the last twosome, Woods two-putted from 25 feet and West-wood stayed alive with a seven-foot par putt after splashing from a bunker.

Mediate failed to extend his lead on 18. A 573-yard par five on the scorecard, it was playing 527 in this round, giving him a better chance to reach in two. However, he drove into the left rough, forcing a lay-up. The wedge third shot wasn't easy to get close, with a pond in front of the green and a front pin. Rocco's approach finished 30 feet past the hole, and he wound up two-putting a for a par. Now, there was nothing he could do but wait to see if Woods or Westwood could tie him with a birdie—or beat him with an eagle.

An eagle wasn't out of the question, especially for Woods, who had made three eagles during the week, including one at 18 on Saturday. It would require a drive in the fairway, or perhaps the light rough. Instead, he pulled it into a fairway bunker on the left side. Westwood hit his drive into a fairway bunker on the right. They would have to make birdie the hard way.

Westwood laid up into the fairway short of the pond. Woods chose a nine-iron and, as soon as he hit it, he shouted in disgust and slammed his club. The ball sailed too far right and landed in the rough.

Tiger was left with 101 yards to the hole on the right front of the green. It was a good yardage for a 56-degree wedge, but he didn't think he could keep it from bounding past, so he decided to swing hard with his 60-degree wedge. Coming in from the right rough wasn't all bad—the water wasn't in his direct line. He had ended up in a tricky lie, not a divot hole, but a slight depression where a shot had been played. It might have even helped put more spin on the ball than if it were in thicker grass. The ball landed pin-high near the right edge of the green, took one bounce forward, then spun back and rolled a few feet down a slope toward the hole, stopping 12 feet from the cup.

Westwood's 74-yard shot from the fairway finished 20 feet past the hole, so he was the first to try a potentially tying putt. It started on a good line, but he didn't hit the left-to-right breaker hard enough and it finished six inches below the hole.

Now, it was down to Woods.

Tiger's reputation as a clutch player—and, most notably, clutch putter—was well established. Still, a 12-foot putt is no sure thing for anyone. Also of note, the greens at Torrey Pines had become bumpy, especially at the end of the day. The ball wasn't rolling smoothly, and even a good putt might be bumped offline.

"I kept telling myself to make a pure stroke. If it bounces in or out, so be it, at least I can hold my head up high," Woods said after the round.

The read was also important. Woods read his aiming point as two-and-a-half balls to the right of the hole. He started it on that line. The ball bounced a bit but took the break as it approached the hole, heading toward the right edge of the cup. It caught the inside of the right lip, rolled around to the back edge, and fell. Tiger leaned back and did a double-fist pump, raised up and slapped hands with caddie Steve Williams, and let loose with a primal howl drowned out by a long, raucous roar of the gallery.

An NBC camera and microphone caught Mediate's reaction as he watched the TV in the scoring area. "Unbelievable. I knew he'd make it," Rocco said in a statement that was literally contradictory but nonetheless true.

Woods had shot a final-round 73 that represented a rally from his awful start. Not a great round, but one that included a heroic finish that enabled him to live for another day. As for Mediate, who shot a 71, he didn't have the Open title, but he did finally have the chance to play in a twosome with Woods. He had asked for it the last two days, now he would meet Tiger in the most pressure-packed of circumstances, an 18-hole playoff for the U.S. Open.

It appeared to be a lopsided match-up. Woods was ranked No. 1 in the world; Mediate 158th. Rocco had made 138 PGA Tour starts since his last victory; Tiger had won 41 times in his last 138 starts. The 32-year-old Woods was hunting down his 14th major championship. Mediate, who at 45 would be the oldest U.S. Open champion if he won, was looking for his first.

If there were any factor weighing the other way, it was Woods's problem knee and the possible rust of a 10-week layoff that might have contributed to his up-and-down play during the week. But after limping early in the final round, the knee seemed to get better on Sunday, with Woods implying afterward that he had taken medication mid-round. There was also the inherent unpredictability of golf, especially in a single 18-hole round, but that had never seemed to apply to Tiger Woods when a major championship was on the line.

Woods famously wore a red shirt and black pants in every final round. Mediate had only one clean shirt left for the Monday playoff, and it happened to be a red one. Tiger apparently packed an extra red shirt, just in case, because he wore his lucky red for the playoff, and good-naturedly ribbed Mediate when Rocco walked onto the practice range before the round. "Nice [bleeping] shirt!" said Tiger. "I thought you only wore red on Sunday," responded Rocco, who did sport a bit of a different look with a black sweater vest.

The playoff turned out to be an epic, back-and-forth battle. It should be noted, though, that the first 12 holes weren't very well played. Woods hit only four of the first 12 greens while Mediate hit six. Both hit five of the nine fairways in that span. Through 12, Woods was two-over and Mediate three-over.

Woods got past the first hole alright this time, hitting the fairway and green and two-putting from 25 feet for a par. He quickly went one stroke ahead when Mediate found the right bunker with his approach, thumped out to five feet, and missed the putt. Both scrambled for pars on the second hole, Woods making a seven-foot putt and Mediate holing a four-footer.

Rocco put a jolt in the proceedings when he nearly holed a six-iron on the par-three third, playing at 188 yards, with the ball finishing a foot behind the hole after rolling an inch past the right lip. Woods, by contrast, hit his tee shot into a buried lie in the front bunker, came out to 12 feet, and two-putted for a bogey to fall to one-over and one behind after the two-stroke swing.

Both parred the tough fourth, Woods with a chip to a foot and Mediate with a two-putt from 60 feet. Rocco fell back to one-over and a tie when he bogeyed the fifth with a drive into a fairway bunker on the right, a second shot way left, a pitch, and two putts from 12 feet, while Tiger made a routine par.

Woods surged two strokes ahead with birdies on Nos. 6 and 7, with an eight-iron to six feet on the sixth, where Mediate had to save par from six feet, and a pitching wedge to 10 feet on the seventh.

As in the fourth round, just when it looked like Tiger had gotten into a good groove, it turned the other way. After those two birdies, Woods played the next five holes in three-over, failed to birdie a par five, and needed a long putt to par the other hole. The sour stretch started with a bad decision on the par-three eighth. After a deliberation, he switched to more club, a seven-iron, then sailed it over the green to a buried lie in the back bunker. The bunker shot was virtually impossible to even keep on the green, and he ended up chipping on and making a five-foot bogey putt. Mediate missed the green and saved par from four-and-a-half feet.

Woods's tee shot on the par-five ninth drew his first pained grimace, though his ball did find the fairway. He reached a greenside bunker with a three-wood, but chunked the bunker shot short of the green. Instead of a birdie chance, he ended up making a four-foot putt for a par. Woods stunningly gained a stroke when Mediate three-putted from 20 feet, missing a three-foot par putt to the right. For the front nine, it was an even-par 35 for Woods and a 37 for Mediate.

Rocco's sloppy play continued on the 10th where he chunked an easy chip and missed an eight-foot par putt. Woods was looking at a likely bogey himself when he hit his drive way to the right into deep rough and could only hack out with his second shot to 69 yards short of the hole. His third shot finished 18 feet from the hole on the fringe—and he holed out from there with a putter. When Rocco missed his shorter putt, the margin was three.

One would think a three-stroke lead with eight to play would be a lock for Tiger, but he bogeyed the next two holes, and the margin was sliced to one as Rocco made a pair of two-putt pars. Woods hit into a bunker on the par-three 11th and missed a 12-foot putt. He drove into a fairway bunker on the 12th, missed the green, and failed to make a 14-foot par putt.

The par-five 13th was set up generously at 539 yards, and both players birdied. Mediate drove into the fairway 261 yards from the hole, reached the front bunker with a three-wood, got out to four feet, and made the putt. Woods drove into the rough but caught a good lie 223 yards from the hole and hit the green from there with an iron, then two-putted from 30 feet.

The 14th was again set up as a very reachable par four. It was 269 yards to the hole after being set at 267 on Sunday. The tee was farther back in the playoff, but with the hole location on the very front, a narrow portion of the green that lined up with an opening between the bunkers. With the wind against the players, Mediate hit a three-wood that came up about 10 yards short of the green in the fairway. The hurting wind enabled Woods to go for it this time instead of laying up, but his three-wood landed right of the narrow neck of fairway and settled in the rough short of the green. Tiger pitched to seven feet from the hole and his birdie attempt lipped out. Mediate's pitch finished a foot from the hole for a birdie. The two were tied with four holes to go.

Woods's tee shot sailed to the right on the 15th hole, so errant that it found a bunker on the adjacent ninth hole. He had a clear shot, yet with an awkward lie, with the ball well below his feet. No problem for Tiger, apparently. His seven-iron shot landed on the front of the green and rolled up to 10 feet from the hole. Mediate, meanwhile, had hit the fairway and green and had a 20-foot birdie putt.

Moments before Mediate hit his putt, Miller said on NBC, "Is it possible someone could steal the scene from Tiger, maybe a guy like Rocco could roll this thing in and Tiger miss? We've seen the other exchange over and over again."

That unlikely scenario is exactly what happened. Mediate rolled his right-to-left putt in the center of the hole for a birdie. Woods's putt missed on the high side. Mediate, with his third consecutive birdie, now led Tiger by one with three holes to play.

The crowd was going crazy. Some 25,000 people had poured into the gates to watch this twosome battle it out. It was a good golf crowd, with hearty cheers for both players from the outset. By the 15th hole, the crowd seemed to turn in Rocco's favor, judging from the decibel levels he drew. And the duel was grabbing the attention of a national television audience as well. During the last two hours of the playoff, trading volume on the major Wall Street indices was way down.

Mediate's tee shot on the par-three 16th came up short in the fairway in front of the green. He used a putter to knock it within a foot of the hole for a par. Woods hit a four-iron 35 feet from the hole. His putt was on a perfect line and pulled up an inch short of falling in the center of the hole. Still one behind.

Woods came up six inches short on a 20-foot birdie putt on 17. Mediate hit the green 40 feet from the hole and ended up making a nervous three-footer for his second putt. For the second straight day, Woods headed to the 18th hole one behind Mediate. Only now they were playing together.

The finishing hole was again set up as very reachable in two at 525 yards. Mediate made good contact with his drive but started his draw down the center of the fairway instead of the right side as intended. The ball bounced into a fairway bunker; he would have to lay up. Woods winced on his tee shot, a reminder of his ailing knee; nonetheless, he hit one of his best drives of the week, leaving only a four-iron second shot. Tiger hit the green, leaving a 45-foot eagle putt. With the hole in a more accessible location than on Sunday, Mediate hit his wedge third shot to 15 feet.

In an electric atmosphere in front of a packed grandstand—where spectators had been waiting for hours since securing their seats in the early morning—Woods ran his eagle putt to the right and past the hole by four feet. Rocco had a 15-foot putt that would win the Open.

"Every kid who has ever played golf has dreamed of that moment. Make this putt, win the U.S. Open. I'd dreamed it a million times," Mediate said in his book. "Now it was real, right there. I told myself, 'Whatever you do, don't leave it short.'"

The putt was too far left all the way and went three feet past. Now both players faced knee-knockers to stay alive. Woods was unsure of the read on his four-footer, and called in caddie Williams for help, something he rarely did. Neither saw any break, so Woods played the putt straight and knocked it in for a birdie. Mediate was more nervous than he had been on any putt all week. "Three-putting for a bogey would have been a horrible way to lose," he said. Fortunately, he was steady enough to hole the putt.

Both players completed 18 holes with even-par 71s. For the third time, the U.S. Open champion would be decided in sudden death (Hale Irwin won in 1990; Els in 1994). The extra-hole playoff would begin on the seventh hole, given its proximity to the 18th green. There would be a pause while the players checked and signed their scorecards—a requirement for their 18-hole round—and then a further delay when Woods needed to go to the bathroom. He went to the closest facility—a porta-john for NBC personnel next to the 18th-hole tower.

The seventh-hole start of sudden death was a bad break for Mediate. It was a left-to-right bending hole, which would pose a challenge to Rocco, given his natural right-to-left draw. Playing first, determined by lot, Woods hit a perfect tee shot—unsurprisingly pulling off a long fade around the corner (of course, he also would have been able to handle a right-to-left hole, because he could hit a draw equally well.)

As on the 18th, Mediate didn't start his draw on the proper line, and it bounced into the left bunker. From there, he pulled his second shot so badly that it ended up against the grandstand. After a free drop, he was left with a tricky pitch shot from the rough and knocked it 20 feet past. Woods had a birdie putt just slightly longer than that. He left it a couple of inches short, and tapped in for a par. A hush fell over the crowd as Mediate prepared for the putt he needed in order to extend the playoff. He sent the ball rolling, and it slid past the hole an inch from the right edge, drawing a low moan from the gallery. Rocco's bid was over, and Tiger had secured his third U.S. Open title.

Woods extended his right hand to Mediate for a handshake. But Mediate felt that the end of this contest deserved more, and extended his arms for a hug. The two combatants exchanged heartfelt congratulations in an embrace.

In a greenside television interview, Mediate's mood was admirably upbeat, despite the outcome: "They wanted a show, they got one. I can't really complain, I did the best I could. I never quit. I got what I wanted, a chance to beat the best player in the world, and came up just a little short, but I think I had him a little scared once. He just said, 'Great fight,' to me and that means a lot."

For his part, Woods thought back on all that had happened during the week. "This has probably been the greatest tournament I've ever had," he asserted.

Eight days later, Woods had reconstructive surgery on his left knee, and wouldn't play in another tournament for eight-and-a-half months.

TOP-10 FINISHERS		
1	Tiger Woods	72-68-70-73—283*
2	Rocco Mediate	69-71-72-71—283
3	Lee Westwood	70-71-70-73—284
T4	Robert Karlsson	70-70-75-71—286
T4	D.J. Trahan	72-69-73-72—286
T6	Miguel Angel Jimenez	75-66-74-72—287
T6	John Merrick	73-72-71-71—287
T9	Eric Axley	69-79-71-69—288
T9	Geoff Ogilvy	69-73-72-74—288
T9	Heath Slocum	75-74-74-65—288
T9	Brandt Snedeker	76-73-68-71—288
T9	Camilo Villegas	73-71-71-73—288

*Woods won playoff on first sudden death hole after both shot 71

2021

RAHM'S HAPPY ENDING

Two weeks before the U.S. Open, as he strode off the 18th green on Saturday at the Memorial Tournament, Jon Rahm learned that he had tested positive for the COVID-19 virus and that he would need to withdraw under the PGA Tour's pandemic protocols.

The consequences were abysmal. Rahm had just shot a 64 to take a six-stroke lead at 18-under par. The winner the next day finished at 13-under par, thus depriving the 26-year-old Spaniard of a virtually certain victory.

To add to his woes, his parents were on their way from Spain to spend the following week with him and to see his 10-month old son for the first time. While Rahm managed to return to his Scottsdale, Arizona home in an air ambulance (rather than isolating in Columbus, Ohio), he was stuck in home quarantine, unable to share time with family.

His U.S. Open participation and preparation were cast in doubt, as his 10-day isolation period ended on the Tuesday of Open week. Fortunately, Rahm remained asymptomatic (he had been subject to testing after coming in contact with someone who had COVID). After testing negative for two consecutive days, Rahm was permitted to leave isolation early, on the Saturday before the Open.

During the week at home, his practice had been limited to hitting balls on a golf simulator. Once unconfined, he dove into his typical U.S. Open practice regimen with relish. And in some more good news, the championship was being played at Torrey Pines in San Diego, where, as a rookie in 2017, Rahm had scored his first tour victory by holing a 40-foot eagle putt on the 72nd hole. The positive vibes of the place went beyond that. In 2018, he proposed to his then-girlfriend Kelley in the adjacent Torrey Pines reserve. Now, she was his wife and mother to his son.

Despite the uncertainty surrounding his preparedness on the heels of the enforced downtime, Rahm was nevertheless one of the favorites. He rose to No. 1 in the world ranking the previous summer. While he since had slipped to No. 3, his play through 54 holes at the Memorial stamped him as a threat to recapture the top spot.

Dustin Johnson and Justin Thomas were 1-2 in the world ranking, but the headliners entering the event were Bryson DeChambeau and Brooks Koepka. DeChambeau was the defending champion, having won the pandemic-delayed U.S. Open in September of 2020 at Winged Foot in New York. He added a victory at the Arnold Palmer Invitational in March of 2021, and led the money list for the 2020-21 season, which started the previous fall. Koepka's recent U.S. Open record was nearly impeccable. He won in 2017, won again in 2018, and finished second in 2019 before missing the event in 2020 due to knee surgery.

A leaked video of an unaired Golf Channel interview with Koepka a couple weeks before the Open raised the temperature of a budding Koepka-DeChambeau rivalry. During the interview, which went viral, Koepka rolled his eyes and made a snide comment as DeChambeau walked past. The two clearly weren't fond of each other, and golf fans chose sides.

Koepka's U.S. Open prowess continued in the first round, as he got to four-under par through 11 holes. He bogeyed two holes coming in for a two-under 69—remarkably, his sixth straight U.S. Open round in the 60s. Four other players reached four-under during the round, and two managed to stay there: Russell Henley and Louis Oosthuizen, sharing the lead with 67s. Torrey Pines annually hosts an event on the PGA Tour, but the 31-year-old Henley had only played it once. In 2014, in his second year on tour following a brilliant college career at the University of Georgia, he shot a 79 on Torrey Pines' South Course in the Farmers Insurance Open (in the first two rounds of the tournament, competitors play one round each on the South Course and the North Course), missing the cut. He decided that henceforth he would skip that week on tour and hadn't played at Torrey Pines since. "I only remember leaving the course feeling like I got beat up," he said in 2021. Henley made a 40-foot birdie putt on the 18th hole in 2014 to break 80. This time he made a 33-foot birdie putt on 18 to shoot a four-under round.

The round started poorly with a bogey on the first hole, before Henley recovered with four birdies in a six-hole stretch starting on the fifth, all on medium-range putts. A bogey on 12 was followed by birdies on 15 and 18. Henley had played in 26 majors with no top-10 finishes. His last of three tour victories was in 2017, but, after slumping in 2018-19, he was recovering his game. He squeaked into the Open field with a world ranking of 59th at the late-May cutoff date, when the top 60 received exemptions.

Oosthuizen had a considerably better record in majors. The 38-year-old South African won the 2010 British Open and since then had the dubious—but creditable—distinction of completing a career second-place Slam by finishing runner-up in all four majors. In fact, he had five seconds in majors, having notched a second runner-up showing in the PGA Championship a month earlier. He also owned a third-place finish in the 2020 U.S. Open.

Like Henley, Oosthuizen was one-over early in his round with a bogey on 11 (he started on the back nine). He made five birdies the rest of the way, including three in a row on Nos. 16-18. There had been a 90-minute fog delay in the morning, and Oosthuizen was one of the players unable to complete his first round on Thursday, finishing it with two pars on Friday morning.

Rory McIlroy, the 2011 champion and four-time major winner (but none since 2014), rushed to finish his round on Thursday, his group teeing off on 18 while the group ahead hadn't completely cleared the fairway. McIlroy birdied the hole for a 70.

Rahm was in good shape with a 69 after a wildly up-and-down start, carding his first par on the seventh hole. Starting on the back nine, he had three birdies and three bogeys on holes 10-15. A two-putt birdie on the par-five 18th, a birdie on the short par-four second, and four par saves on the front nine—all on putts of five feet or less—brought him in at two-under and a chance to make up for the Memorial. Another of the six players at 69 was a local favorite, San Diego native Xander Schauffele, owner of four PGA Tour wins at age 27.

Henley again finished as the co-leader after Round 2, missing a chance to be the sole leader when he three-putted his last hole, the ninth, from 17 feet. It was his only bogey of the day against two birdies in a steady round of 70.

The story of the day was Englishman Richard Bland, the man who tied Henley at 137. The 48-year-old had just claimed his first European Tour victory a month earlier at the British Masters and was playing in only his fourth major championship and second U.S. Open (the other was in 2009). His 67 included seven birdies and made him the oldest player ever to hold a share of the 36-hole lead at a U.S. Open. It was just a one-day story, though, as Bland shot 77-78 on the weekend.

Another good story was Matthew Wolff, returning to the tour after taking a seven-week break due to what he said were mental health issues triggered by his failure to meet expectations after a sterling start to his career. Turning pro at age 20 in 2019, Wolff won a tournament that summer and in 2020 finished T4 at the PGA Championship and second in the U.S. Open. He skipped the 2021 PGA Championship during his time off in May.

Wolff's first round back was a wild one at Torrey Pines with eight birdies, two double bogeys, and three bogeys for a 70. He was steadier in the second round with four birdies and one bogey for a 68 and a 138 total, one off the lead. He admitted that he still sometimes wanted to stay in bed in the morning, but was "getting closer to feeling more comfortable." Wolff was tied at 138 with Oosthuizen, who hit only nine greens but limited the damage to two bogeys in a round of 71.

Rahm also had a scrambling 71 to stay in touch at 139. He pointed to a key stretch of par-saving putts on 10, 11, and 12, the first two from 14 and eight feet for bunker saves and the third from five-and-a-half feet on a second putt. "Things could have taken a turn for the worse," said Rahm, who was encouraged by his solid ball-striking on the last four holes, hoping it was a good sign for the weekend. A holed bunker shot on 14 for one of his two birdies on the day also helped.

Joining Rahm at 139 was Bubba Watson, one of four players to share the low round of 67, along with Bland, Mackenzie Hughes, and Collin Morikawa.

Hughes had a dream start on a tough stretch of holes—he birdied the 10th from 55 feet, chipped in for a birdie at the 11th, and sank a 20-foot putt to birdie the 12th. For good measure, after a three-under 33 on the back nine, he made a 40-foot birdie putt at the second and a 12-footer at the seventh against a lone front-nine bogey. While the long-range putts allowed him to go low, his ball-striking lent solid support, with 15 greens hit in regulation, marking a rediscovery of form by a player who had missed his last five cuts. In the first round, he eagled the 18th hole for a 73, and now sat at 140 along with Schauffele.

Morikawa's 67 was a recovery from a first-round 75 that had been brightened only by an eagle on 18, while otherwise including bogeys on all four par threes, three three-putts, and a double bogey. After a bogey on the first hole of the second round, the 2020 PGA champion was just looking to make the cut. He did better than that, saying that he figured something out on his swing on the third hole. He made birdies on Nos. 2, 6, 7, 8, and 9 for a four-under 31 on the front nine and parred every hole on the back.

Koepka and DeChambeau were also at 142, Koepka with 69-73 and DeChambeau with 73-69. For the second day, Koepka reached four-under for the championship with birdies at the second and fourth. However, he had five bogeys and just one birdie the rest of the way in a round in which he hit only seven greens in regulation.

DeChambeau had spent time on the practice range in near darkness after his erratic first-round 73. He didn't find a cure there but shared that he had woken up in the middle of the night with a swing fix in his head. It didn't work right away—he bogeyed two of his first three holes (Nos. 10 and 12) to stand at four-over overall. When it kicked in, he rallied with birdies on 13 and 16 and an eagle from 24 feet on 18 for a two-under back nine. An even-par front nine left him within striking distance entering the weekend, though it would require a strong move.

The 2020 champion indeed made his move on Saturday by eliminating bogeys, so that three birdies were enough for a 68 and a 210 total, two strokes behind tri-leaders Henley, Oosthuizen, and Hughes. DeChambeau, who had gained weight specifically to add to his already considerable distance off the tee, won the previous fall at Winged Foot with a bomb-and-gouge strategy. The fairways there were so narrow that everyone had trouble hitting them, so DeChambeau figured he had an advantage with shorter shots into the greens even if they were from the rough.

The course setup at Torrey Pines wasn't as extreme, but DeChambeau's strategy still held merit. While he found only five fairways in the third round, he hit 15 greens in regulation. All three of his birdie putts were from seven feet, while one of his par saves (No. 14) was from 20 feet. The lack of accuracy did hurt him on the 18th, however, where a drive in a fairway bunker prevented going for the par five in two, and he ended up settling for a par.

McIlroy also cut down on bogeys, making only one on Saturday after having seven in a second-round 73. He had five birdies for the second consecutive day, but this time the result was a 67 that matched the best round of the day and moved him into a tie with DeChambeau, two behind.

Hughes and Oosthuizen each decorated their rounds with long eagle putts in a two-man display reminiscent of Tiger Woods' one-man eagle show in the third round in 2008. Hughes sank a 62-foot putt for an eagle on 13 to highlight a 68. Waiting until the end, Oosthuizen holed a 52-foot eagle putt on 18 to gain his share of the lead. He also made a 30-foot putt at the 16th in going from two-over for the round through 15 holes to shooting a one-under 70. Henley didn't do anything so dramatic in a round of 71 that included four birdies and four bogeys, making them in alternating fashion, each birdie followed by a bogey on his next deviation from par.

Rahm had a relatively quiet 72, with a three-putt from 15 feet for a double bogey on the 14th striking a sour note somewhat assuaged by a two-putt from 80 feet for a birdie on 18 to end up three strokes out of the lead at 211. Also at that figure were Wolff (73) and Scottie Scheffler (70).

There were 20 players within three strokes of the lead through 54 holes, including such luminaries as Johnson (68 with birdies on the last two holes), Morikawa (70), and Schauffele (72) four strokes back at 212 and Paul Casey (67), Koepka (71), and Thomas (72) at 213, all of them still in the mix.

Rahm burst out of the gate on Sunday with a birdie on the first hole on a 10-foot putt and another on the second from two-and-a-half feet after a big drive and an approach from 58 yards on the 387-yard hole. That pulled him within one stroke of the leaders, who had yet to tee off. When the last twosome of Oosthuizen and Hughes reached the first tee, there were nine players within two shots (including the three co-leaders) and nine more three shots back.

It would get even tighter on the front nine, reaching a congestion point when four players were tied for the lead at four-under and six were at three-under. The quartet in front were Henley, Oosthuizen, DeChambeau, and McIlroy. Henley bogeyed the first hole, birdied the par-three third with a tee shot to two feet, and bogeyed the fifth. Oosthuizen bogeyed the fourth. They were caught by McIlroy and DeChambeau each going one-under in the early going, McIlroy thanks to a 35-foot, downhill, sliding birdie putt at the fourth, and DeChambeau with a four-foot birdie putt at the fifth.

Rahm slipped back to three-under with a bogey at the fourth, where he drove into a fairway bunker. The others at three-under were Casey (birdies on 7, 8, and 9 for a 32 on the front), Koepka (birdies on 2, 8, and 9 for a 32 on the front), Morikawa (birdies at 2 and 4), Wolff (bogey at 1, birdies on 4 and 6), and Hughes (bogeys on 1 and 5).

DeChambeau put his nose in front with an exquisite tee shot on the 173-yard eighth, depositing the ball an inch from the hole. A hole-in-one really would have put a charge into the air; but, in any case, it was a birdie for the defending champion to take the solo lead. Moments later, McIlroy missed a chance to join him when his seven-foot birdie attempt slid by the hole on the seventh.

The next significant traffic jam occurred when the last twosome made the turn. Oosthuizen birdied the ninth hole with a 16-foot putt after laying up in two to tie DeChambeau for first at five-under, with five players tied at four-under: Morikawa, Rahm, McIlroy, Koepka, and Hughes.

Morikawa became the third player to post a 32 on the front nine, adding a third birdie at the ninth. It could have been even better. He was firing on all cylinders, hitting all nine greens in regulation and missing birdie putts of seven and four feet on the sixth and eighth holes.

Rahm posted a 33 on the front nine. After the two starting birdies, he made par saves of six and five feet on the third and fifth around his bogey on No. 4. Two-putt pars followed on the next three holes, and then he got a break on the ninth. His drive hooked wildly into a staging ground beyond a temporary fence. Rahm feared it was out of bounds, but, since that area was on course property and in bounds for general play, it wasn't O.B. John Wood, who was walking with the group for NBC television, reported that Rahm broke into a smile when informed that the ball was in bounds, and he would be granted a free drop near the fence. He was able to hit a second shot far enough down the fairway for a wedge third shot into the par-five green. That approach landed on the left edge of the green about 12 feet past the hole, then caught a slope that brought it back to within three feet of the cup. Rahm holed it for birdie.

McIlroy settled for a par on the ninth. He couldn't get up and down after reaching the vicinity of the green in two, completing an eight-par, one-birdie front nine of 34. Hughes recovered from three early bogeys with birdies on 7 and 9 to get back to four-under. Up ahead, Koepka had fallen to two-under with a three-putt bogey on the 12th, then fought back with birdies on 13 (11 feet) and 15 (16 feet) to reach four-under in his bid for a third U.S. Open title.

That bid suffered a severe blow when Koepka pulled his tee shot into a bunker on the 223-yard 16th, yielding a bogey after he missed a 15-foot putt. Behind him, DeChambeau bogeyed the other par three on the back nine, No. 11, with a tee shot far right of the green and a miss from 10 feet after pitching on.

Moments later, Oosthuizen birdied the 10th with a 28-foot putt, a two-stroke swing between the erstwhile co-leaders giving the South African a two-stroke lead. On a day when three players started at five-under, Oosthuizen was the first player to reach six-under.

It didn't last long. Oosthuizen soon bogeyed the 11th by the same route DeChambeau had, with a tee shot to the right and a missed 10-footer. Suddenly and incongruously, a pall descended upon the play as some of the game's greatest golfers became simultaneously unglued as they tackled the back nine at Torrey Pines.

McIlroy followed a three-putt bogey on 11 with a double bogey on the 501-yard, par-four 12th. His second shot was badly pushed to the right into a downhill, plugged lie on the side of the bunker away from the green, from where he inevitably took two strokes to get on the putting surface. At one-under, he was suddenly out of it.

On the 616-yard, par-five 13th, Morikawa visited the right rough on each of his first two shots, then bladed a 56-yard wedge shot well over the green, leaving a devilish downhill pitch shot that he couldn't keep on the green. A double bogey dropped him to two-over, which is where he would finish after a back-nine 39 for a 71. A second major title in his young career would wait until a month later, when he captured the British Open.

Whereas DeChambeau and Oosthuizen missed the 11th green to the right, Hughes suffered a worse fate when he missed to the left. His shot bounced off a cart path up into the branches of a tree—and the ball stayed there. He took a penalty drop under the unplayable-ball rule underneath the spot where the ball rested, pitched on, and two-putted for a double bogey. His downfall continued with bogeys on 12, 14, and 15.

DeChambeau had gone 30 holes without a bogey before his bogey on 11. He followed with another on 12, where he missed the fairway by a wide margin to the right. He did well to reach the front of the green with his second shot from the deep rough but three-putted from 60 feet. Worse was to come.

DeChambeau's foot slipped on his tee shot at the 13th, causing another miss to the right. He didn't make good contact on his second shot, leaving a 190-yard third shot from a lie nestled in the right rough. That one finished in a bunker well short of the green, and, from there, he skulled it considerably over the green, coming to rest against a carton of beer. He got relief from standing on an adjacent cart path (and moved the carton), but there was no way to get a pitch close from that spot and he ended up two-putting from 40 feet for a double bogey.

The 11th and 12th played as the two toughest holes for the week, so troubles there were understandable—Casey had earlier fallen there by going bogey-double bogey. But for Morikawa and DeChambeau to both double bogey a par five to practically end their chances was almost inexplicable. In DeChambeau's case, he had now played a stretch of three holes in four-over. For good measure, he made a quadruple bogey on the par-four 17th, hitting his tee shot into an adjacent hazard to the left, taking a penalty drop, hitting a shot close to the green, and then shanking one from a tricky lie in the rough. A par on the 18th left him with a bizarre scorecard of 33-44—77 and a T26 finish in a tournament he had led heading into the back nine of the final round. DeChambeau hit only three fairways in the final round. This time, the bomb-and-gouge strategy failed.

His rival, Koepka, narrowly missed a birdie putt at the 17th and came to 18 needing a birdie to post four-under, which might give him a chance. Instead, he made a bogey, hitting his second shot right of the green, then dumping that one into a bunker. A round of 32-37—69 left him at two-under.

Shortly thereafter, Harris English birdied the 18th to finish at three-under, having also birdied 14 and 17 in a round of 68. When all was said and done, he ended up in third place and with some cause for regret—while flying under the radar at the beginning of the round, he had made three bogeys and a birdie on the first four holes before heating up.

Italy's Guido Migliozzi also emerged from the shadows with a 68 to finish at two-under. Although 11 players were three-under or better at some point of their final round, the two-under finish earned a T4. That was ahead of elite players Johnson, Thomas, Schauffele, and Scottie Scheffler—all of whom reached two-under at some point of their round, yet ended up worse.

What had once seemed a wide-open Open ultimately resolved itself to a two-man fight between Oosthuizen and Rahm down the stretch. A string of pars under the considerable demands of a U.S. Open is often a good thing, and it was especially good on this day. Rahm parred every hole from the 10th through 16th, staying at four-under. He made a bunker save on the 11th with a nice escape to three feet. He drove into a fairway bunker on 13, but avoided the problems that befell others there by hitting his second into the fairway, wedging on, and missing a 12-foot birdie putt.

A wedge to the 14th gave him another birdie chance, but he missed from 10 feet. (Unlike in the 2008 Open at Torrey Pines, No. 14 played at its scorecard yardage of 434 all four days instead of being converted to a drivable par four for a round.) He nearly birdied the 15th, where his 40-foot putt hit the hole and spun out. The 16th was more routine, with a two-putt from 20 feet.

Oosthuizen maintained a one-stroke lead at five-under with a five-foot second putt after a slippery birdie attempt at 12. Just as so many others, he ended up in the right rough after his second shot on 13. He distinguished himself from Morikawa and DeChambeau by making a hard-earned par. He gouged his third shot onto the front fringe, 60 feet from the hole, used a putter to go six feet past, and made that.

By that time, Rahm had reached the 17th hole. The Spaniard's tee shot drifted into a fairway bunker on the right, leaving a not-so-nettlesome shot from 122 yards, which he hit to 24 feet left of the hole. Rahm allowed for some eight feet of break on the left-to-right putt. His read and his stroke were perfect, and the ball dropped into the hole for a birdie that tied him with Oosthuizen at five-under.

Rahm proceeded to the 18th and lashed a drive of 331 yards, leaving a four-iron to the green and a reasonable chance for a birdie. The birdie prospect dimmed, however, when his second shot finished in a bunker to the right of the green. With a green tilting downhill toward a pond in front, Rahm didn't dare aim at the hole. Instead, he played a safe shot, 18 feet to the right of the cup.

It was another left-to-right putt, this one breaking about three feet.

On the same hole he had eagled to win a tour event four years before, Rahm felt confident as he surveyed the putt and stood over it. He again had the perfect line, with the ball rolling down the slope and into the hole for a second straight birdie. The gallery roared, and Rahm answered with a gleeful fist pump and an exultant shout into the din.

Rahm's birdie-birdie finish vaulted him to six-under, leaving Oosthuizen one behind as he played the 15th hole. Louis successfully made it past the tough 15th and 16th with pars, the latter on an eight-foot putt.

The 17th fairway was guarded tightly by an overgrown, shallow seaside canyon on the left. Many players, guarding against a miss to the left, which would incur a penalty stroke, missed to the safer right side, including Rahm. Oosthuizen, pressing for a birdie, took a big swing with his driver and pulled it to the left, into the penalty area—a disastrous mistake, unless he were to make a par with the penalty stroke. He made a valiant effort after his drop, hitting a 130-yard approach shot to 10 feet from the hole. He missed the putt, though, and now needed an eagle on the 18th to force a playoff.

His chances went from slim to almost none when he drove into the left rough. With no way to re ach the green in two, he ended up needing to hole a 69-yard third shot for a tie, and couldn't perform that miracle. He finished by making a birdie putt for a 71 to finish one stroke behind—yet another agonizing near miss in a major championship, his sixth runner-up finish in the game's biggest events. Incredibly, the 2010 British Open remained his only win on the PGA Tour, though he did have 14 victories on the European and South African tours.

Rahm's closing 67 matched the best score of the final round and of the championship, and his spectacular finish marked the first time a player birdied the last two holes to win a U.S. Open by one stroke.

The victory was all the sweeter given his misfortunes two weeks earlier at the Memorial. It also burnished his legacy at Torrey Pines, a place where he said he and his family were always happy.

"It felt like such a fairy tale story that I knew was going to have a happy ending," Rahm told the press afterward. "I knew there was something special in the air. I could just feel it. That's why I played as aggressive as I did because I was just like, man, this is my day."

TOP-10 FINISHERS		
1	Jon Rahm	69-70-72-67—278
2	Louis Oosthuizen	67-71-70-71—279
3	Harris English	72-70-71-68—281
T4	Brooks Koepka	69-73-71-69—282
T4	Guido Migliozzi	71-70-73-68—282
T4	Collin Morikawa	75-67-70-70—282
T7	Daniel Berger	71-72-72-68—283
T7	Paul Casey	71-75-67-70—283
T7	Branden Grace	72-70-74-67—283
T7	Rory McIlroy	70-73-67-73—283
T7	Xander Schauffele	69-71-72-71—283
T7	Scottie Scheffler	72-69-70-72—283

ACKNOWLEDGMENTS

T his was a research-driven book, so it was built on the reporting and writing of chroniclers of golf through the decades, particularly chroniclers of the U.S. Open. The published forms of this work include newspapers, magazines, books, and websites.

Newspapers were a primary source with their on-site reporting of U.S. Opens. Fortunately, newspapers.com has a collection of archives of many of the papers that have covered the championship through the years. A list of newspapers and news services used in the research appears at the end of these acknowledgments.

The coverage of U.S. Opens in periodicals also formed an important source. From the first half of the 20th century, those included *The American Golfer*, *Golf*, and *Golf Illustrated*. From the 1950s onward, there have been *Sports Illustrated*, *Golf World*, *Golf Digest*, *Golf* magazine, *Golfweek*, and the USGA's *Golf Journal*, and more recently their associated websites and also pgatour.com.

The next layer is books. General books about the U.S. Open are *The U.S. Open*, by Robert Sommers; *The Official U.S. Open Almanac*, by Salvatore Johnson; *Greatest Moments of the U.S. Open*, by the USGA, *Tiptoeing Through Hell*, by John Strege; and my book, *Golf Courses of the U.S. Open*. Books about particular U.S. Opens are *The Greatest Game Ever Played*, by Mark Frost about 1913; my book *Miracle at Merion* about 1950; *The Upset*, by Al Barkow about 1955; *The Longest Shot*, by Neil Sagabiel about 1955; *Golf's Greatest Championship*, by Julian I. Graubart about 1960; *Chasing Greatness*, by Adam

Lazarus and Steve Schlossman about 1973; *Payne At Pinehurst*, by Bill Chastain about 1999; and *Are You Kidding Me?*, by Rocco Mediate and John Feinstein about 2008.

Biographies and autobiographies that touch on U.S. Opens include *A Game of Golf,* by Francis Ouimet; *Thirty Years of Championship Golf,* by Gene Sarazen with Herbert Warren Wind; *Sir Walter and Mr. Jones,* by Stephen R. Lowe; *Down the Fairway,* by Robert T. Jones and O.B. Keeler; *Golf Is My Game,* by Bobby Jones; *The Immortal Bobby,* by Ron Rapoport; *How I Played the Game,* by Byron Nelson; *Slammin' Sam,* by Sam Snead with George Mendoza; *Ben Hogan,* by James Dodson; *Hogan,* by Curt Sampson; *American Triumvirate,* by James Dodson; *A Golfer's Life,* by Arnold Palmer with James Dodson; *My Story,* by Jack Nicklaus with Ken Bowden; *Arnie & Jack,* by Ian O'Connor; *They Call Me Super Mex,* by Lee Trevino with Sam Blair; *Payne Stewart: The Authorized Biography,* by Tracey Stewart; and *In Search of Tiger,* by Tom Callahan.

Books about the tour or golf in general that touch on U.S. Opens include *The Story of American Golf,* by Herbert Warren Wind; *Present-Day Golf,* by George Duncan and Charles Darwin; *Mostly Golf: A Bernard Darwin Anthology,* edited by Peter Ryde; *Triumphant Journey,* by Dick Miller; *Merion: The Championship History,* by Jeff Silverman; *The Age of Palmer,* by Patrick Hand; *The Eternal Summer,* by Curt Sampson; *Tour '72,* by Michael D'Antonio; *Following Through,* by Herbert Warren Wind; *The Spirit of Pinehurst,* by Lee Pace; and various annual editions of *The World of Professional Golf,* by Mark H. McCormack. Some excerpts of the above books were accessed through *One Week in June: The U.S. Open,* a compendium of published work on various U.S. Opens.

The USGA library was useful for access to periodicals, books, U.S. Open programs, and club histories. This library research was mostly done for my earlier book, *Golf Courses of the U.S. Open.* Fortunately, I kept files of photocopies of relevant pages that I used for research of this book.

Transcripts of interviews at the U.S. Open in recent decades have been done by ASAP Sports and are found on asapsports.com. I also used my own notes and USGA notes from U.S. Opens that I covered.

The PGA Tour database was a resource for results, player records, and statistics.

The book owes its existence to publisher Chris Sulavik of Tatra Press. It was his idea, and I am very grateful for the opportunity to execute it. Chris also provided helpful editing and proofreading, as did Emily Church. The cover design was handled by Mimi Bark, with thanks to Oakmont Country Club for providing the photo. Page design and additional proofreading were done by Isabella Piestrzynska and Maria Ilardi. Many thanks to all.

NEWSPAPERS

Atlanta Journal

Atlantic City Press

Berkeley Gazette

Boston Evening Transcript

Boston Globe

Brooklyn Daily Eagle

Brooklyn Times-Union

Charlotte Observer

Chicago Tribune

Daily Telegraph (London)

Durham Herald-Sun

The Evening World

Greensboro News and Record

The Times of London

Los Angeles Times

Minneapolis Star-Tribune

New Jersey Record

New York Daily News

New York Times

New York Tribune

New York/Long Island Newsday

Oakland Tribune

Orlando Sentinel

Philadelphia Bulletin

Philadelphia Daily News

Philadelphia Inquirer

Pittsburgh Press

Pittsburgh Post-Gazette

Raleigh News & Observer

Reading Times

San Fransico Examiner

Washington Post

Winston-Salem Journal

NEWS SERVICES

Associated Press

Knight News Service

North American Newspaper Alliance

United Press International

USA Today Network